"Barber has contributed a fascinating volume to Baker Academic's distinguished series A Catholic Biblical Theology of the Sacraments. Barber's profound exploration challenges us to think about anointing of the sick more biblically. This exemplary work of theology leads us into the biblical vision of being anointed in Jesus Christ the Lord, our King, Priest, and Prophet, for our healing. Highly recommended!"

—**Andrew Hofer, OP**, The Dominican House of Studies

Praise for the Catholic Biblical Theology of the Sacraments series

"This series shows tremendous promise and ambition in laying out the multiple living connections between the Scriptures and the sacramental life of the Church. Taken together, these books could accomplish what Jean Daniélou's *The Bible and the Liturgy* accomplished for a previous generation of biblical and theological scholarship. And like that work, this series gives to students of the Bible a deeply enriched view of the mesh of relationships within and between biblical texts that are brought to light by the liturgy of the sacraments."

—**Jennifer Grillo**, University of Notre Dame

"In recent years, theological exegesis biblical commentary by theologians has made a significant contribution. This series turns the tables: explicitly theological reflection by biblical scholars. The result is a breakthrough. Theologically trained, exegetically astute biblical scholars here explore the foundations of Catholic sacramental theology, along paths that will change the theological conversation. This series points the way to the theological and exegetical future."

—**Matthew Levering**, Mundelein Seminary

"The sacraments come to us clothed in images that carry their mystery and propose it to our hearts. These images come from Scripture and are inspired by the Holy Spirit, who wills to transfigure us each into the full measure of Christ. The books in this series, by situating the sacraments within the scriptural imagery proper to each, will over time surely prove themselves to be agents in this work of the Spirit."

—**John C. Cavadini**, McGrath Institute for Church Life, University of Notre Dame

SERIES EDITORS

Timothy C. Gray
John Sehorn

ALSO IN THE SERIES

The Bible and Baptism: The Fountain of Salvation
Isaac Augustine Morales, OP

The Bible and Marriage: The Two Shall Become One Flesh
John S. Bergsma

The Bible and the Priesthood: Priestly Participation in the One Sacrifice for Sins
Anthony Giambrone, OP

The Bible and Reconciliation: Confession, Repentance, and Restoration
James B. Prothro

The Bible and the Anointing of the Sick

Healing in Christ

Michael Patrick Barber

Baker Academic
a division of Baker Publishing Group
Grand Rapids, Michigan

Published by Baker Academic
a division of Baker Publishing Group
Grand Rapids, Michigan
BakerAcademic.com

Printed in the United States of America

Library of Congress Cataloging-in-Publication Data
Names: Barber, Michael Patrick, author.
Title: The Bible and the anointing of the sick : healing in Christ / Michael Patrick Barber.
Description: Grand Rapids, Michigan : Baker Academic, a division of Baker Publishing Group, [2025] | Series: A Catholic biblical theology of the sacraments | Includes bibliographical references and indexes.
Identifiers: LCCN 2024052137 | ISBN 9781540960993 (paper) | ISBN 9781540968616 (casebound) | ISBN 9781493449194 (ebook) | ISBN 9781493449217 (pdf)
Subjects: LCSH: Unction. | Unction—Biblical teaching. | Catholic Church—Doctrines.
Classification: LCC BX2292 .B37 2025 | DDC 265/.7—dc23/eng/20250216
LC record available at https://lccn.loc.gov/2024052137

In accordance with CIC 827, permission to publish has been granted on February 13, 2025, by the Most Reverend Mark S. Rivituso, Auxiliary Bishop, Archdiocese of St. Louis. Permission to publish is an indication that nothing contrary to Church teaching is contained in this particular work. It does not imply any endorsement of the opinions expressed in the publication, or a general endorsement of any author; nor is any liability assumed by this permission.

Unless indicated otherwise, Scripture translations are those of the author.

Cover painting from Bigorski Monastery Saint John the Baptist / Zvonimir Atletić / Alamy Stock Photo

Baker Publishing Group publications use paper produced from sustainable forestry practices and postconsumer waste whenever possible.

25 26 27 28 29 30 31 7 6 5 4 3 2 1

For Uncle Pete

With endless gratitude for your priestly ministry, through which you have anointed countless members of the faithful in their hour of darkness, and for the innumerable ways you have helped to deepen my faith in and love for the Anointed One, Christ Jesus. I can never thank you enough.

Contents

Sidebars

Series Preface

> But one of the soldiers pierced his side with a spear, and at once there came out blood and water.
>
> —John 19:34 (ESV)

The arresting image of Jesus's pierced side has fed the spiritual imagination of countless believers over the centuries. The evangelist tells us that it "took place that the Scripture might be fulfilled" (John 19:36 ESV). Extending this line of thought, St. Thomas Aquinas goes so far as to compare the opened heart of Christ to the Scriptures as a whole, for the passion reveals the secret depths of God's trinitarian love latent in the Word, both written and incarnate. The Fathers of the Church—Latin, Greek, and Syriac alike—also saw in the flow of blood and water a symbol of the sacraments of Christian worship. From the side of Christ, dead on the cross, divine life has been dispensed to humanity. The side of Christ is the fount of the divine life that believers receive, by God's grace, through the humble, human signs of both Word and Sacrament.

Recognition of the life-giving symbiosis between Scripture and sacrament, so richly attested in the teaching of the Fathers of the Church, has proved difficult to maintain in the modern world. However much the Church has insisted upon the unity of Word and Sacrament, "the faithful are not always conscious of this connection," and so "there is great need for a deeper investigation of the relationship between word and sacrament in the Church's pastoral activity and in theological reflection" (Benedict XVI, *Verbum Domini*

53). This series seeks to contribute to that "deeper investigation" by offering a biblical theology of each of the seven sacraments.

One classic definition of theology is "faith seeking understanding." Catholic theology operates with the conviction that the deposit of faith—that which theology seeks to understand—has been brought to completion in Jesus Christ, is reliably transmitted in Scripture and Tradition, and is authentically interpreted by the Church's teaching office (see *Dei Verbum* 7–10). Accordingly, the teaching of the Catholic Church is the *initium fidei* or starting point of faith for theological reflection. The series does not aim primarily to demonstrate the truth of Catholic sacramental doctrine but to understand it more deeply. The purpose of the series, in short, is to foster a deeper appreciation of God's gifts and call in the sacraments through a renewed encounter with his Word in Scripture.

The volumes in the series therefore explore the sacraments' deep roots in the revelation of the Old and New Testaments. Since the study of Scripture should *always* be "the soul of sacred theology" (*Dei Verbum* 24), the expression "biblical theology" is used to indicate that the series engages in a theological reading of the Bible in order to enliven our understanding of the sacraments. The guidelines for such theological interpretation of Scripture are specified in *Catechism of the Catholic Church* 112–14 (cf. *Dei Verbum* 12): attention (1) to the entire content and unity of Scripture, (2) to the living Tradition of the whole Church, and (3) to the analogy of faith. A few words on each of these criteria are in order.

In keeping with the series' character as "biblical theology," the content and unity of Scripture is the criterion that largely governs the structure of each volume. The *Catechism* provides a helpful summary of the series' approach to this criterion. Following "the divine pedagogy of salvation," the volumes attempt to illuminate how the meaning of the seven sacraments, like that of all liturgical signs and symbols, "is rooted in the work of creation and in human culture, specified by the events of the Old Covenant and fully revealed in the person and work of Christ" (*CCC* 1145). Each volume explores (a) the Old Testament threads (including but not limited to discrete types of the sacraments) that (b) culminate in the ministry and above all in the paschal mystery of the incarnate Christ.

The series' acceptance of the Church's sacramental teaching ensures that the Church's Tradition plays an integral role in the volumes' engagement with the Bible. More directly, sidebars offer specific illustrations selected from the teaching and practice of the postbiblical Church, showing the sometimes surprising ways in which Tradition embodies the Church's ongoing reception of the biblical Word.

In the case of the sacraments, attention to the analogy of faith means, among other things, keeping always in mind their origin and end in the eternal life of the Blessed Trinity, their relationship to the missions of the Son and the Spirit, their ecclesial context, their doxological character, their soteriological purpose, their vocational entailments, and their eschatological horizon.

The series' intended readership is broad. While the primary audience is Catholics of the Roman Rite, it is hoped that Catholics of the non-Roman rites as well as Eastern Christians who are not in full communion with the Bishop of Rome, whose sacramental theory and practice are very close, will find much to appreciate. Protestant Christians, of course, vary widely in their views of sacramental worship, and their reception of the series is likely to vary similarly. It is our hope that, at the very least, the series helps Protestant believers better understand how Catholic sacramental teaching is born of Scripture and animated by it.

We pray that all those who read these volumes will together delight in the rich food of God's Word (cf. Isa. 55:2), seeking the unity in faith and charity to which we are called by our common baptism into the life of the Blessed Trinity. To him be the glory.

Timothy C. Gray
John Sehorn

Abbreviations

AB Anchor Bible
ABRL Anchor Bible Reference Library
ACD Ancient Christian Doctrine
ACT Ancient Christian Texts
ACW Ancient Christian Writers
AER *American Ecclesiastical Review*
AGJU Arbeiten zur Geschichte des antiken Judentums und des Urchristentums
AJEC Ancient Judaism and Early Christianity
ANF *Ante-Nicene Fathers*
AYB Anchor Yale Bible
BBR *Bulletin for Biblical Research*
BCBC Believers Church Bible Commentary
BCOT Baker Commentary on the Old Testament
BECNT Baker Exegetical Commentary on the New Testament
BIS Biblical Interpretation Series
BNTC Black's New Testament Commentaries
BTB *Biblical Theology Bulletin*
BTCB Brazos Theological Commentary on the Bible
BTS Biblical Tools and Studies
BZNW Beihefte zur Zeitschrift für die neutestamentliche Wissenschaft
CBTS A Catholic Biblical Theology of the Sacraments
CC Continental Commentary
CCC *Catechism of the Catholic Church*
CCSS Catholic Commentary on Sacred Scripture
CEJL Commentaries on Early Jewish Literature
CHR *Catholic Historical Review*
CIC *Codex Iuris Canonici* (*Code of Canon Law*)
CTC Christian Theology in Context
DCLS Deuterocanonical and Cognate Literature Studies
DSSSE *The Dead Sea Scrolls Study Edition*. Edited by Florentino García Martínez and Eibert J. C. Tigchelaar. 2 vols. Leiden: Brill, 1997–98
ECC Eerdmans Critical Commentary
ExpTim *Expository Times*
FC Fathers of the Church
GLS Gorgias Liturgical Studies
GSECP Gorgias Studies in Early Christianity and Patristics

ICC	International Critical Commentary
ITQ	*Irish Theological Quarterly*
JBL	*Journal of Biblical Literature*
JSNT	*Journal for the Study of the New Testament*
JSNTSup	Journal for the Study of the New Testament Supplement Series
JSOTSup	Journal for the Study of the Old Testament Supplement Series
JTS	*Journal of Theological Studies*
LCL	Loeb Classical Library
LHBOTS	Library of Hebrew Bible / Old Testament Studies
LNTS	Library of New Testament Studies
LXX	Septuagint
MT	Masoretic Text
NCBC	New Cambridge Bible Commentary
NIGTC	New International Greek Testament Commentary
NovT	*Novum Testamentum*
NovTSup	Supplements to Novum Testamentum
NPNF[1]	*Nicene and Post-Nicene Fathers*, Series 1
NPNF[2]	*Nicene and Post-Nicene Fathers*, Series 2
NTL	New Testament Library
NTR	New Testament Readings
NTS	*New Testament Studies*
OECT	Oxford Early Christian Texts
OTL	Old Testament Library
OTP	*Old Testament Pseudepigrapha*. Edited by James H. Charlesworth. 2 vols. New York: Doubleday, 1983, 1985
PG	Patrologia Graeca [= *Patrologiae Cursus Completus* Series Graeca]. Edited by J.-P. Migne. 162 vols. Paris, 1857–86
PL	Patrologia Latina [= *Patrologiae Cursus Completus* Series Latina]. Edited by J.-P. Migne. 217 vols. Paris, 1844–64
PPS	Popular Patristics Series
RSV	Revised Standard Version
SBLMS	Society of Biblical Literature Monograph Series
SCT	Sources of Christian Theology
SJOT	*Scandinavian Journal of the Old Testament*
SNTSMS	Society for New Testament Studies Monograph Series
SP	Sacra Pagina
STDJ	Studies on the Texts of the Desert of Judah
SVTP	Studia in Veteris Testamenti Pseudepigraphica
TENTS	Texts and Editions for New Testament Study
TS	*Theological Studies*
VTSup	Supplements to Vetus Testamentum
WBC	Word Biblical Commentary
WSA	The Works of Saint Augustine: A Translation for the 21st Century
WUNT	Wissenschaftliche Untersuchungen zum Neuen Testament

1

Introduction

The Bible and the Anointing of the Sick

[The twelve apostles] cast out many demons, and they *anointed with oil* many who were sick and healed them.

—Mark 6:13

It is no exaggeration to say that anointing of the sick has been the most misunderstood . . . of the seven sacraments of the Church.

—Charles Gusmer[1]

At the heart of Jesus's public ministry is his proclamation of the kingdom. According to all four of the canonical Gospels, the apostles began sharing in this work even prior to Jesus's passion and resurrection (Matt. 10:1–42; Mark 6:7–13; Luke 9:1–6; cf. John 4:1–2). Paul also seems aware of this tradition (1 Cor. 9:14).

The Gospel of Mark provides us with an arresting detail about the apostles' initial mission, however, that is often overlooked. While spreading the word

1. Charles W. Gusmer, *And You Visited Me: Sacramental Ministry to the Sick and the Dying*, rev. ed., Studies in the Reformed Rites of the Church 6 (Collegeville, MN: Liturgical Press, 1989), 181.

about the need for repentance, the apostles also healed the sick by *anointing them with oil.*

> And Jesus called to himself the twelve, and he began to send them out two by two, and he gave them authority over the unclean spirits. . . . And the twelve went out and proclaimed repentance. And they cast out many demons, and they *anointed with oil* many who were sick and healed them. (Mark 6:7, 12–13)

This intriguing report is often passed over without much reflection.[2] This is a mistake. Jesus's commissioning of his disciples to heal others by anointing them with oil is not inconsequential.

That anointing people with oil was significant for early Christians is also evident from the New Testament letter of James. Like the apostles in Mark 6, the early followers of Jesus continued to minister to the sick with oil. James writes:

> Is anyone among you sick? He should call for the elders of the church, and have them pray over him, anointing him with oil in the name of the Lord. (James 5:14)

Citing James's instructions, various early sources indicate that unction (oil) was used in ministering to the sick in early Christianity. Catholic and Orthodox Christians would eventually come to identify anointing of the sick as one of the seven sacraments. Other Christians, even those who do not embrace a "sacrament" of unction, nevertheless have continued to use oil in ministering to the sick in accordance with James's directive.[3]

Yet, as with Mark 6:13, there are subtleties in James 5 that raise many questions. To mention a few:

- Who exactly are the "sick"? The Greek word used by James is a verb, *astheneō*, "to be sick." Is this a reference to physical infirmity or spiritual weakness?
- Why should *elders* come? Who are these figures? Are they merely elderly Christians? And why is it important that the anointing is done by *them*?

2. Take, for instance, Timothy J. Geddert, *Mark*, BCBC (Scottdale, PA: Herald, 2001), 137–38, which never even mentions the Twelve's use of oil.

3. See, e.g., Huldrych Zwingli, *Writings*, vol. 2, *In Search of True Religion: Reformation, Pastoral and Eucharistic Writings*, trans. H. Wayne Pipkin (Eugene, OR: Pickwick, 1984), 102.

- What precisely does the oil do? What does the oil accomplish that prayer alone does not?

This study is going to address these and other related questions.

The Aims of This Study

Although this book is written in a series that has Catholics as its primary audience, it is hoped that this study will benefit both Catholics and non-Catholic Christians. Its title is *The Bible and the Anointing of the Sick*. That the "Bible" comes first is deliberate—this study is first and foremost about unpacking the riches of the scriptures, which all Christians accept as containing the inspired word of God.

It is also, of course, about anointing of the sick. As we have mentioned, long before the Protestant Reformation, Christians in both the East and the West had celebrated anointing as a sacramental rite. At the time of the Reformation, this was not a new practice; they had done so *for centuries*. Even today, like Catholic Christians,[4] Orthodox Christians observe anointing of the sick as a liturgical rite.[5] In addition, though not recognizing it as a "sacrament" or a liturgical rite like Catholics and Orthodox Christians, many Protestant Christians use oil in ministering to the sick as well.[6]

For all of these traditions, anointing is seen not as an "addendum" to Scripture but as a practice mandated by it. The practice of anointing the sick, then, *returns* us to the biblical text. The use of oil on the infirm ensures that we focus our attention on aspects of the biblical text that we might otherwise overlook. How often, for example, is the apostles' use of oil in their initial work

4. I deliberately avoid the language of "Roman Catholic." The term is problematic because it obscures the fact that there are many Eastern Rite Christians who are in communion with Rome but who have their own theological, liturgical, and canonical traditions. While this author is Latin Rite, like the majority of Catholics in the West, I hope this book will also be of help to Catholics of other rites.

5. For theological treatments of the rite from an Orthodox perspective, see Paul Meyendorff, *The Anointing of the Sick*, The Orthodox Liturgy 1 (Crestwood, NY: St. Vladimir's Seminary Press, 2009); David G. Bissias, *The Mystery of Healing: Oil, Anointing, and the Unity of the Local Church* (Rollinsford, NH: Orthodox Research Institute, 2008).

6. For example, the history of the use of anointing oil in the Anglican tradition alone is too complex to discuss here. For a classic discussion of the sacrament from an Anglican perspective, see Frederick W. Puller, *The Anointing of the Sick in Scripture and Tradition* (London: SPCK, 1904).

overlooked? A study of anointing of the sick is not simply needed for ecumenical purposes; it is needed *because it helps us better understand the biblical texts.*

Moreover, by focusing on Scripture, this study hopes to make a contribution to Catholic systematic theology. Sadly, the biblical bases for the sacraments in general—and anointing of the sick in particular—are often treated in only a cursory manner or understood in a superficial way. Works on sacramental theology often begin by mentioning the key biblical passages related to the sacrament being studied but then seldom look carefully at the exegetical issues they raise. This is a problem. It reinforces the perception that Catholic systematic theology is weakly rooted in the scriptures. What is more, I would contend that approaches that only superficially treat the scriptural bases of the sacraments are *profoundly* misguided because they fundamentally misconstrue the very nature of the theological task itself.

Theology versus "Theologianology"

One recent Church document—a work that Pope Francis says "remains fundamental for our communities"[7]—insists that "where theology is not essentially the interpretation of the Church's Scripture, such a theology no longer has a foundation."[8] Theology must "essentially" involve "the interpretation of the Church's Scripture." Here we find a restatement of the Second Vatican Council's teaching about the nature of theology: "The study of the sacred page should be the very soul of sacred theology."[9] This articulation uses the language of Christian tradition, which views the soul as that which "animates" or "gives life to" the bodies of living things.[10] In sum, the Second Vatican Council is saying that to do theology apart from "the study of the sacred page" is to commit to a *dead* theology. From an authentically Catholic perspective, a nonbiblical approach to theology is not properly "theology" at all.[11] Catholic theology

7. Francis, *Aperuit illis* (He Opened Their Minds), Apostolic Letter Instituting the Sunday of the Word of God (September 30, 2019), §2.

8. Benedict XVI, *Verbum Domini* (The Word of the Lord), Post-synodal Apostolic Exhortation on the Word of God in the Life and Mission of the Church (September 30, 2010), §35; cf. Francis, *Aperuit illis* 2.

9. Second Vatican Council, *Dei Verbum* (The Word of God), Dogmatic Constitution on Divine Revelation (November 18, 1965), §24. Translation from Austin Flannery, *Vatican Council II: The Basic Sixteen Documents, Constitutions, Decrees, Declarations*, rev. ed. (Collegeville, MN: Liturgical Press, 2014), 113.

10. See, e.g., Tertullian, *The Soul* 6: "It is the soul itself which makes the body either animate, if it be present to it, or else inanimate, if it be absent from it" (*ANF* 3:185).

11. This present study appears in a series entitled "A Catholic Biblical Theology of the Sacraments." The term "biblical theology," however, is defined in different ways by different

cannot simply consist of studying different theologians' opinions. That would be "theologianology," not "theology" properly speaking. To ensure that God himself remains the living subject of theology—"the study of God"—the Church wisely instructs that priority be given to the study of Scripture, which is recognized as containing God's inspired word (2 Tim. 3:16).

This conviction that theology must first and foremost be anchored in the Bible is rooted in Christian tradition. For example, writing in the late 300s, Cyril of Jerusalem insists, "For in regard to the divine and holy mysteries of the faith, not even a casual statement should be delivered without the Scriptures."[12] He therefore writes that the articles of the creed represent "the most important points collected from the Scriptures."[13] Later Church Fathers and Doctors would echo this sentiment. Thomas Aquinas—officially recognized by popes with the honorific term "the Common Doctor," due to his lasting legacy in Catholic theology[14]—himself emphasized the centrality of the scriptures. While he held that it is appropriate to draw from other authorities, for Thomas, Scripture remained the primary source for theological study. For example, Thomas writes: "Sacred doctrine . . . *properly uses the authority of the canonical Scriptures as an incontrovertible proof*, and the authority of the doctors of the Church as one that may properly be used, *yet merely as probable*."[15]

To be clear, I do not mean to suggest that sacramental theology is *only* the result of exegetical engagement with biblical texts. That the study of sacramental theology involves something more than that is manifest from the fact

---

people, and I am not particularly fond of it. Indeed, one is hard-pressed to imagine an authentic Catholic approach to theology that would be truly "unbiblical."

12. Cyril of Jerusalem, *Catechetical Lectures* 4.17; translation from Cyril, *The Works of Saint Cyril of Jerusalem*, trans. Leo P. McCauley and Anthony A. Stephenson, 2 vols., FC 61–62 (Washington, DC: Catholic University of America Press, 1969–70), 1:127.

13. Cyril of Jerusalem, *Catechetical Lectures* 5.12; translation from Cyril, *Works of Saint Cyril*, 1:146.

14. See, e.g., Pius XI, *Studiorum ducem* (The Supreme Guide), Encyclical Letter on St. Thomas Aquinas (June 29, 1923), §11; Francis, "Address to the Participants in the International Thomistic Congress" (September 22, 2022).

15. Thomas Aquinas, *Summa Theologiae* I, q. 1, art. 8, ad 2. Translation from *Summa Theologiae, Prima Pars, 1–49*, trans. Laurence Shapcote, Latin/English Edition of the Works of St. Thomas Aquinas 13 (Lander, WY: The Aquinas Institute for the Study of Sacred Doctrine, 2012), 12 (emphasis added). For more on the centrality of Scripture in the Church Fathers and Thomas Aquinas, see Michael Patrick Barber, "The Bible, the New Ressourcement, and Peter's Priestly Keys," *New Ressourcement* 1, no. 2 (2024): 271–313; Barber, "Thomas Aquinas's Exegesis of Paul and the Eucharist as *Panis Angelicus*: Typology and Transubstantiation," in *Thomas Aquinas and the Eucharist*, ed. Michael A. Dauphinais, Andrew Hofer, and Roger W. Nutt (Ave Maria, FL: Sapientia Press, 2025).

that the very word "sacrament" is derived from a Latin term, *sacramentum*. The biblical books were written not in Latin but in Hebrew, Aramaic, and Greek. Nevertheless, a genuinely Catholic approach to anointing of the sick must accept that theology is "essentially the interpretation of the Church's Scripture." As we will see, the sacrament is understood to draw us into mysteries testified to by biblical texts themselves. Pope Francis therefore insists, "Sacred Scripture and the sacraments are thus inseparable."[16]

New Light on Anointing of the Sick

Despite its long history, many have noted that the theology of the sacrament of anointing of the sick remains underdeveloped. In his comprehensive study of the sacrament, Charles Gusmer writes, "It is no exaggeration to say that anointing of the sick has been the most misunderstood . . . of the seven sacraments of the Church."[17] This should not be surprising. As we have seen, from a Catholic perspective, a proper understanding of the sacrament must be anchored in Scripture. Yet, as far as I know, Gusmer's is the only monograph-length study on the biblical roots of the sacrament. Indeed, many studies focus on Mark 6 and James 5 and then say little if anything more about other biblical passages that might shed light on the sacrament. It is therefore no wonder that the theology of the sacrament is perceived to be underdeveloped. This book responds to the call of Pope Benedict XVI, who wrote: "This sacrament deserves greater consideration today both in theological reflection and in pastoral ministry among the sick. . . . Anointing of the Sick should not be held to be almost 'a minor sacrament' when compared to the others."[18]

The scriptural bases for anointing of the sick involve much more than merely Mark 6 and James 5. This is especially true in light of the Second Vatican Council's teaching about the sacrament, which marked a watershed moment in the history of the Church's understanding of anointing of the sick. In addition to the traditional passages used to explain it—that is, Mark 6 and James 5—the council explains the sacrament by citing biblical passages *never used by previous magisterial sources to articulate the sacrament of anointing*

16. Francis, *Aperuit illis* 8.

17. Gusmer, *And You Visited Me*, 181.

18. Benedict XVI, Message of the Holy Father on the Occasion of the Twentieth World Day of the Sick (February 11, 2012), §3, https://www.vatican.va/content/benedict-xvi/en/messages/sick/documents/hf_ben-xvi_mes_20111120_world-day-of-the-sick-2012.html.

of the sick's meaning. By studying the implications of the council's use of these texts, I will make the case that we can have a deeper understanding of the sacrament. As a result, I will advocate an approach to the sacrament that goes beyond (though not against) previous articulations.

Specifically, what we will discover when we read James 5 in light of other texts used by the Church to explain the sacrament of anointing is this: true healing involves more than mere biological health. Ultimately, true healing entails conformity to the crucified and risen Lord. This occurs through being "in Christ"—that is, through union with the "Anointed One" in the Spirit. This conformity is first realized at baptism but reaches maturity as one more fully unites oneself to Christ by love that is expressed in suffering in union with him. In uniting themselves to Christ's death through faithful suffering in love, believers participate in Christ's royal, priestly, and prophetic identity and thus look in hope to share also his resurrection. With this outlook, then, the Church can look to the scene of Jesus's own anointing at Bethany as a sort of icon for understanding the sacrament of anointing of the sick. As Jesus was anointed to prepare his body ahead of his suffering and death, believers—as members of that body—also share in what sacral anointing signifies: the life-giving power and strengthening of the Spirit. The Spirit, then, enables them to share in his dominion over sin and its effects (Rom. 5:17), to present their bodies as part of one "living sacrifice" in Christ (Rom. 12:1), and to bear suffering in a prophetic way in the world, faithfully giving testimony to Jesus (Rev. 19:10).

Yet, while the Church's understanding of anointing of the sick is rooted in many different biblical texts, James 5 has long been identified as the key text at the heart of the theology of the practice. We therefore turn to look at the core questions raised by James's instruction and how they have been answered in Christian tradition. This discussion sets the stage for the study to follow.

2

James's Instructions and Christian Tradition

Questions about the Theology of the Anointing of the Sick

> Is anyone among you sick? He should call for the elders of the church, and have them pray over him, anointing him with oil in the name of the Lord.
>
> —James 5:14

> This [passage about anointing the sick in James 5] ought to be received and understood as referring to the faithful who are ailing for they are able to be anointed with the holy oil of chrism, which has been made by the Bishop.
>
> —Pope Innocent I (ca. AD 416)[1]

As we will see, the practice of anointing the sick is especially anchored in James 5. Although we have already quoted from it above, it is necessary to

1. Innocent I, *Letter to Decentius* 8; translation from Martin Connell, *Church and Worship in Fifth-Century Rome: The Letter of Innocent I to Decentius of Gubbio*, GLS 50 (Piscataway, NJ: Gorgias, 2010), 47.

read James's teaching regarding anointing the sick in its immediate context. We are told:

> Is anyone among you sick? He should call for the elders of the church, and have them pray over him, anointing him with oil in the name of the Lord. And the prayer of faith will save the one who is sick, and the Lord will raise him up. And if he has committed sins, he will be forgiven. Therefore, confess your sins to one another and pray for one another, that you may be healed. The prayer of the righteous has great power in its effects. (James 5:14–16)

At first glance, this passage seems rather straightforward: the sick should be anointed, the prayer of faith will "save" the sick person, sins are to be confessed, and believers are to pray for one another. The more we reflect on James's[2] instructions, however, the more questions emerge. Catholic theologians will often cite the passage in treating the sacrament of anointing of the sick without engaging the various issues interpreters have raised about the text. This is unhelpful. To do sacramental theology without serious consideration of the exegetical questions involved with the passage is irresponsible.

This chapter sets the table for the rest of the study. We will not be able to answer all the questions raised by James 5:14–16 until the end of this book. In this chapter, we identify some of the key interpretive issues we will have to examine. Yet we cannot ignore the way Christian history has received James's instructions. It is necessary to look at the way the passage has been read by Christians through the ages. Long before the Protestant Reformation, James's teaching came to be read as describing an important liturgical rite. This not only is true of the West but applies to the ancient Eastern church as well. The Protestant Reformers, however, resisted a sacramental reading of this passage. Here we cover that history, looking briefly at the development of the sacrament and debates about it up to recent times. Moreover, we will see how the Second Vatican Council offered an approach to the sacrament of anointing that involves reading James 5 in light of biblical texts never before used to explain the sacrament in Christian history.

2. Following the standard scholarly convention, I simply refer to the author of the epistle as "James" without prejudice to debates about the author's identity. For different perspectives on that matter, see Dale C. Allison Jr., *James*, ICC (London: Bloomsbury T&T Clark, 2013), 1–30; David A. deSilva, *The Jewish Teachers of Jesus, James, and Jude: What Earliest Christianity Learned from the Apocrypha and Pseudepigrapha* (Oxford: Oxford University Press, 2012), 45–54. I use the same convention for other biblical books: Isaiah, Matthew, Mark, and so on.

Core Questions about Anointing the Sick in James 5

James 5 mandates that the sick should be anointed with oil by the "elders of the church." But what does this involve exactly? Here we need to consider critical interpretive questions that emerge from a careful reading of the passage.

Who Are Proper Recipients and Ministers of Anointing?

In James, we are told that the "sick" should be prayed over and anointed by "the elders" (James 5:14). But who are the "sick," and who are the "elders"? Let us take these one at a time.

First, as to the identity of the recipients of anointing in James 5, interpreters have arrived at a general consensus: there can be little doubt that James specifically has in mind the physically infirm. The Greek verb he employs, *astheneō*, typically refers to bodily sickness, especially in Christian literature.[3] In addition, James speaks of the "one who is sick" (*kamnonta*) being "saved" or "healed" (*sōsei*). The Greek terms here are often used to describe sick people who are restored to physical health.[4] Moreover, oil was often used as a healing agent (e.g., Isa. 1:6; Luke 10:34).[5] As we have seen, Mark 6 depicts the apostles using oil on the those with physical sicknesses. It stands to reason that James envisions a similar scenario. Furthermore, that the elders are to be summoned by the sick and to go to them suggests that the intended recipients are so unhealthy they are homebound. It appears, then, that James has in mind those who are gravely ill, not merely people with minor sicknesses.[6]

The meaning of the "elders," however, is less clear. The Greek noun translated "elder," *presbyteros*—which is sometimes also rendered in English as "presbyter"—could simply refer to people who are of advanced biological age. Yet James's instruction can also be read against the background of other New Testament books where the word is applied to appointed leaders in the

3. Allison, *James*, 754: "The Jesus tradition . . . , as we know it, uses *astheneō* exclusively of bodily illness." Allison cites Matt. 10:8; 25:36, 39; Mark 6:56; Luke 4:40; John 4:46; 5:3, 7; 6:2; 11:1–3, 6; Acts 9:37; 19:12; 2 Tim. 4:20; *Testament of Zebulun* 5:2, 4; *Testament of Joseph* 3:5; 9:4; *1 Clement* 59:4.

4. Allison, *James*, 754; Peter H. Davids, *James*, NIGTC (Grand Rapids: Eerdmans, 1982), 192.

5. See, e.g., Josephus, *Jewish Antiquities* 17.172; *Jewish War* 1.657; Philo, *On Dreams* 2.58; Pliny, *Natural History* 23.39–40. This application of oil will be discussed in more detail in this chapter as well as in chap. 3.

6. See, e.g., Ralph P. Martin, *James*, WBC 48 (Dallas: Word, 1988), 206; Davids, *James*, 192.

churches (Acts 14:23; 15:2, 4, 6, 22, 23; 16:4; 20:17; 21:18; cf. 1 Pet. 5:1). Does James have a similar meaning in mind? This is a question we will have to take up in greater detail later (see chap. 6). In this chapter, however, we will look at data that indicates that early postbiblical Christians came to identify the "elders" with ordained ministers.

What Is the Significance of the Use of Oil?

As in Mark's description of the apostles' mission, James connects oil with healing. But why is oil itself important? To attribute to the oil itself healing power apart from God or faith would be superstitious.[7] Why should oil, then, be used? For James, the efficacy of anointing is ascribed first and foremost to "the Lord," in whose name it is performed. So, why use oil at all?

Oil was commonly used in the ancient world as a natural healing agent. For example, in the story of the good Samaritan, it is used to dress the wounds of the man left beaten by the side of the road (Luke 10:34). Nevertheless, being anointed with oil has additional resonances in Scripture. Among other things, it is associated with reception of God's Spirit. A powerful example of this is found in the scene of King David's royal anointing. When the prophet Samuel anoints David, we are told, "The Spirit of the LORD came mightily upon David" (1 Sam. 16:13). The connection between anointing and the power of the Spirit is also found in Isaiah: "The *Spirit of the Lord GOD* is upon me, because the LORD has *anointed* me" (Isa. 61:1).

The obvious question here is this: Are these traditions connecting oil to the Spirit somehow related to the practice of anointing the sick? Or is oil used in Mark 6 or James 5 simply as a kind of natural healing agent with no spiritual meaning intended? These are questions we will have to think through below.

In What Way Does Anointing Bring about Healing?

A final question raised by James's instructions is this: What connection is there between physical healing and forgiveness? The two ideas are frequently associated in Jewish and Christian literature. Among other places, in the canonical Gospels bodily healing and remission of sins are linked, perhaps most prominently in the Synoptic accounts of Jesus's healing of a paralytic (Matt. 9:2–8//Mark 2:1–12//Luke 5:17–26). Let us briefly review the story as it appears in Mark.

7. See CCC 2111.

A paralyzed man is brought to Jesus, and Jesus announces to him, "Child, your sins are forgiven" (Mark 2:5). Hearing this, the Jewish scribes are astonished. They think to themselves, "Why does this man speak in this way? He is blaspheming! Who can forgive sins except the one God?" (Mark 2:7). Jesus, knowing their thoughts (Mark 2:8), asks them, "Which is easier to say to the paralytic, 'Your sins are forgiven' or 'Rise, and pick up your stretcher, and go home'?" (Mark 2:9). Jesus then heals the man in order to demonstrate that "the Son of Man has authority on earth to forgive sins" (Mark 2:10). We will return to this story later, but for now we can simply highlight that the core of the story affirms that Jesus heals the man *in order to prove that he has forgiven a man's sins*. Physical healing is a sign of spiritual healing.

Still, questions remain about both the story of Jesus's healing and James 5. Why is physical healing connected with forgiveness of sins? Does forgiveness of sins bring about a cure of physical ailments? We will return to these matters later (chap. 5). In addition, another question can be asked about James 5: What does the passage mean when it says that the sick person will be "saved"? Is it simply speaking of physical well-being, or is it also referring to spiritual salvation? Again, we will consider this in greater detail below. Specifically, early Christians appear to have linked anointing to *both* physical and spiritual healing.

James 5 and Anointing the Sick in the Early Church

When we look at Christian tradition regarding anointing the sick, we find differences in the way the practice has been both celebrated and interpreted. Nevertheless, what cannot be disputed is this: from the earliest times, the practice of anointing the sick with oil was "catholic"—that is, "universal"—inasmuch as it was practiced by ancient Christians of both East and West.

Anointing and Forgiveness of Sins

It is not difficult to account for the fact that anointing the sick came to be associated with forgiveness of sins. Such an interpretation emerged directly from James's epistle. After all, James moves from ministering to the sick with oil to the concept of forgiveness of sins (James 5:13–16). Remarkably, our earliest source witnessing to the reception of James's directives specifically connects anointing to *spiritual* healing.

In the third century, the early Christian writer Origen quotes from James's directives for ministering to the sick. He explicitly interprets this passage as providing the basis for priests' ability to forgive sins.

> [The penitent] is not ashamed to make known his sin to the priest of the Lord and *to seek a cure* according to the one who says, "I said, 'I will proclaim to the Lord my injustice against myself,' and you forgave the impiety of my heart" [Ps. 31:5 LXX]. What the Apostle James said is fulfilled in this: "But if anyone is sick, let that person call the presbyters of the Church, and they will place their hands on him, anointing him with oil in the name of the Lord. And the prayer of faith will save the sick person, and if he is in sins, they will be forgiven him" [James 5:14–15].[8]

Origen makes a striking change to James's instructions, specifying that the presbyters will "place their hands on" the sick person rather than simply praying over the sick, as James describes. Is Origen speaking of a rite in which the sick are anointed, or does he know of a separate rite involving forgiveness of sins that he sees as having precedence in James's instructions? This is unclear.[9]

What is indisputable, however, is that Origen connects seeking a "cure" to the penitent's responsibility to "make known his sin to the priest"; the "cure" is found in oral confession of sins. Aside from the words from James, Origen speaks of no physical ailment. Instead, he moves from speaking of a "cure" to the psalmist's words about the Lord forgiving "the impiety of my heart." Whether Origen has any physical infirmity in mind here is not specifically stated. For our purposes, the upshot of Origen's statement is this: James's instructions about anointing and healing refer to something *more* than restoration of biological health.

Another source worth mentioning is the letter of Polycarp, which is even earlier than the passage from Origen, likely dating to the early part of the second century. Polycarp speaks of how the "elders" should "be compassionate . . . visiting all the sick."[10] Though Polycarp never mentions anointing the sick, one wonders if we nonetheless have here an allusion to James 5,

8. Origen, *Homilies on Leviticus* 2.4.5; translation from Origen, *Homilies on Leviticus 1–16*, trans. Gary Wayne Barkley, FC 83 (Washington, DC: Catholic University of America Press, 1990), 47–48.

9. Advocates for both positions can be found. See John J. Ziegler, *Let Them Anoint the Sick* (Collegeville, MN: Liturgical Press, 1987), 35.

10. Polycarp, *To the Philippians* 6:1, in Michael W. Holmes, *The Apostolic Fathers: Greek Texts and English Translations*, 3rd ed. (Grand Rapids: Baker Academic, 2007), 287 (modified).

which also assigns to the "elders" the task of attending to the sick. That James 5 informs Polycarp's description receives further support from the next line, which speaks of *forgiveness of sins*: "Therefore if we ask the Lord to forgive us, then we ourselves ought to forgive."[11] James 5 also moves from a description of the elders visiting the sick to forgiveness of sins. If James 5 is in the backdrop of Polycarp's words, it would seem to suggest that Polycarp—like Origen—gave special emphasis to the *spiritual* dimension of James 5.[12]

Some have suggested that the spiritual emphasis of sources like Polycarp and Origen emerged because miraculous physical healings receded from view. This theory, however, lacks supporting evidence.[13] While some in the early Church did seem to speak of a cessation of miraculous works, others adamantly rejected such a claim. Augustine directly rebuts the notion that miracles have ceased, insisting that "even now miracles are being worked in Christ's name, either through his sacraments or through the prayers or relics of his saints."[14] More to the point, there are no data to support the claim that views of anointing changed in response to perceptions that healings had failed to occur. To the contrary, throughout the centuries we find the use of oil linked to physical healing. Here we can give a few examples.

Anointing and Miraculous Healing

Writing in the 200s, the Latin writer Tertullian relates a story about a pagan named Severus who expressed gratitude to a Christian named Proculus who had "cured him by anointing."[15] Stories like these served as powerful witnesses against heretics like the Gnostics, who believed that the material world was inherently evil. Yet, notably, even the Gnostics were said to have used oil. In his famous work *Against Heresies*, Irenaeus (d. 202) reports that they had the practice of pouring oil out on a person's body at death, not in order to

11. Polycarp, *To the Philippians* 6:2, in Holmes, *Apostolic Fathers*, 289.

12. This evidence is overlooked by those who downplay the use of James 5 in connection with the early Christian practice of ministering to the sick. See, e.g., Joseph Martos, *Deconstructing Sacramental Theology and Reconstructing Catholic Ritual* (Eugene, OR: Wipf & Stock, 2015), 150.

13. Frederick W. Puller, *The Anointing of the Sick in Scripture and Tradition* (London: SPCK, 1904), 200–203.

14. Augustine, *City of God* 22.8; translation from Augustine, *The City of God*, trans. William Babcock, WSA I/7 (Hyde Park, NY: New City Press, 2012–13), 506. This represents a reversal from his earlier view (see Augustine, *On True Religion* 16.34).

15. Tertullian, *To Scapula* 4.

heal the body but to enable the soul to leave it behind.[16] Some have suggested that the Gnostics' use of oil at death was the result of a perversion of the practice described by James. Whereas orthodox Christians followed James in maintaining that anointing could be associated with bodily healing, the Gnostics may have adopted the practice of anointing to celebrate "escape" from the body.[17]

In the *Acts of Thomas*, a work that dates to the early 200s, we find oil used in connection with baptism.[18] However, there is an episode involving anointing a man's wife who "was not well in body" (*Acts of Thomas* 67).[19] She ends up being anointed with "the oil of life." The anointing is accompanied by a prayer: "Lord of all orders of creation . . . anoint [the deacon Xanthippius's] flock with your oil of life, and cleanse it of its disease." Later, the apostle speaks of "holy oil, which was given to us for unction," within the context of a prayer to Jesus that speaks of "life and health and remission of sins" (*Acts of Thomas* 121). A woman is then anointed while the apostle prays: "Heal her old wounds, and wash away from her sores, and strengthen her weakness" (*Acts of Thomas* 121). These stories, however, are not presented as liturgical acts related to the instructions in James 5.

That anointings were occurring in the West in liturgical contexts is evident from a document known as the *Apostolic Tradition*. The historical development of this work remains a complicated issue.[20] For our purposes, it is worth noting that we find in it a liturgical blessing over oil that can be dated to the fourth century. The prayer indicates that the oil is meant to be administered to the sick with the hope of bringing physical healing to them:

> O God, sanctify this oil: *grant health* to all who are anointed with it and who receive it, and as you anointed kings, priests, and prophets, so may

16. Irenaeus, *Against Heresies* 1.21.5.

17. See Cyprian Vagaggini, *Theological Dimensions of the Liturgy: A General Treatise on the Theology of the Liturgy*, trans. Leonard J. Doyle and W. A. Jurgens, rev. ed. (Collegeville, MN: Liturgical Press, 1976), 422; Paul F. Palmer, *Sacraments and Forgiveness: History and Doctrinal Development of Penance, Extreme Unction and Indulgences*, SCT 2 (Westminster, MD: Newman Press, 1959), 275.

18. See, e.g., *Acts of Thomas* 27.

19. On the dating of this work and the translation used here, see A. F. J. Klijn, *The Acts of Thomas: Introduction, Text, and Commentary*, 2nd rev. ed., NovTSup 108 (Leiden: Brill, 2003).

20. For a discussion of the text's development and provenance, see Paul F. Bradshaw, Maxwell E. Johnson, and L. Edward Phillips, *The Apostolic Tradition*, Hermeneia (Minneapolis: Fortress, 2002), 1–18.

> it *give strength* to all who consume it and *health* to all who are anointed with it.[21]

Note here that the prayer specifically connects the oil to that used to anoint kings, priests, and prophets. This will be important later in our study.

The *Sacramentary of Serapion*, a fourth-century Egyptian work, contains a more expansive prayer over holy oil. Though somewhat lengthy, it is worth quoting in full:

> We call upon you who have all authority and power, O Savior of all human beings, Father of our Lord and Savior Jesus Christ, and we ask you to send healing power from the heights of heaven, from the only Son, upon this oil in *order that it may remove all sickness and infirmity* far from those who are anointed with it . . . that it may serve them as an antidote against every demon; that it may expel every unclean spirit from them, banish every evil spirit, dispel every fever and chill and sickness; *that it may grant them good grace and forgiveness of sins*; that it may be for them *a remedy for life and salvation* and bring them health and integrity of soul, body, and spirit, a perfect constitution.[22]

This remarkable invocation indicates that oil was associated not only with bodily healing but also with spiritual benefits—namely, the reception of "good grace" and "forgiveness of sins."[23] Dale Allison notes that the Greek text includes phrases that mirror the language of James 5, making it the likely source text for the sacramentary's prayer.[24]

More evidence regarding early Christian beliefs about anointing the sick can be found in the works of John Chrysostom. Writing at the end of the fourth century, Chrysostom explicitly cites James 5:

21. *Apostolic Tradition* 5:2; translation from Hippolytus of Rome, *On the Apostolic Tradition*, trans. Alistair Stewart-Sykes, 2nd ed., PPS 54 (Yonkers, NY: St. Vladimir's Seminary Press, 2015), 90 (emphasis added).

22. Translation from Paul Meyendorff, *The Anointing of the Sick*, Orthodox Liturgy Series 1 (Crestwood, NY: St. Vladimir's Seminary Press, 2009), 35 (emphasis added). On the dating and provenance of this work, see Everett Ferguson, *Baptism in the Early Church: History, Theology, and Liturgy in the First Five Centuries* (Grand Rapids: Eerdmans, 2009), 460.

23. Puller argues that the references to "good grace" and "forgiveness of sins" are a later interpolation, though he lacks textual evidence (*Anointing of the Sick*, 95–100).

24. See Allison, *James*, 747–48. Allison doubts this is due to direct dependence but suggests the use of wider liturgical traditions that are also shaped by James, which he dates to the second century. The postulation of additional liturgical traditions seems far more speculative than simply accepting direct dependence in this case.

> God has given greater power to priests than to natural parents, not only for punishment, but also for help. . . . Parents bring us into this life; priests into the life to come. Parents cannot avert bodily death nor drive away the onset of disease; priests have often saved the soul that is sick and at the point of death, by making the punishment milder for some, and preventing others from ever incurring it, not only through instruction and warning, but also through helping them by prayer. They have the authority to remit sins, not only when they make us regenerate, but afterwards too. "Is any among you sick? . . ."[25]

Chrysostom goes on to quote the passage from James in full. What is notable here is that the ancient bishop evidently believes that James's teaching means ecclesial ministers have the power to bring about physical healing and forgiveness of sins. Chrysostom is not alone. Ambrose also appears to connect laying hands on the sick with the issue of forgiveness of sins.[26]

Writing in about 416, Pope Innocent I quotes James's instructions, adding:

> There is no doubt that this [James 5:13–16] ought to be received and understood as referring to the faithful who are ailing for they are able to be anointed with the holy oil of chrism, which has been made by the Bishop. In case of emergency, this anointing is permitted not only for priests but even for all Christians.[27]

The Church's ministry to the sick with oil was thus seen as fulfilling the instructions found in the Letter of James. It is worth mentioning that Innocent here seems to recognize that non-priests can administer sacred oil in "emergency" circumstances.[28]

In addition, a notable blessing over oil is found in a work known as the *Testament of Our Lord Jesus Christ*, which likely has its origin in the fourth

25. John Chrysostom, *On the Priesthood* 3.6; trans. Graham Neville, PPS (Crestwood, NY: St. Vladimir's Seminary Press, 1964), 74. Whether Chrysostom knew of separate rites for anointing the sick and penance is unknown. See Ziegler, *Let Them Anoint the Sick*, 35–36.

26. Ambrose, *On Repentance* 1.8.36. Ambrose seeks to underscore the inconsistency of the Novatians, who do not permit forgiveness of sins of the lapsed, though their own priests are understood to have the power to effect forgiveness of sins through baptism.

27. Innocent I, *Letter to Decentius* 8; translation from Connell, *Church and Worship*, 47. Connell examines other textual variants, explaining why the version quoted is to be preferred (*Church and Worship*, 48).

28. See Puller, *Anointing of the Sick*, 278. Notably, Caesarius of Arles (d. 543) moves from speaking of lay anointing to a quotation from James 5. However, it is not clear that he equates lay healings with James 5 strictly speaking. See Palmer, *Sacraments and Forgiveness*, 284–85.

Adam and Priestly Anointing

A fascinating tradition regarding the use of oil on the sick is found in *The Testament of Adam*, which can be dated sometime between the second and fifth centuries AD. In the second chapter, Adam details the way the different hours of the day are linked to important liturgical realities. We read: "At that hour [the tenth hour of the day] the waters are taken up and the priest of God mixes them with consecrated oil and *anoints those who are afflicted* and *they are restored and healed*."[a] These lines are recognized by scholars as reflecting early Christian practice and therefore suggest that such anointing was understood both as bringing about *physical healing* and *as the work of priests*.[b]

a. *Testament of Adam* 2:10, in *OTP* 1:993 (slightly revised and emphasis added).

b. See, e.g., John M. Scholer, *Proleptic Priests: Priesthood in the Epistle to the Hebrews*, JSNTSup 49 (Sheffield: JSOT Press, 1991), 27.

century.[29] The blessing is said to be for "oil for the healing of those who suffer." The prayer asks God to consecrate the oil so that "it may deliver those who are diseased, and [that] it may *heal the sick* and *sanctify* those who return, as they draw near to your faith." Here once again the oil is linked not only with the hope of healing of sickness but with a spiritual benefit—sanctification.

Likewise, in the sixth century, Caesarius of Arles urges the faithful not to trust in sorcerers for healing but to come to the Church to receive both the eucharist and sacred oil.

> How much more correct and salutary it would be to hurry to the church, to receive the body and blood of Christ, and with oil that is blessed to anoint in all faith themselves and their dear ones; for according to what James the Apostle says, *not only would they receive health of body, but also remission of sins*.[30]

29. See the introduction to Grant Sperry-White, trans., *The Testamentum Domini*, GLS 22 (Piscataway, NJ: Gorgias, 2010). The translation of the blessing is taken from this source, though I have added italics.

30. Caesarius of Arles, *Sermon* 279.5 (attributed to Augustine in PL 39:2273). Translation taken from Palmer, *Sacraments and Forgiveness*, 285 (emphasis added).

Caesarius goes on to quote directly from James 5 in the following lines. Once again, as with Pope Innocent, the possibility of lay anointing is mentioned. Nevertheless, the connection to the Church's ministers is clearly affirmed—even if the laity can administer the oil to others, it still must be blessed by the Church's ministers. What is especially notable is that Caesarius connects anointing to both physical and spiritual healing.[31]

The seventh-century writer Bede explicitly ties Mark 6 together with James 5. Commenting on James's instructions, Bede alludes to Mark 6, saying:

> We read in the Gospel that the apostles did this. And now the custom of the Church holds that those who are sick be anointed with consecrated oil by the presbyters, with the prayer that goes with this, *that they may be cured*. Not only presbyters, but, as Pope Innocent writes, even for all Christians it is lawful to use the same oil for anointing at their own necessity or that of their [relatives], but the oil may be consecrated only by the bishops.[32]

He then explains:

> Many persons on account of sins committed in the soul are struck with sickness or even death of the body. . . . If, therefore, the sick [have committed] sins and have confessed them to the presbyters of the Church and have sincerely tried to leave them behind and to amend, *these will be forgiven them*. But sins cannot be forgiven without a firm promise of amendment.

For Bede, then, we see that the practice of anointing the sick is understood to be rooted in both Mark 6 and James 5. Moreover, for Bede, anointing is indisputably linked to healing; specifically, it heals physical infirmities that are due to sin. This healing is not "magical" or "automatic." It can result only from genuine repentance that is expressed in sincere confession of sins and firm purpose of amendment. For Bede, physical and spiritual healing are both associated with anointing, which is in turn understood as continuing the apostolic practice as attested in the Gospel of Mark and the Letter of James. In addition, following Innocent, Bede acknowledges the possibility of being

31. A very similar quotation is found in the seventh-century writer Eligius of Noyon, *On Correctness of Catholic Conduct* 5 (PL 40:1172–73). See Palmer, *Sacraments and Forgiveness*, 285–86.

32. Translation here and below taken from Bede the Venerable, *Commentary on the Seven Catholic Epistles*, trans. Dom David Hurst (Kalamazoo, MI: Cistercian Publications, 1985), 61–62 (emphasis added).

anointed by a lay person, though this must be done with oil consecrated by the bishop. Forgiveness of sins through confession, however, is solely linked with priestly ministry.

Distinctions among Anointings and the Seven "Sacraments"

In the third-century work *Acts of Thomas*, Thomas instructs a nurse to continue to anoint a sick woman with the unction he has already used on her (*Acts of Thomas* 121). Various other texts report stories of holy men and women—often but not always lay monastics or ascetics—performing miraculous healings with oil. These include Pachomius (d. 292), disciples of Antony, Hilarion (d. 371), Symeon Stylites (d. 460), Geneviève of Paris (d. 502), and Austreberta, who was Abbess of Pauilly (d. 703).[33] The sources that relate these healing stories typically make no mention of James's instructions.[34] The ability of these figures to perform miracles, then, appears to have more to do with unique spiritual gifts for healing than the implementation of James's prescriptions. One thinks, for example, of Paul's affirmation that some believers are given the "spiritual gift" (*charisma*) of healing (1 Cor. 12:9, 28, 30).

As more emphasis was placed on unction's association with forgiveness of sins—a power especially seen as reserved to ordained clergy—there was also an increased emphasis on the importance of receiving anointing from an ordained priest. Stress was put on James's statement that anointing should be carried out by the "elders," a term that was understood as a reference to ordained ministers. The Council of Chalon II (813) thus produced the following canon: "According to the document of the Apostle James, with which the documents of the Fathers are also in agreement, *the sick ought to be anointed by presbyters* with oil which is blessed by the bishop."[35] James's reference to "elders" (*presbyteroi*) is explicitly interpreted as referring to clergy.

But what, then, of anointings performed by nonclergy? Theologians began making distinctions between different types of sacred anointings. Theodulf of Orléans (d. 821), for example, explains that while there are fifteen different

33. See Puller, *Anointing of the Sick*, 149–89; Thomas M. Izbicki, "Saint Geneviève and the Anointing of the Sick," *CHR* 104, no. 3 (2018): 393–414.

34. The *Penitential of Cummean* (seventh century) speaks only broadly of saints healing people in reference to James. See John T. McNeill and Helena M. Gamer, *Medieval Handbooks of Penance* (1938; repr., Cambridge: Cambridge University Press, 1990), 100. Whether this refers to lay saints is unclear.

35. Council of Chalon II, Canon 48; translation from Palmer, *Sacraments and Forgiveness*, 290–91.

Jerome on the Multifaceted Significance of Anointing

In a homily dated to sometime between AD 391 and 392, Jerome explains that the different kinds of anointing in Scripture have different meanings, all of which must be carefully understood. He uses this to call to mind the importance of properly reverencing sacramentals used by the Church, implicitly connecting the holy rites and objects used in the Church to the use of oil in the biblical traditions.

> We have read in Exodus the account of how oil is prepared for the anointing of the priest; we have read, too, of the different kind of balm used to anoint kings. There was still another unguent for prophets. What more is there to say? All these oils of unction were different, each with its own spiritual symbolism. Do we have the proper reverence for sacramentals (*de sanctis*)?[a]

a. Jerome, *Homily on Psalm* 132. Translation from Jerome, *The Homilies of Saint Jerome (1–59 on the Psalms)*, trans. Marie Liguori Ewald, FC 48 (Washington, DC: Catholic University of America Press, 1964), 334.

kinds of unctions, the apostles employed only three of those that had come to be known.[36] According to Theodulf, most anointings practiced by Christians were seen as unrelated to James's instructions.

Distinctions among the different ecclesial anointings were also made in connection with the development of the concept of sacraments. Here we cannot offer a detailed discussion of that history. Suffice it to say that, for centuries, Latin theologians simply adopted Augustine's definition of a sacrament: "Signs . . . are called sacraments when they are applied to divine things."[37] In other words, according to Augustine, a sacrament is essentially a visible sign of an *invisible* reality.[38] This was a rather broad definition, however. By 1131, following Augustine's terminology, Hugh of St. Victor would identify no fewer

36. Theodulf of Orléans, *Capitulare* 2 (PL 105:221). See Bernard Poschmann, *Penance and the Anointing of the Sick*, trans. Francis Courtney (New York: Herder & Herder, 1964), 247.

37. Augustine, *Letter* 138.7; translation from Augustine, *Letters: Volume 3 (131–164)*, trans. Wilfrid Parsons, FC 20 (Washington, DC: Catholic University of America Press, 1953), 40.

38. See Augustine, *City of God* 10.5. For further discussion of Augustine's views and their influence on later sacramental theology, see William A. Van Roo, *The Christian Sacrament*, Analecta Gregoriana (Rome: Editrice Pontificia Università Gregoriana, 1992), 38–43.

than thirty "sacraments"![39] These included not only baptism and the eucharist but other pious practices such as the use of holy water and the application of blessed salt. Hugh's interest in God's use of material realities to impart blessing was probably occasioned by the emergence of the Albigensians, a heretical group who, like the Gnostics of old, rejected the goodness of the material world.[40] Hugh was therefore driven to show the various ways God uses physical things in the economy of salvation.

The first to speak of seven principal sacraments was the twelfth-century theologian Peter Lombard, whose work *On the Sentences* became a focal point for medieval theological studies. Interestingly, Master Simon, a contemporary of Lombard, arrived at the same number of sacraments. From this time on—in both the West *and* the East—the enumeration of seven sacraments became standard. Importantly, both Lombard and Simon included anointing of the sick among the seven. In these writers' works, the sacrament of anointing was not connected to physical healing but was understood as preparation for death.[41] Indeed, Lombard is the theologian credited with dubbing the sacrament "extreme unction," signifying its connection with life's end.[42] This, however, opened the door for debate: How could James's teaching, which emphasizes physical healing, be viewed as a sacrament whose goal is preparation for death?

Debates over Anointing the Sick and Recent Developments

In his oft-cited study on the sacrament, Charles Gusmer writes, "One reason why so few theologians have attempted to write on the anointing of the sick is the uneven and complicated tradition of the sacrament."[43] Andrew Cuschieri likewise says, "The theology of the Anointing of the Sick is the least developed in comparison with that of other sacraments."[44] Due to frequent

39. See Hugh of St. Victor, *On the Sacraments of the Christian Faith*.

40. See Thomas M. Finn, "The Sacramental World in the *Sentences* of Peter Lombard," *TS* 69 (2008): 567.

41. See Palmer, *Sacraments and Forgiveness*, 298; Charles W. Gusmer, *And You Visited Me: Sacramental Ministry to the Sick and the Dying*, rev. ed., Studies in the Reformed Rites of the Church 6 (Collegeville, MN: Liturgical Press, 1989), 29.

42. For the development of this term, see Paul F. Palmer, "The Purpose of Anointing of the Sick: A Reappraisal," *TS* 19 (1958): 328–29.

43. Gusmer, *And You Visited Me*, 41.

44. Andrew Cuschieri, *Anointing of the Sick: A Theological and Canonical Study* (Lanham, MD: University Press of America, 1993), iii.

neglect of it, one writer has even referred to it as "the forgotten sacrament."[45] Here, to help lay the groundwork for the discussion in the rest of this book, I will briefly look at some of the major issues that have emerged in discussions of the sacrament.

Healing, Preparation for Death, or Both?

As we have seen, anointing of the sick has been viewed as having both physical and spiritual benefits, including physical healing and forgiveness of sins. But how are these different effects to be integrated? Over time, greater attention was given to the spiritual effects of the sacrament than to physical healing. Liturgical prayers accompanying administration of the sacrament eventually dropped references to hope for physical restoration.[46]

The emphasis on the sacrament's ability to remit sins also came with a significant side effect. Lest the faithful begin to take sin too lightly, it was believed that ecclesial practices involving the remission of sins should be limited.[47] It was common, then, for the sacrament of penance to be delayed until death.[48] By the eighth century, the use of holy unction on the sick was generally restricted in the West to those who were about to die. A theological dilemma began to emerge out of this. The sacrament had been traditionally anchored in the text of James, which speaks not of the death of the anointed person but of their healing. How could the sacrament involve a hope for healing if it was to serve as preparation for death?

Different explanations of the precise effects of the sacrament emerged; we cannot examine all of them here. The medieval thinker who would prove the most influential, however, is Thomas Aquinas (d. 1274). It is necessary briefly to consider his contribution to this debate. Thomas finds a way to connect the sacrament of unction to the possibility of physical healing, while *also* maintaining its ability to effect spiritual healing. His thought on this matter, however, seems to mature over time.

45. William J. Bausch, *A New Look at the Sacraments*, rev. ed. (Mystic, CT: Twenty-Third Publications, 1983), 202.

46. Joseph Martos, *Doors to the Sacred: A Historical Introduction to Sacraments in the Catholic Church* (Garden City, NY: Doubleday, 1981), 379; John F. Cheriavely, "25th Year of the Rite of Anointing of the Sick: Challenges and Perspectives," *Questions liturgiques* 78 (1997): 164–75.

47. See, e.g., Ambrose, *On Penance* 2.10.95 (*NPNF*^{2} 10:357).

48. See Palmer, *Sacraments and Forgiveness*, 118.

In his *Summa Contra Gentiles*, Aquinas explains that sins can affect not only the soul but the body as well. In addition, he explains that in some cases physical ailments can be borne in such a way that they are penitential. Still, he maintains that physical illness can also become an obstacle to virtue. Quoting James 5, Thomas argues it was therefore fitting for there to be a remedy for sicknesses that are due to sin:

> Bodily infirmity is sometimes a hindrance to the health of the soul insofar as it is an obstacle to virtue. It was therefore fitting that a spiritual remedy should be applied against sin, insofar as sin is an occasion of bodily infirmity, and sometimes this remedy heals the bodily ailment (that is to say, when it is good for the soul's health).[49]

In this, Thomas affirms that the sacrament can involve physical healing.

Nevertheless, Thomas goes on to note that the sacrament of unction will not always bring about a physical cure—after all, at some point, all die. Yet, even in cases where physical healing does not occur, Aquinas insists that the sacrament still provides a spiritual form of healing—*it heals through forgiveness of sins*. This raises an obvious question. With other medieval thinkers, Thomas affirms the existence of a sacrament specifically ordered to the forgiveness of sins—namely, the sacrament of penance. Why would *another* sacrament involving the forgiveness of sins be needed if the Church already celebrates the sacrament of penance? In his answer to this question, Thomas notes that people cannot be fully aware of *all* the sins they have committed over the course of a lifetime. Extreme unction, he says, serves to address these forgotten sins.[50]

Thomas writes again of the sacrament of unction later in his *Summa Theologiae*. Sadly, he died before he could write the question specifically devoted to the sacrament of unction. The only place where he treats the sacrament in this work is in his general discussion of the seven sacraments.[51] Here Thomas observes that an analogy can be made between spiritual and physical health. In regard to the latter, health is restored in stages: (1) one is cured of sickness; (2) after one is cured of an infirmity, the person must regain their vigor. Penance

49. Thomas Aquinas, *Summa Contra Gentiles* 4.73. Translation from Thomas Aquinas, *Summa Contra Gentiles, Books III–IV*, trans. Laurence Shapcote, Latin/English Edition of the Works of St. Thomas Aquinas 12 (Green Bay, WI: The Aquinas Institute for the Study of Sacred Doctrine, 2018), 507.

50. Thomas Aquinas, *Summa Contra Gentiles* 4.73.

51. Thomas Aquinas, *Summa Theologiae* III, q. 65, art. 1.

is compared to the first stage, while unction is identified with the second. While theologians will sometimes claim that Thomas deliberately moves away from his earlier position,[52] caution is required. It might be that, as with his treatment of other sacraments, Thomas offered different but complementary models for understanding unction.[53] Had Thomas lived to write a section specifically focused on the sacrament, he might have said something closer to what is found in the *Summa Contra Gentiles*.

There is, however, a question dedicated to the sacrament of unction in the Supplement to the *Summa Theologiae*, a section of the work that was completed not by Thomas himself but by his students. The treatment on unction draws entirely from Thomas's earlier treatment in the *Commentary on the Sentences* and so predates the material in the *Summa Contra Gentiles*. It maintains that the sacrament of anointing is a remedy for the "remains" of sin.[54] This might be taken as a reference to the residual effects of sin, understood as inclinations to sin. There is also evidence, however, that the "remains of sin" refers to physical infirmities that result from sin. In the Supplement, we are told that since the infirmities of children "are not caused by actual sin, as in adults," the sacrament of unction "does not apply to children." These infirmities are expressly identified as "remnants of sin" (*peccati reliquiae*). This parallels Thomas's teaching in the *Summa Contra Gentiles* that physical ailments can be due to sin in adults and that it is these that constitute the "remains of sin" that are addressed through unction.[55]

Thomas's teaching on the sacraments in general and on extreme unction in particular shaped the decrees of later Church councils.[56] The official decree

52. See John F. Boyle, "Saint Thomas Aquinas on the Anointing of the Sick (Extreme Unction)," in *Recovering Aquinas and the Sacraments: Studies in Sacramental Theology*, ed. Matthew Levering and Michael Dauphinais (Chicago: Hillenbrand Books, 2009), 76–84.

53. For example, in his general treatment of the sacraments in the *Summa Theologiae*, Thomas explains that the sacrament of confirmation can be related to strength due to maturity (III, q. 65, art. 1). Later, however, he insists that this analogy should not be pressed too far, arguing that spiritual strength need not correspond to physical age (III, q. 72, art. 8). He goes on to liken the sacrament to the mark received by a soldier (III, q. 72, art. 9).

54. For what follows, see Thomas Aquinas, *Summa Theologiae*, Supplement, q. 32, art. 4.

55. Notably, elsewhere Thomas affirms that "often bodily diseases are caused by spiritual sins." *Commentary on the Gospel of Matthew* 715; translation from Thomas Aquinas, *Commentary on the Gospel of Matthew, Chapters 1–12*, trans. Jeremy Holmes and Beth Mortensen, Latin/English Edition of the Works of St. Thomas Aquinas 33 (Lander, WY: The Aquinas Institute for the Study of Sacred Doctrine, 2013), 263.

56. See John C. Kasza, *Understanding Sacramental Healing: Anointing and Viaticum* (Chicago: Hillenbrand Books, 2007), 51–52; Romanus Cessario, *The Seven Sacraments of the Catholic Church* (Grand Rapids: Baker Academic, 2023), 133–34.

on unction from the Council of Florence (1441–49) affirms that James 5 refers to the sacrament. It maintains the sacrament's capacity to bring both spiritual and physical restoration, saying that the effect of the sacrament is "to cure the mind and, in so far as it helps the soul, also the body."[57] Nevertheless, by the sixteenth century, theologians in the West were downplaying the sacrament's connection to physical healing and emphasizing its role as preparation for death. This set the stage for controversy. Enter the Protestant Reformers.

The Protestant Reformation and the Catholic Response

In his work *On the Babylonian Captivity of the Church*, Martin Luther argues that James links unction to the restoration of physical health.[58] This, the former monk argues, is at odds with the theology of the sacrament of anointing, which—especially in his day—was understood primarily as final preparation for death. Moreover, he makes the case that James connects healing and forgiveness of sins not to the oil but to the prayer of faith.[59]

Other Protestant writers followed Luther's critique. In his writings, John Calvin agrees with Luther that the miraculous healing power of oil was limited to the New Testament period. Calvin even goes as far as calling the Catholic practice of anointing the sick "play acting."[60] Catholic theologians had to consider how to respond to Protestant objections. Different approaches were taken.

The great commentator on Thomas Aquinas's work, Thomas de Vio "Cajetan" (d. 1534), comes to a surprising conclusion. Contrary to what earlier theologians had held, Cajetan argues that James's instructions should *not* be seen as describing the sacrament of holy unction at all. He agrees with Luther that, for James, anointing is primarily aimed at physical healing. Cajetan concedes that the sacrament of extreme unction is *not* about the restoration of bodily health. Instead, he explains, its goal is preparation for death.[61]

57. Council of Florence, Session 8, Bull of Union with the Armenians (November 22, 1439); translation from Norman Tanner, ed., *The Decrees of the Ecumenical Councils*, 2 vols. (Washington, DC: Georgetown University Press, 1990), 1:549.

58. Martin Luther, *On the Babylonian Captivity of the Church*, in *Luther's Works*, vol. 36, trans. A. T. W Steinhäuser, F. C. Ahrens, and A. R. Wentz (Philadelphia: Fortress, 1959), 118–19.

59. Luther, *On the Babylonian Captivity*, 121.

60. John Calvin, *Institutes of the Christian Religion* 4.18, ed. John T. McNeill, trans. Ford Lewis Battles, 2 vols. (Philadelphia: Westminster, 1960), 1466.

61. Thomas Cajetan, *Commentary on James* 370b.

Other Catholic theologians of the time, including some of those gathered as consultants to the Council of Trent, would follow Cajetan.[62]

The Council of Trent's teaching on the sacrament's relationship to Mark 6 and James 5 ends up being carefully nuanced. Trent maintains that the sacrament of anointing is "insinuated" in Mark 6 but "promulgated" by the Letter of James.[63] Moreover, contrary to Cajetan, Trent's teaching recognizes *various* effects of the sacrament. The council affirms that the reality of the sacrament consists of

> the grace of the Spirit, whose anointing takes away sins, if there are any still to be expiated, and the remains of sin [*reliquiae peccati*], and comforts and strengthens the soul of the sick person, by arousing in him great trust in the divine mercy; supported by this the sick person bears more lightly the inconveniences and trials of his illness, and resists more easily the temptations of the devil who lies in wait for his heel [Gen. 3:15]; and sometimes he regains bodily health when it is expedient for the salvation of his soul.[64]

We can note that Trent affirms that the sacrament can bring physical healing, though this is mentioned only at the end and is carefully qualified—physical restoration occurs only "sometimes" and only in cases "when it is expedient for the salvation of his soul." Nevertheless, given the earlier debates, it is remarkable that Trent affirms that the sacrament can have *both* spiritual and physical effects.

Moreover, Trent's use of the language of the "remains of sin" in connection with unction would become a focal point for later theological debates. Trent never specifically explains the precise meaning of the phrase. Theologians would subsequently engage in debates about its meaning.[65] The controversy became so heated that Benedict XIV (d. 1758) eventually intervened with a cease-and-desist order, stating that the nuances insisted upon by theologians had become so fine they were no longer helpful.[66]

62. See Ziegler, *Let Them Anoint the Sick*, 134–43.

63. Council of Trent, Session 4, Chapter 9.1.

64. Council of Trent, Session 14, Chapter 2; translation from Tanner, *Decrees of the Ecumenical Councils*, 2:710.

65. Stanislaus J. Brzana, *Remains of Sin and Extreme Unction according to Theologians after Trent* (Rome: Catholic Book Agency, 1953).

66. See James L. Empereur, *Prophetic Anointing: God's Call to the Sick, the Elderly, and the Dying* (Wilmington, DE: Michael Glazier, 1982), 71; Poschmann, *Penance and the Anointing of the Sick*, 254. By making a plenary indulgence available to the dying, Benedict XIV helped to

Developments in the Theology of Anointing and Ongoing Questions

The Second Vatican Council (1962–65) marked a landmark moment in the development of Catholic theology.[67] Leading up to the council, there was much discussion about how trends in theological studies could enrich the Church's view of the sacraments.[68] As with other areas of doctrine, the council's teaching on the sacrament of unction involved some aspects that should be recognized as genuine developments of doctrine.

First, while the council's constitution on sacred liturgy still refers to "Extreme Unction," it nevertheless holds that the sacrament is "more fittingly" called "Anointing of the Sick."[69] In addition, we are told that it is "not a sacrament intended only for those who are at the point of death."[70] The sacrament is not to be administered to those with only minor sicknesses, but it is also not to be withheld until the sick person is on the brink of death. The latter had become the norm; the council fathers, however, wanted to emphasize that the sacrament should, if at all possible, be given to those who could be conscious of receiving it.

The council also offers biblical support for the sacrament. While the James 5 passage is cited, what is especially remarkable is that the sacrament is tied to New Testament passages that speak in different ways about the believer's participation in Christ's suffering.

> By the sacred Anointing of the Sick and the prayer of the priests, the whole Church commends those who are ill to the suffering and glorified Lord that he may give them relief and save them (see James 5:13–16). And indeed, she exhorts them to contribute to the good of the people of God by freely uniting

make the debate unnecessary by providing a way to deal with both sins and the effects of sins. On the question of the relationship between the "remains of sin" and temporal punishment, see Brzana, *Remains of Sin*, 110–11.

67. See, e.g., the comments by Richard R. Gaillardetz, "Preface," in *The Cambridge Companion to Vatican II*, ed. Richard R. Gaillardetz (Cambridge: Cambridge University Press, 2020), xv.

68. See Bernard Leeming, "Recent Trends in Sacramental Theology," *ITQ* 23 (1956): 195–217.

69. Second Vatican Council, *Sacrosanctum Concilium* (The Holy Council), Constitution on the Sacred Liturgy (December 4, 1963), §73; translation from Austin Flannery, *Vatican Council II: The Basic Sixteen Documents, Constitutions, Decrees, Declarations*, rev. ed. (Collegeville, MN: Liturgical Press, 2014), 141. This follows a trajectory from Pius XII, who spoke of the sacrament as "sacram infirmorum unctionem." See Pius XII, *Mystici Corporis* (The Mystical Body), Encyclical on the Mystical Body of Christ (June 29, 1943), §19.

70. Second Vatican Council, *Sacrosanctum Concilium* §73, in Flannery, *Vatican Council II*, 141.

> themselves to the passion and death of Christ (see Rom. 8:17; Col. 1:24; 2 Tim. 2:11–12; 1 Pet. 4:13).[71]

This christological emphasis on the sick person's union with the suffering and glorified Lord is a very important development in official magisterial teaching about the sacrament.[72] *No previous ecclesiastical definition of the sacrament included citations of biblical texts that speak of participation in Christ's suffering.*

In one sense, the teaching on the sacrament at the Second Vatican Council reiterates what was taught by previous councils. Like other magisterial decrees, it roots the sacrament in James 5. Anointing is said to be for the purpose of asking the Lord to "save" the sick. At the same time, the council's teaching on the sacrament of anointing of the sick represents an enrichment of the Church's understanding. Not only does the sacrament involve a petition that the sick be "saved," it also indicates that through it the sick are able somehow to "contribute" to the body of Christ by "uniting themselves to the passion and death of Christ." On one level, this sounds like previous Church documents; the sacrament is seen as a preparation for death. Yet here we find something more.

At the end of the paragraph cited above, we find references to four biblical texts. Let us take a preliminary look at them.

> [We are] heirs of God and fellow heirs with Christ, if indeed we suffer together with him so that we may also be glorified together with him. (Rom. 8:17)

> Now I rejoice in my sufferings for you, and I fill up in my flesh what is lacking of the afflictions of Christ for his body, which is the church. (Col. 1:24)

> This word is trustworthy: For if we died with him, we will also live with him. (2 Tim. 2:11)

> But rejoice insofar as you share in the sufferings of Christ, so that at the revelation of his glory you may also rejoice. (1 Pet. 4:13)

71. Second Vatican Council, *Lumen gentium* (The Light of the Nations), Dogmatic Constitution on the Church (November 21, 1964), §11; slightly adapted from Flannery, *Vatican Council II*, 15–16.

72. The emphasis on the christological nature of the sacraments has been a feature of recent magisterial Catholic teaching. See Dominic Langevin, *From Passion to Paschal Mystery: A Recent Magisterial Development concerning the Christological Foundation of the Sacraments* (Fribourg: Academic Press Fribourg, 2015).

Note first that all of the verses cited in some way speak of the believer's union with Christ. In addition, the passages from Romans, 2 Timothy, and 1 Peter all appear to indicate that sharing in Christ's glory is in some way contingent on suffering with him. How can this be? Is not salvation based on God's free gift of grace? What is more, the passage from Colossians appears even more mysterious. How can Paul be described as indicating that his sufferings are "for you"? Is not Christ himself the redeemer? How could it be that Paul's suffering redounds for the benefit of the Church? Most important for our conversation, how does any of this relate to being anointed with oil? All of this will be discussed below.

Since Vatican II, further insight into the nature of the sacrament has been offered in two important ecclesiastical documents—namely, the reformed rite of the sacrament and the *Catechism of the Catholic Church*. Nonetheless, as John Kasza observes, anointing of the sick continues to be "one of the least understood of the sacraments."[73] In part, confusion over the nature of the sacrament can be traced to broader trends in theological research. Theologians have often sought to reframe sacramental theology altogether.[74]

Instead of offering a full overview of contemporary discussions that would inevitably tax the reader,[75] let us simply make the following observation: many of the core questions that emerge in contemporary treatments of the sacrament of the anointing of the sick take us back to the issues involved with interpreting James's instructions raised at the beginning of this chapter.

First, *what is the significance of the use of oil?* Since the Protestant Reformation, this question has remained a major issue in ecumenical conversations. Is the use of oil merely symbolic, or is the oil instrumental to the healing?

Second, *who are the proper recipients and ministers of anointing?* If the sacrament of unction is best viewed as Vatican II has taught—namely, as "anointing of the sick" rather than simply a sacrament for the dying—who should receive it? How sick need someone be to qualify for it? What about young children? Significantly, there is a discrepancy in Catholic practice on

73. John C. Kasza, "Anointing of the Sick," in *The Oxford Handbook of Sacramental Theology*, ed. Hans Boersma and Matthew Levering (Oxford: Oxford University Press, 2005), 558.

74. See, e.g., Godfried Danneels, "Current Challenges for Sacramental Theology," *Antiphon* 5, no. 2 (2000): 44–45; David N. Power, Regis Duffy, and Kevin Irwin, "Sacramental Theology: A Review of Literature," *TS* 55 (1994): 657–705.

75. See the excellent treatment in Matthew Levering, *Dying and the Virtues* (Grand Rapids: Eerdmans, 2018), 135–47.

this matter. In the Latin Rite, which encompasses most Catholics in the West, only those who have attained the age of reason may receive the sacrament.[76] There is no such restriction, however, in the *Code of Canon Law for Eastern Churches*. Catholics belonging to Eastern rites, therefore, can and do administer the sacrament of anointing to young children. In addition, who are the proper ministers of this sacrament? If lay people performed anointings with oil in the past, should not the laity be permitted to administer the sacrament of anointing of the sick today? The Council of Trent specified that only ordained ministers could administer the sacrament. It has been argued, however, that Trent's ruling was not a matter of doctrine but a response to the Protestant Reformers' rejection of the Church's authority to regulate the practice of the sacrament. In other words, this view holds that Trent's teaching should be understood as a response to the denial of the Church's *juridical* authority over the administration of the sacraments and not as a solemn definition about the *nature* of the sacrament itself.[77]

Third, *how are the physical and spiritual effects of the sacraments related?* Vatican II views the sacrament in terms of participation in Christ's passion and resurrection. Yet how is this dimension of anointing of the sick to be integrated with the sacrament's identity as a "sacrament of healing"?[78] Furthermore, while sacramental theologians have long identified the visible aspect of the sacrament (the *sacramentum tantum*) with oil and the invisible reality of the sacrament (the *res tantum*) as spiritual strengthening and healing from sin and its effects, what can be said about the third dimension of the sacrament, the abiding dimension of the sacrament (the *res et sacramentum*)? This dimension has remained a matter of speculation in theological works on the sacrament of anointing of the sick.

Since "the study of the sacred page" must be "the very soul of sacred theology,"[79] to address the theological questions effectively we must pay closer attention to the biblical text. This does not simply mean looking at the passages from Mark 6 and James 5. Here we must also pay attention to the biblical traditions that inform the relevant New Testament passages. Theological discussions about the sacrament have been woefully thin on the biblical

76. *CIC* 1004.

77. This interpretation is advanced by Ziegler, *Let Them Anoint the Sick*, especially 22–25, 144–53.

78. A designation for this sacrament found in CCC 1421.

79. Second Vatican Council, *Dei Verbum* (The Word of God), Dogmatic Constitution on Divine Revelation (November 18, 1965), §24, in Flannery, *Vatican Council II*, 113.

data, often implying that exegetical discussions need no more than a chapter to cover the issues responsibly. This, I believe, is why there has been such little theological discussion on the sacrament of anointing of the sick. To begin with, let us look more carefully at the passage that has usually been understood as the central passage for the sacrament: James's prescription. James prescribes not only that the sick be anointed with oil but that they be anointed "in the name of the Lord" (James 5:14). Here James draws deeply from Israel's scriptures.

3

The Lord of Life and the Significance of Oil

Christ as the Source of Healing

> You anoint my head with oil,
> my cup overflows.
> —Psalm 23:5

> Anoint yourself with blessed ointment of incorruptibility.
> —*Joseph and Aseneth* 15:4[1]

As we have seen, the Letter of James calls for elders to come and "pray over" the sick and anoint them "in *the name of the Lord*" (James 5:14). James adds: "And the prayer of faith will save the one who is sick, and *the Lord* will raise him up" (5:15). In all of this we see that the oil and the elders' prayer are not the ultimate source of healing. For James, the healing power of the anointing involves something more than mere folk medicine. The sick person is "raised up" due to the power of the "Lord." James's text and the practice of anointing itself turn our attention to the God of Israel. What "saves" is not the oil but

1. Translation from *OTP* 2:226.

the Lord, who is somehow working through the anointing. This conviction, then, must remain central to any theology of the sacrament.

In using the language of anointing the sick "in the name of the Lord," James is drawing on Jewish traditions. While the nations worship many different gods, the scriptures explain that Israel is to trust in one—the LORD. In Scripture, the LORD is uniquely worthy of trust. Israel's LORD is the creator of the cosmos, the sustainer and savior of life. The LORD also ensures human flourishing. This dimension of the identity of Israel's God is especially linked to the provision of oil, which is often described as a sign of God's care and the Lord's gift of strengthening. These beliefs are central for the New Testament authors, who proclaim Jesus as the "Lord." Moreover, when the Letter of James instructs believers to anoint the sick "in the name of the Lord," these traditions are in the background.

The LORD as the Life-Giving God

In the book of Exodus we find the famous list of commands known as the Ten Commandments. They begin: "I am the LORD your God, who brought you out of the land of Egypt. . . . You shall have no other gods before me" (Exod. 20:2–3). The passage makes a vitally important point: Israel's redeemer is not just any deity; Israel's God is "the LORD." In the scriptures, Israel's LORD is revealed to be the Creator God, the true sustainer and savior of life.

Israel's One LORD

The revelation of God's holy name occurs early in the book of Exodus. At the burning bush, God tells Moses:

> This is what you shall say to the Israelites: "The LORD, the God of your fathers, the God of Abraham, the God of Isaac, and the God of Jacob, has sent me to you." This is my name forever, and this is my title for all generations. (Exod. 3:15)

It is important here to understand why English Bibles put the word "LORD" in small capital letters. In the original Hebrew, which does not use vowels, God's name is given as four Hebrew letters. Transliterated into English, these letters are usually given as "YHWH." Out of reverence for God's holiness, ancient Jews developed the practice of refraining from pronouncing the divine name.[2] This helped to ensure that Israel would keep God's commandment, "You shall not take the name of YHWH your God in vain" (Exod. 20:7). Over time, then, the Hebrew word for "Lord," *Adonai*, was used as a substitute for the divine name.[3]

Early evidence for this practice can be found in the Dead Sea Scrolls.[4] By the first century BC, we find evidence that Jewish authors who wrote in Greek used the Greek term for "Lord," *kyrios*, as a substitute for the divine name. This convention is found throughout the Septuagint (abbreviated as "LXX"), the ancient Greek version of the Old Testament. English Bibles today continue this tradition. In passages where the Hebrew text has "YHWH," most English Bibles have "LORD." Therefore, the commandment against taking the divine name in vain is usually translated: "You shall not take the name of the *LORD* your God in vain" (Exod. 20:7).

The books of the Bible refer to the names of other gods, such as Baal (Judg. 6:25), Chemosh (Judg. 11:24), and Molech (1 Kings 11:7). In some texts, there are references to the belief that there was a divine council of sorts (Ps. 82:1). However one accounts for the historical development of popular beliefs about God among the people of Israel,[5] what matters for our discussion here is this: various scriptures indicate that YHWH is the one God to be worshiped. For example, in Psalm 95, Israel's God is described as "a great King above all the gods" (Ps. 95:3). In the Greek version of Deuteronomy, the other gods are told to "worship" (*proskyneō*) the LORD (Deut. 32:43). Other deities are said to be "false gods" (Ps. 40:4). In some texts, they are even identified as "demons" (Deut. 32:17; Ps. 106:37; Bar. 4:7; cf. 1 Cor. 10:19–20).

Most famously, Israel's faith in one LORD is proclaimed in a passage in Deuteronomy that became central to the daily Jewish prayer, the *Shema* (in Hebrew, "Hear"): "Hear, O Israel: The LORD is our God, *the LORD is one*" (Deut. 6:4). The prayer is meant to emphasize that Israel is to have one God: YHWH, "the LORD." This idea is emphasized in numerous other passages (e.g., Deut. 4:39;

2. See Josephus, *Jewish Antiquities* 2.275–76; Philo, *On the Life of Moses* 2.114; *Mishnah Sotah* 7:5–6.

3. For a helpful reflection on the meaning of the divine name, see Thomas Joseph White, *Exodus*, BTCB (Grand Rapids: Brazos, 2016), 39–44.

4. See Sean M. McDonough, *Yhwh at Patmos: Rev 1:4 in Its Hellenistic and Early Jewish Setting*, WUNT 2/107 (Tübingen: Mohr Siebeck, 1999), 74.

5. The biblical texts themselves frequently refer to the fact that people in Israel—even, at times, what seems to be a majority of the nation—fall into sins of idolatry and worship other gods (e.g., 1 Kings 14:9; 2 Kings 17:7; 22:17; 1 Chron. 5:25; 2 Chron. 11:15; 13:8–12; 28:23–25; 33:15; 34:25; Isa. 42:17; Jer. 1:16; 2:11; Hosea 3:1).

2 Kings 19:15; 1 Chron. 17:20). But what makes the LORD so unique? Among other things, according to the scriptures, Israel's God is the Creator God.

Israel's LORD as the Creator God

In the scriptures the name YHWH is specifically bound up with the God of Israel's identity as Creator. In Genesis, YHWH is shown to be the Creator God, the maker of humanity: "The LORD God made the earth and the heavens. . . . Then the LORD God formed the man of dust from the ground and breathed into his nostrils the breath of life" (Gen. 2:4, 7). Likewise, the identity of YHWH as the maker of heaven and earth is emphasized in the book of Isaiah:

> For thus says the *LORD*,
> *who created the heavens*,
> he is God,
> *who formed the earth and made it.*
> *He established it*;
> he did not create it empty
> —*he formed it* to be inhabited.
> I am the LORD, and *there is none beside me*. (Isa. 45:18)[6]

All creation belongs to Israel's God, since YHWH is the Creator. The language of the LORD not creating the earth "empty" (*tohu*) likely evokes Genesis 1. Isaiah's text uses the same term found in Genesis 1:2: "The earth was *without form* [*tohu*] and void."[7] The teaching of Deuteronomy 10:14—"For to the LORD your God belong heaven and the heaven of heavens, the earth with all that is in it"—is affirmed in the Psalms (Pss. 24:1; 50:10–12; etc.).

The LORD as the Savior and Sustainer of Life

For Israel, YHWH is not merely the one who first fashioned the world but also the one who sustains, upholds, and saves lives. This idea is expressed in countless ways. Consider the following passages:

6. See also Isa. 44:24: "I am the *LORD*, *who made all things*, who spread out the heavens *alone*, who spread out the earth—*who was with me*?" The question here is a rhetorical one; when YHWH asks, "Who was with me?" the implied answer is, "No one." This is clarified in Isa. 45:18: the LORD created all things with no one by his side.

7. See Klaus Baltzer, *Deutero-Isaiah*, trans. Margaret Kohl, Hermeneia (Minneapolis: Fortress, 2001), 246.

Who among all these does not know
that the hand of the LORD has done this?
In his hand is the life of every living thing
and the breath of all human flesh. (Job 12:9–10)

You *save* humans and animals alike, O LORD.
. . . For with you is the fountain of life. (Ps. 36:6, 9)

I lie down and sleep,
I wake up again, for *the* LORD *sustains me*. (Ps. 3:5)

All of these passages emphasize the same essential idea: the LORD is the source of life. Ecclesiastes thus speaks of "the life God gives us" (Eccles. 5:18; cf. 8:15). Life comes from Israel's God. In 2 Maccabees, Israel's God is referred to as "the Lord of life" (2 Macc. 14:46).

The scriptures therefore explain that one should turn to YHWH for help when life is threatened. In the Psalms, the LORD is presented as the "Savior."

Turn, O LORD, *rescue my life*;
save me for the sake of your steadfast love. (Ps. 6:4)

But you, O LORD, do not be far off!
O you my help, come quickly to my aid!
Deliver my life from the sword,
my only life from the power of the dogs!
Save me from the mouth of the lion! (Ps. 22:19–21a)

Israel's God is the one who saves and preserves life. This idea is echoed in other biblical traditions outside of the Psalter (1 Kings 1:29; 2 Kings 14:27; 2 Chron. 20:9; etc.).

The LORD's faithfulness in preserving life is especially evident in the exodus story, where God saves the people of Israel from slavery and then continues to nourish them in the wilderness. Looking back on this part of Israel's past, the book of Nehemiah recalls, "Forty years you provided for them in the desert, and they lacked nothing. Their clothes did not wear out and their feet did not become swollen" (Neh. 9:21). God not only protects the people but does so in miraculous and extravagant ways.

Moreover, YHWH does not simply provide the necessities of life but is said to bring *fullness* of life. For instance, the giving of the manna to Israel in the wilderness is seen as a sign of God's gracious care for Israel. In Wisdom of Solomon, the manna is contrasted with ordinary crops of the unrighteous land:

> Instead of these things you fed your people *food of angels*,
> and without their toil you gave them bread from heaven ready to eat,
> providing every pleasure and suited to every taste. (Wis. 16:20)

The manna is understood to be the "food of angels" (in Jerome's Latin Vulgate, *panis angelicus*). It is no ordinary bread. It contained "every pleasure" and was somehow "suited to every taste." Later Jewish and Christian interpreters would explain that the bread would taste however one wished, like "the taste of fish, the taste of locusts, the taste of all the delicacies in the world."[8] All of this emphasizes the LORD's extravagant provision for Israel.

God's abundant goodness is stressed in other biblical books. For instance, the psalmist declares that the LORD shows "the path of life" and that the LORD's way leads to "fullness of joy" and "pleasures forever" (Ps. 16:11). Likewise, in Ezekiel, the LORD reminds the people of Jerusalem, "*I made you flourish* like a plant of the field" (Ezek. 16:7). Closer to the time of the New Testament, the book of Sirach, which was written between 185 and 175 BC,[9] says, "The blessing of the Lord is in the wage of the pious, and *God quickly causes his blessing to flourish*" (Sir. 11:22). The LORD is the source of rich blessings, which causes Israel to flourish.

The LORD and the "Oil of Gladness"

The LORD's identity as the giver and sustainer of life is not merely understood in an abstract way in the scriptures. For our purposes, it is worth noting that *God's abundant provision is often connected to the gift of oil*, which was understood as having numerous applications, including basic sustenance. Oil

8. *Mekilta de-Rabbi Ishmael*, Amalek 3 (*Mekilta de-Rabbi Ishmael*, ed. and trans. Jacob Z. Lauterbach, 3 vols. [Philadelphia: Jewish Publication Society of America, 1933], 2:174); see also Ephrem, *Commentary on Exodus* 16:3.

9. See, e.g., A. Jordan Schmidt, *Wisdom, Cosmos, and Cultus in the Book of Sirach*, Deuterocanonical and Cognate Studies 42 (Berlin: De Gruyter, 2019), 5.

thus serves as a fitting and powerful image of the LORD's role as the source and maintainer of life.

Oil in the Ancient World

Oil was seen as necessary for subsistence in the ancient world. Sirach refers to oil as "basic to all the needs of human life" with other elements, such as water, fire, iron, salt, flour, milk, honey, and clothing (Sir. 39:26). Here it is important to understand what "oil" in the Bible refers to—that is, what physical substances are in view.

The single English word "oil" is used to translate different Hebrew terms. Typically, when English translations of Old Testament books use the word "oil," it is rendering the Hebrew term *shemen*. This type of oil represented an essential ingredient in the diet of ancient peoples. Cakes of flour made with oil were inexpensive to make and therefore served as the basic meal eaten by ordinary people (Num. 11:8). This, for example, was the only food item the poor widow at Zarephath could afford (1 Kings 17:12–13). When Leviticus makes exceptions for the poor to bring sacrifice, it is understood that even they can bring offerings with oil (Lev. 14:21). When Sirach speaks of oil being among life's necessities, *shemen* is what the author has in mind.

Because oil was necessary for sustenance, it is closely tied to health and vitality in various biblical passages. The psalmist speaks of the way oil (*shemen*) causes one's face to "shine," going on to speak of how "bread" is given "to strengthen the human heart" (Ps. 104:15). This same sort of oil was also used for medicinal purposes (Isa. 1:6). As we have already mentioned, this application of oil is on display in the famous story of the good Samaritan: the protagonist shows compassion to the wounded man on the side of the road by dressing his wounds with wine and *oil* (Luke 10:34).

Yet oil was not just important for daily life; it also had important liturgical purposes. The word *shemen* is used for the "sacred anointing oil" (Exod. 30:25)—that is, the specific substance that was part of Israel's sacred rites and priestly anointings (e.g., Exod. 30:22–28; Lev. 10:7). The sacral anointing oil was a compound mix of various sweet-smelling ingredients, the base of which was oil (Exod. 30:23–24). Given its aromatic features, it is sometimes called a "perfume" (Exod. 30:25). Since this particular type of oil was reserved for sacred applications, the laity's use of it was punishable by death

(Exod. 30:31–33). Along with animals for sacrifice, wheat, salt, and wine, oil is even understood to be "required" for Israel's liturgical life (for examples, see Lev. 2:1, 5; 6:15; 9:4; cf. Ezra 6:9).

The Oil of Gladness

Oil is connected to happiness and rejoicing. Addressing the king on his wedding day, Psalm 45 describes how God has "*anointed* you with the oil of *gladness*" (Ps. 45:7). Likewise, in Psalm 133 the pleasantness of God's people dwelling in unity is compared to "*the precious oil* on the head, running down upon the beard, the beard of Aaron, running down over the collar of his robes" (Ps. 133:2). Similarly, when Job recalls his days of prosperity and joy, he speaks of not only his children surrounding him and his path being "washed with milk" but also how "the rock poured out for me streams of oil!" (Job 29:6).

In times of mourning or repentance, the use of oil is suspended (2 Sam. 12:20; 14:2; Dan. 10:3; *Apocalypse of Abraham* 9:7). In the New Testament, Jesus explains that while hypocrites disfigure their appearance when they fast, his disciples must not look sad. Rather, he says, "*Anoint your head* and wash your face, so that your fasting may not be seen by others" (Matt. 6:17–18). The verb translated "anoint," *aleiphō*, is used in the Greek Old Testament in contexts involving oil (Exod. 40:15; 4 Kgdm. 4:2). While the verb could refer to something other than the use of oil, given its properties, it is hard to think that oil is not referred to in Jesus's words. The unstated assumption is that the use of oil is associated with vigor and joy.

Oil was thus tied to living a good and happy life. In Micah, being unable to anoint oneself is associated with other trials, such as "gnawing hunger" or having one's savings pillaged (Mic. 6:14–15). Oil is so appealing it can lead to excess. Proverbs sets up a parallelism, warning about the one who "loves pleasure" and the one who "loves wine and oil" (Prov. 21:17). Proverbs also describes the seductive words of an immoral woman as "smoother than oil" (Prov. 5:3). Oil was also used by women for cosmetic purposes (Ezek. 16:18; Esther 2:12).

In Ecclesiastes, oil is bound up with joy and merriment: "Go, eat your bread with joy and drink your wine with a merry heart, for God has already approved your deeds. Let your garments be white always. *Never let oil be lacking on your head. Enjoy life* with the wife whom you love" (Eccles. 9:7–9).

Something similar is found in Psalm 92, where the psalmist celebrates the LORD's deliverance of him from his enemies. The psalm explains that while the wicked perish, the righteous thrive due to God's goodness. This deliverance and flourishing of the righteous is bound up with the metaphor of God pouring oil on the psalmist: "But you have exalted my horn like that of a wild ox; you have poured fresh *oil* on me. . . . The righteous flourish like the palm tree, and grow like a cedar in Lebanon" (Ps. 92:10, 12). In biblical literature, the horn is a symbol of power and strength. The next line then speaks of how the LORD "poured fresh oil on me." Thus, being strengthened by God is metaphorically described in terms of being anointed. Going on, we read that the righteous thrive, which is ultimately ordered to the proclamation of the righteousness of the LORD. So, to summarize: to flourish and to be strengthened by God is all associated with being anointed.

Oil as a Blessing from the LORD

Another word translated as "oil" in English Bible translations is the Hebrew term *yitshar*, which refers to fresh oil that is made from recently picked olives. This was the most precious type of oil, which the book of Numbers calls "the finest of the oil" (Num. 18:12). It was considered a valuable commodity and therefore was given as a tithe to the priests (Neh. 10:37). This oil often appears in contexts where the LORD's blessing is in view.

When the LORD blesses the people with the gift of rich land, it is this oil that is explicitly mentioned. Consider the following from the book of Deuteronomy. Moses tells the people:

> [The LORD] will love you, bless you, and multiply you. He will bless the fruit of your womb and the fruit of your ground, your grain, your wine, and *your oil*, the increase of your cattle and the young of your flock, in the land that he swore to your fathers to give you. You will be the most blessed of peoples. (Deut. 7:13–14)

Chief among God's blessings is the land of Israel, which is specifically said to provide an abundance of precious *oil* (*yitshar*). With grain and wine, this oil is frequently mentioned as one of the great gifts of the land (see Deut. 11:14; 12:17; 18:4; 28:51; 2 Kings 18:32; 2 Chron. 31:5; 32:28; Neh. 5:11; 10:39; 13:5, 12; Hosea 2:8, 22; Joel 2:19, 24; Hag. 1:11).

In Jeremiah, the gift of oil (*yitshar*) is also said to be among God's future blessings in the coming new covenant age:

> They will be radiant over the goodness of the Lord,
> over the grain, the wine, *and the oil* . . .
> I will make *a new covenant* with the house of Israel and the house of Judah. (Jer. 31:12, 31)

Likewise, in the book of Joel, the future day of Israel's deliverance is associated with the gift of "grain, wine, and oil" and the promise that "you will be satisfied" (Joel 2:19). A similar promise is made in Isaiah 61, which, using the other word for oil discussed above, speaks of how those in Zion will be given "the oil [*shemen*] of gladness instead of mourning" (Isa. 61:3).

Later Jewish works not found in the Bible develop the idea that eschatological salvation involves the gift of oil. One example may be found in *2 Enoch*, where we read about Enoch being taken up into the heavenly realm and glorified by being anointed with a supernatural oil:

> And the Lord said to Michael, "Go, and extract Enoch from his earthly clothing. And anoint him with my delightful oil, and put him into the clothes of my glory." And so Michael did, just as the Lord had said to him. He anointed me and he clothed me. And the appearance of that oil is greater than the greatest light, and its ointment is like sweet dew, and its fragrance myrrh; and it is like the rays of the glittering sun. And I looked at myself, and I had become like one of his glorious ones, and there was no observable difference. (*2 Enoch* 22:8–10)[10]

Within the book, it seems likely that this oil is associated with "the paradise of Eden" (*2 Enoch* 8:6), located in "the third heaven" (*2 Enoch* 8:1). Some have suggested that this scene reflects early Christian initiations, but this seems unlikely given the lack of other Christian imagery.[11]

Likewise, the Jewish work *Joseph and Aseneth*—which most scholars think was written between 100 BC and AD 115 and which may or may not reflect Christian influence—repeatedly indicates that the righteous will receive a

10. *OTP* 1:138.

11. See note *o* by F. I. Andersen in *OTP* 1:138–39. Similar imagery of angelic transformation is found in the Dead Sea Scrolls (e.g., *1QRule of the Community* [1QS] 4:6–8, 11–13; *1QWar Scroll* [1QM] 12:1–7).

supernatural anointing.[12] For example, when Aseneth turns to the God of Israel in repentance and humbles herself in prayer, an angel appears to her, saying: "Behold, from today, you will be renewed and formed anew and made alive again, and you will eat blessed bread of life, and drink a blessed cup of immortality, and *anoint yourself with blessed ointment of incorruptibility*" (15:4).[13]

Jesus as LORD and Anointing the Sick in James

With the discussion above as background, we can now turn back to James. The Letter of James is not merely shaped by biblical traditions in general. It is written by an author convinced that Jewish hopes for a Messiah are fulfilled in Jesus. When James indicates that the infirm are to be anointed with oil "in the name of the Lord" and that "the Lord" will "raise up" the sick, he is undoubtedly drawing together many of the ideas we have looked at above. Here let us unpack some of these connections.

Anointing the Sick "in the Name of the Lord"

The recognition of Jesus as the "Christ"—the Messiah—is rooted in a Jewish outlook. The first followers of Jesus believed that what happened in Christ had been "in accordance with the scriptures" (1 Cor. 15:3–4)—namely, the scriptures of Israel. They did not see themselves as "former Jews" but understood that Israel's hopes had been realized in Jesus. When Paul recalls his conversation with Peter at Antioch, he remembers how he said to the fisherman, "We *are* Jews" (Gal. 2:15). Notice, Paul does not say, "We *were* Jews."[14] Elsewhere Paul explains that he is "an Israelite, a descendant of Abraham, a member of the tribe of Benjamin" (Rom. 11:1). We read in Acts that the early Church was viewed as a "sect" (*hairesis*) within Judaism (Acts 24:5, 14). Other Jewish groups such as the Pharisees and Sadducees were identified by this same term.[15]

12. For discussion of the provenance and date of this work, see Kirsten Marie Hartvigsen, *Aseneth's Transformation*, DCLS 24 (Berlin: De Gruyter, 2018), 21–31.

13. *OTP* 2:226 (emphasis added).

14. On Paul's identity as a new covenant Jew, see Brant Pitre, Michael P. Barber, and John A. Kincaid, *Paul, a New Covenant Jew: Rethinking Pauline Theology* (Grand Rapids: Eerdmans, 2019).

15. See Josephus, *Life* 10; 12; 191; *Jewish Antiquities* 13.171; 20.199.

The Letter of James is likewise best read as written by a genuinely *Jewish* writer. For example, it seems that James assumes his readers attend synagogue meetings. Using the normal Greek word that means "synagogue" in other Jewish literature as well as in the New Testament, he writes, "If a man wearing a gold ring and fine clothes comes into your *synagogue* [*synagōgēn*] . . ." (James 2:2).[16] Suffice it to say, as Dale Allison writes, "The broadly Jewish character of James is not in dispute."[17]

When James writes that the sick person will be saved by "the Lord" (*kyrios*), he is writing in the way Jews would commonly speak about the God of Israel. Moreover, that the sick person is to be anointed "in the name of the Lord" likewise reflects Jewish traditions. The Jewish scriptures frequently speak of invoking "the name of YHWH," or "the name of the LORD."

> [Abram] built there an altar to the LORD and *called on the name of the LORD*. (Gen. 12:8; cf. 26:25)

> May *the LORD* answer you in the day of distress!
> May *the name of the God* of Jacob protect you! (Ps. 20:1)

> Our help is in *the name of the LORD*,
> who made heaven and earth. (Ps. 124:8)

Blessings are pronounced on others "in the name of the LORD" (e.g., Deut. 21:5; 2 Sam. 6:18; 1 Chron. 16:2). Some passages even explicitly link being "saved" to "calling upon the name of the LORD."

> Then I called on *the name of the LORD*:
> "O LORD, I pray, *save* my life!" (Ps. 116:4)

> For everyone who calls on *the name of the LORD* shall be *saved*. (Joel 2:32)[18]

James's teaching that "the prayer of faith will *save* the one who is sick, and *the Lord* will raise him up" (James 5:15) therefore draws deeply from the biblical traditions that identify YHWH as the "Savior."

16. See, e.g., Josephus, *Jewish War* 2.285, 289; 7.44; *Jewish Antiquities* 19.300, 305; Matt. 4:23; 6:2, 5; 9:35; 10:17; 12:9; 13:54; 23:34; Mark 1:39; 3:1; 6:2; 13:9; Luke 4:15; 6:6; 12:11; 21:12; John 18:20; Acts 22:19; 26:11.

17. Dale C. Allison Jr., *James*, ICC (London: Bloomsbury T&T Clark, 2013), 8.

18. The versification of this passage in some English Bibles is different and appears as Joel 3:5.

Ancient Commentary on the Symbolism of Oil

An ancient collection of commentary on the Gospel of Mark known as the *Catena in Marcum*, which likely first emerged in the sixth century, discusses the significance of the apostles' use of oil in Mark 6 and the instructions to use oil in James 5. We read:

> And the oil also heals pain and is a cause of light and a source of cheerfulness. Therefore, *the oil used in anointing indicates also the mercy that comes from God*, and *the healing of disease*, and *the illumination of the heart*, for it is manifest to anyone anywhere that prayer brings about everything; and the oil, so I suppose, is a symbol of these things.[a]

Oil is not simply understood as superfluous in Mark's narrative. The physical use of oil is understood to symbolize spiritual truths—namely, the mercy of God, physical healing ("the healing of disease"), and spiritual "illumination."

a. Translation from William R. S. Lamb, ed., *The Catena in Marcum: A Byzantine Anthology of Early Commentary on Mark*, TENTS 6 (Leiden: Brill, 2012), 294 (emphasis added).

Furthermore, that James refers to using oil in ministering to the sick is also not unusual for a Jewish writer. Oil, as we have seen, served as a medicinal remedy, so for that reason alone its application makes sense. However, we should recognize that its potential healing properties are never mentioned as part of the rationale for its use in James 5. Rather, the sick are to be anointed with oil "in the name of the Lord." In addition, this anointing is to be carried out in connection with confession of sins and prayer.

The use of oil therefore cannot be separated out from hope in "the Lord." Anointing, then, is best understood as bound up with traditions that recognize the goodness of Israel's God, who strengthens and blesses. James appears to use the kind of imagery we found in Psalm 92 above: "You have poured over me fresh *oil*. . . . The righteous flourish like the palm tree" (Ps. 92:10, 12). *Being anointed signifies being empowered by God*. It is not simply *oil* used in a naturalistic way that one should hope in, but it is "the Lord" who raises up the sick. The anointing, then, is a sign of the power of God, who can raise up the sick, just as the psalmist's "horn" was "exalted" by God (Ps. 92:10).

The point is not that the oil *itself* heals but that the oil signifies the healing power of the Lord.

Moreover, as we have seen, oil was specifically linked not only to God's blessing in general but to eschatological realities. In light of this, the use of oil in James is not at all surprising, nor is the apostles' use of oil in their initial ministry in Mark 6. Jesus sends them out against the backdrop of his proclamation that the kingdom of God is "at hand" (Mark 1:15).

Jesus as "Lord"

In the New Testament, the Greek term for "Lord," *kyrios*, is applied to Jesus himself. While the word could be used for a variety of human rulers, there are several passages where it is best seen as pointing to Jesus's divinity. This is especially evident in the writings of Paul, widely recognized as the earliest New Testament writer. For example, in Romans 10, Paul quotes the book of Joel: "Everyone who calls on the name of the *Lord* [*kyrios*] will be saved" (Rom. 10:13; cf. Joel 2:32).[19] In context, Joel uses "Lord" (*kyrios*) to refer to the God of Israel. Paul applies this passage to Jesus, indicating that he is the divine Lord spoken of by Joel. Paul points to Jesus's divinity in many other ways. For example, the apostle speaks of idolatry not just as a sin against the God of Israel but as a sin "against Christ" (1 Cor. 8:12). The scriptures do not equate idolatry with sins against the royal sons of David. Rather, idolatry is a sin against Israel's God.[20]

The Fourth Gospel especially emphasizes that Jesus is the God who appeared at the burning bush. Jesus declares: "Before Abraham was, I am [*egō eimi*]" (John 8:58). Here Jesus applies the divine name to himself.[21] Because of this, Jesus's contemporaries seek to kill him for blasphemy, understanding that "he was calling God his own Father, thus *making himself equal with God*" (John 5:18). Jesus is therefore not only the "Word" and "Son" but nothing less than, as the apostle Thomas exclaims, "My Lord and my God" (John 20:28).

Jesus is also identified as the divine Lord in the Synoptic Gospels. For example, Jesus asks, "Why do you call me '*Lord, Lord*,' and do not do what I tell

19. In some translations, this passage appears as Joel 3:5.

20. For a fuller discussion of Paul's divine Christology and responses against the arguments presented here, see Pitre, Barber, and Kincaid, *Paul, a New Covenant Jew*, 102–28. See also Chris Tilling, *Paul's Divine Christology* (Grand Rapids: Eerdmans, 2015).

21. See Catrin H. Williams, *I Am He: The Interpretation of* 'Anî Hû' *in Jewish and Early Christian Literature*, WUNT 2/113 (Tübingen: Mohr Siebeck, 2000), 275–83.

you?" (Luke 6:46; cf. Matt. 7:21–22; 25:11). Jason Staples has demonstrated that the use of "Lord, Lord" in these verses is most likely an allusion to the divine name.[22] He shows that the double use of "Lord" reflects the way the Hebrew scriptures were translated into Greek. Where the Hebrew Bible has "Adonai YHWH"—"the Lord YHWH"—the ancient Greek translation of the scriptures has "*kyrie, kyrie*" (e.g., Deut. 3:24; Ps. 108:21 LXX [109:21 MT]; cf. Ezek. 37:21). By saying others will address him as "Lord, Lord," Jesus thus reveals that he is "the Lord YHWH."

As in the Gospel of John, the Synoptic Gospels also bear witness to Jesus being accused of blasphemy for making divine claims. For example, when Jesus announces his ability to forgive sins, the scribes think: "He is blaspheming! *Who can forgive sins but the one God*?" (Mark 2:7; cf. Matt. 9:3; Luke 5:21). Jesus's divine abilities are further stressed by another aspect of the story: he reads their hearts (Mark 2:8), something only the God of Israel can do (e.g., Ps. 44:21; Prov. 21:2; Jer. 17:9–10). Jesus's divinity is further confirmed by other aspects of the narrative. He goes on to perform other actions uniquely associated with divinity, such as walking on water (Mark 6:48; cf. Job 9:8; 38:16; Hab. 3:15).[23] Moreover, while walking on the water, Jesus even appears to invoke the divine name, applying it to himself: "I am [*egō eimi*]" (Mark 6:50).[24]

The evangelists *reconfigure* beliefs about God in light of Jesus. Jewish New Testament scholar Amy-Jill Levine maintains that Matthew "changed the image of the deity," explaining that the relationship between the Father and Jesus in Matthew involves "something that looks like bitheism."[25] Of course, one cannot simply say Matthew asserts bitheism *per se*; Jesus explicitly quotes from the context in Deuteronomy from which the *Shema* is taken, explaining to Satan that the Lord alone is to be worshiped: "Him only shall you serve" (Matt. 4:10; cf. Deut. 6:13). For Matthew, there are not "*two* LORDS." There is one LORD—yet somehow this involves *both the Father and the Son*.

22. Jason Staples, "'LORD, LORD': Jesus as YHWH in Matthew and Luke," *NTS* 64 (2018): 1–19.

23. Randi Rashkover, "Christology," in *The Jewish Annotated New Testament*, ed. Amy-Jill Levine and Marc Zvi Brettler, 2nd ed. (Oxford: Oxford University Press, 2017), 754.

24. Richard B. Hays, *Echoes of Scripture in the Gospels* (Waco: Baylor University Press, 2016), 73. For a more expansive treatment on these issues, see Brant Pitre, *Jesus and Divine Christology* (Grand Rapids: Eerdmans, 2024).

25. Amy-Jill Levine, "Concluding Reflections: What's Next in the Study of Matthew?," in *Matthew within Judaism: Israel and the Nations*, ed. Anders Runesson and Daniel M. Gurtner, Early Christian Literature (Atlanta: SBL Press, 2019), 452.

Especially notable are Jesus's final instructions to the disciples in Matthew that they should baptize "in the name of the Father and of the Son and of the Holy Spirit" (Matt. 28:19). *Here the Son and the Spirit are identified with "the name" no less than the Father is.* John Meier writes: "One could hardly imagine a more forceful proclamation of Christ's divinity—and, incidentally, of the Spirit's distinct personality—than this listing together, on a level of equality, of Father, Son, and Spirit. One does not baptize people in the name of a divine person, a holy creature, and an impersonal divine force."[26] Meier's explanation evokes Augustine, who held that by speaking of "the name" rather than "the names," Jesus indicates "one substance of godhead in the Trinity."[27]

"The Lord" in James 5 and Anointing the Sick

James says that the sick are to be anointed "in the name of the Lord" (James 5:14). Likewise, we read that "the Lord will raise up" those who have received such anointing (James 5:14–15). If other New Testament authors refer to Jesus as "the Lord," should Jesus also be seen as the specific referent of "the Lord" in James? Such a reading would make sense in light of the opening of the letter, which explicitly identifies Jesus as "the Lord" (James 1:1).

We should be aware that James does not speak with the precision of a systematic theologian. Nevertheless, if we pay close attention, we see that James's use of "Lord" not only refers to God the Father but also points to Jesus's divinity. Just prior to speaking of Job and the Old Testament prophets, James says:

> Be patient, brothers, until *the coming of the Lord*. Behold, the farmer waits for the valuable fruit of the soil, being patient over it until it receives the early and late rains. You must also be patient. Strengthen your hearts because *the coming of the Lord is near*. Do not grumble, brothers, against one another in order that you may not be judged. Behold, the judge stands at the gates. (James 5:7–9)

Who is "the Lord" in this passage?

On the one hand, the language evokes Old Testament texts that describe the Lord God coming in judgment (Isa. 66:15–16; Jer. 2:29–36; Mic. 7:8–10;

26. John P. Meier, *Matthew*, New Testament Message 3 (Wilmington, DE: Michael Glazier, 1980), 371.

27. Augustine, *Sermon* 215.8; translation from Augustine, *Sermons 184–229Z*, trans. Edmund Hill, WSA III/6 (New Rochelle, NY: New City Press, 1993), 164.

etc.). Furthermore, James's description of the patient farmer fits well into this theme, since the day of God's judgment is often described in Jewish sources with harvest symbolism (e.g., Isa. 18:4; Jer. 51:33; Joel 3:13).

On the other hand, by speaking of the "coming of the Lord," James echoes a common aspect of the Church's proclamation—namely, that the Lord Jesus is coming in judgment. For example, in 1 Thessalonians 3:13, Paul writes, "May your hearts be strengthened in holiness so that you may be blameless before our God and Father at *the coming of our Lord Jesus* with all his saints." Here, as in James, being "strengthened" in heart is described as preparation for the coming of the Lord.

What further strengthens the impression that James is describing Jesus's coming is that James appears to echo a teaching of Jesus found in the Gospel of Mark. James's teaching sounds remarkably similar to Mark 13:

> Then they will see *the Son of Man coming with the clouds* with great power and glory. Then he will send out the angels and gather his elect from the four winds, from the end of the earth to the end of heaven. From the fig tree learn the parable: when its branch becomes tender and puts forth leaves, you know that summer is near. So likewise, when you see these things taking place, know that *he is near, even at the gates*. (Mark 13:26–29)

In these lines from Mark, Jesus speaks of the coming of the Son of Man at the final judgment, who is "near" and "at the gates." Moreover, Jesus's saying draws on a seasonal observation about the fig tree and the coming of summer. The parallels with James 5 are truly striking.

The Son of Man's Coming in Mark 13	The Lord's Coming in James 5
"the Son of Man coming [*erchomenon*]" (13:26)	"the coming [*parousias*] of the Lord" (5:7)
Seasonal observation: "summer is near" (13:28)	Seasonal observation: "early and late rains" (5:7)
"is near [*engys*]" (13:28)	"is near [*ēngiken*]" (5:8)
"at the gates [*thyrais*]" (13:29)	"at the gates [*thyrōn*]" (5:9)

That James would cite a teaching from Jesus should not be unexpected since he seems familiar with a number of Jesus's sayings known to us from the Gospels (e.g., compare James 5:12 with Matt. 5:33–37).[28] True, James does

28. See Allison, *James*, 56–62; Patrick Hartin, *James and the Q Sayings of Jesus*, JSNTSup 47 (Sheffield: Sheffield Academic, 1991); D. B. Deppe, *The Sayings of Jesus in the Epistle of James* (Chelsea, MI: Bookcrafters, 1989).

not use all the same Greek words that appear in the saying of Jesus found in Mark 13. Yet, as Allison shows, this is consistent with James's general style. In other places where James cites the Greek Old Testament, he reworks material, substituting synonyms and avoiding verbatim reproduction (e.g., compare James 3:7 with Gen. 1:26–28).[29] Furthermore, that James uses the term *parousias* to describe the Lord's "coming" instead of the word *erchomenon* used in Mark 13 is hardly difficult to explain; *parousia* appears as a technical term for Jesus's return in the New Testament (e.g., Matt. 24:37, 39; 2 Thess. 2:8). On balance, it seems difficult to write off the parallels between James 5 and Mark 13 as merely coincidental. It therefore seems likely that James knew the saying of Jesus that appears in Mark (though I am not necessarily claiming that the author of James knew the Gospel of Mark itself). For him, then, the "Lord" who is coming probably refers in some way to Jesus.

If "the Lord" refers to Jesus in James 5:7—just as it does in the opening line of the letter (James 1:1)—it seems difficult to insist that when James later speaks of the elders anointing the sick "in the name of the Lord" there is no reference to Jesus. James's instructions evoke what is found in Acts, where the apostles heal people in Jesus's "name" (Acts 3:6, 16; 4:10, 12, 30). In Acts, this becomes a matter of great controversy (Acts 4:7, 17–18). Healing people in *Jesus's* name suggests that he is the divine source of healing. Yet that seems to be the point. In Acts, Joel's prophecy that "everyone who calls upon the name of the Lord will be saved" (Joel 2:32) is said to be fulfilled in Jesus (Acts 2:21, 38). Peter even stresses this point by declaring, "*There is salvation in no one else*" (Acts 4:12). The language here brings together biblical traditions of the divine name with Jesus himself, thus emphasizing Jesus's divinity. Jesus is "the Lord."

It seems, then, that James is making a similar theological point to that found in Acts: in ministering to the sick, it is the *Lord*—the God of Israel—who is the source of healing: "And the prayer of faith will save the one who is sick, and *the Lord* will raise him up" (James 5:15). Yet here we can see how the *theology* of anointing is also, at root, *christological*: in healing people in the name of "the Lord," Christians profess that Jesus is the Lord God, the "Author of Life" (Acts 3:15).

I would also suggest that because James views the healing as taking place through Jesus, whom he identifies from the outset as "Christ" (James 1:1), it

29. Allison, *James*, 543.

The Liturgical Prayer for Anointing of the Sick

When the Church celebrates anointing of the sick within the context of eucharistic worship, the minister specifically uses the language of "Lord." For example, when the minister anoints the sick, the following prayer is to be used: "Through this holy anointing may the *Lord* in his love and mercy help you with the grace of the Holy Spirit."[a]

a. Taken from the revised rite approved by the National Conference of Catholic Bishops of America (November 18, 1982) and confirmed by the Vatican's Congregation for the Sacraments and Divine Worship (December 11, 1982), published in *Pastoral Care of the Sick: Rites of Anointing and Viaticum* (Totowa, NJ: Catholic Book Publishing, 1983), 116 (emphasis added).

seems very hard to believe that the use of oil *only* relates to its associations with healing. It seems far more likely that James recognizes a connection between the use of oil and the power of the Anointed One—that is, the "Christ."

Following from all of this, Christian liturgical practice has long retained the custom of addressing Jesus as "Lord." The expression *Kyrie, eleison* ("Lord, have mercy") contains the same Greek word used by the New Testament writers.[30] This prayer is used throughout the rites of anointing of the sick.[31] The same Lord who brought life and healing to Israel now works in the life of the Church. The sacrament, then, makes a crucial theological point—not only is Jesus the Lord, but he is specifically the Lord of life. It is entirely appropriate, then, for the sick to be anointed in the "name of the Lord"—Jesus is the LORD, the source and sustainer of life. The use of oil signifies the gift of life and strength bestowed on the sick person who is anointed, a source and strength that has its origin in the "Christ." This idea also relates to another dimension of James's teaching—namely, the connection between sin and death. To this connection we now turn.

30. *Kyrie* is the way *kyrios* appears in Greek when it is used in a direct address (the vocative form).

31. For the Catholic rites, see *Pastoral Care of the Sick*. For the rites of the Orthodox Church, see Paul Meyendorff, *The Anointing of the Sick*, The Orthodox Liturgy 1 (Crestwood, NY: St. Vladimir's Seminary Press, 2009).

4

Sin, Death, and the Hope for the Oil of Mercy

The New Adam and the Return to Eden

> For as all die in Adam, so all will be made alive in Christ.
>
> —1 Corinthians 15:22

> When he, the Son of God, comes, he himself will be baptized in the river Jordan, . . . then he will anoint from the oil of mercy all who believe in him.
>
> —*Life of Adam and Eve* 42[1]

In James 5:14 we are told that if someone is sick, he or she should call for the "elders of the church," be prayed over by them, and be anointed "with oil in the name of the Lord." We go on to read:

> The prayer of faith will save the one who is sick, and the Lord will raise him up. And if he has committed sins, he will be forgiven. Therefore, confess your sins to one another and pray for one another, that you may be healed. (James 5:15–16)

1. *OTP* 2:274n42a (from a few copies of the Latin version).

If the sick person does *not* confess his or her sins, the person may not be healed and die. This might seem like a forced reading, but other evidence from the Letter of James supports this interpretation.

In the opening chapter of James's letter, we read: "Desire, when it has conceived, gives birth to sin, and sin, when it is fully grown, gives birth to *death*" (James 1:15). For James, sin, sickness, and death are tightly interrelated. This chapter explains that James's teaching on this point reflects a Jewish outlook.

Up front, however, we should acknowledge that the connection between sin and sickness suggested by James's teaching poses pastoral challenges. The scrupulous might wonder if they are sick only because of some forgotten personal sins that they have failed to repent of adequately. They may also entertain false hopes that they might be cured if only they could remember forgotten sins and renounce them. Such thoughts by those who genuinely have repented of sin to the best of their knowledge are unhelpful and may even constitute a failure of faith. Yet these pastoral concerns should not cause us to fail to seriously face up to Scripture's teaching.

At the same time, we must also be vigilant against reading ideas into James's teaching that are not there. James does not say that *all* sickness and death are the result of personal sin. We should recognize that James is aware that even good people die. It is impossible to believe that James is ignorant that Christ died. We can safely assume that James does not believe Christ's death is somehow proof of his sinfulness.

Furthermore, earlier in the epistle, James reminds his readers: "Blessed is the man who endures the test. For when he has been proven sound, he will receive the crown of life [*ton stephanon tēs zōēs*] that God has promised to those who love him" (James 1:12).[2] Notably, the language seems to refer to the rewards of the afterlife. Dale Allison notes that the "crown of life" is often associated with the afterlife or the eschatological age to come in Jewish and Christian texts.[3] Consider the following passages from Wisdom of Solomon, the Dead Sea Scrolls, and the book of Revelation:

> But the righteous live forever,
> and in the Lord is their repayment;
> the Most High takes care of them.

2. The translation "when he has been proven sound" is especially indebted to Luke Timothy Johnson, *The Letter of James*, AB 37A (New York: Doubleday, 1995), 188.

3. Dale C. Allison Jr., *James*, ICC (London: Bloomsbury T&T Clark, 2013), 231–32.

On account of this they will receive a majestic palace
and a beautiful crown [*to diadēma tou kallous*] from the hand of
the Lord. (Wis. 5:15–16)

These are the foundations of the spirit of the sons of truth (in) the world. And the reward of all those who walk in it will be healing, plentiful peace in a long life, fruitful offspring with all everlasting blessings, eternal enjoyment with endless life, and *a crown of glory* with majestic raiment in eternal light. (*1QRule of the Community* [1QS] 4:6–8)[4]

Be faithful until death, and I will give you *the crown of life*. (Rev. 2:10)

Given the language of "testing" and the "crown of life," it is hard to believe that James's instructions on healing the sick express the idea that physical death can be fully avoided. James understands that death cannot be staved off forever.

We are therefore presented with a puzzle. On the one hand, James encourages the sick to seek healing. On the other hand, he also surely would know that anointing would not forever prevent physical death. Passing from this life is not one of many hypothetical outcomes for human beings; barring an unexpected arrival of the eschaton—of which Scripture teaches no one knows the day or hour except the Father (Mark 13:32)—death is inevitable. In this chapter we therefore need to look at the way Jewish tradition connects sin and death. As we will see, Jewish sources ultimately trace the origins of sin and death back to the garden of Eden. In the New Testament, sin and death are conquered by Christ. All of this sheds helpful light on James's teaching.

Sin and Death

New Testament scholar Richard Bauckham explains that the author of James "is a wisdom teacher."[5] The motif of wisdom is explicitly introduced in the first chapter of the letter: "If any of you lacks *wisdom*, let him ask God . . . and it will be given to him" (James 1:5). James's teaching is deeply anchored in Israel's wisdom literature. In chapter 4, James quotes explicitly from the

4. *DSSSE* 1:77.
5. Richard Bauckham, *James*, NTR (London: Routledge, 1999), 30.

book of Proverbs: "God opposes the proud but gives grace to the humble" (James 4:6; see Prov. 3:34 LXX).[6] In other places, without giving direct quotations, James also echoes other passages from the Old Testament's sapiential books.[7] It makes sense, then, that James ties together sin and death, righteousness and life. These connections are made throughout Israel's wisdom books. Yet these traditions also lead us to creation and Edenic traditions. In some Jewish sources, the inception of sin and death is also associated with what happened with Adam and Eve.

Righteousness and the Way of Life in Proverbs

The book of Proverbs frequently connects righteousness to life and evil to death. Consider the following passages:

> Whoever is steadfast in *righteousness* is on the way to *life*,
> but whoever pursues *evil* is on the way to *death*. (Prov. 11:19)
>
> In the way of *righteousness* is *life*,
> and in the way of its path there is *no death*. (Prov. 12:28)
>
> The *righteous one* is delivered from trouble,
> but the *wicked one* gets into it instead. (Prov. 11:8)[8]

An essential theme in Proverbs is that righteous living will result in happiness and human flourishing, while evil will result in sadness, ruin, and misery.

The connection between life and righteousness is further reinforced in another way. In Proverbs, righteousness is bound up with "wisdom" (*hokhmah*). We are told, "The Lord gives *wisdom* [*hokhmah*]" and "stores up *wisdom* for the upright" so that "you will understand *righteousness* [*tsedeq*] . . . for *wisdom* [*hokhmah*] will come into your heart" (Prov. 2:6, 7, 9, 10). Notably, both "the fruit of the righteous" and "wisdom" are spoken of as a "tree of life" (Prov. 3:18; 11:30). This latter image is especially familiar from the well-known story of Adam and Eve. Indeed, we will return to Genesis below. For

6. James has "God" (*theos*) where, notably, the Greek version of Proverbs has "the Lord" (*kyrios*).

7. See Allison, *James*, 51, who notes the following: Prov. 10:12 in James 5:20; elements of Wis. 2 in James 4:13–5:6; elements of Sir. 2 in James 5:10; Sir. 5:11–12 in James 1:13.

8. Other such passages abound. See, e.g., Prov. 2:20–22; 4:11–12, 18–19; 9:9–11; 10:27–31; 11:6–11, 18, 21, 23, 30; 12:6–7, 13; 13:21; 14:32, 34; 15:6; 16:31; 20:7; 21:12, 21; 24:15–16; 29:2.

now, it is enough to underscore that "life" is bound together with "wisdom" and "righteousness" in Proverbs. Later wisdom books will also emphasize the connection between life and righteousness and between evil and death (see Sir. 1:13; 33:14).

On the flipside of the pairing of life and righteousness is another coupling: sin is bound up with death. Proverbs specifically connects *disobedience* to death:

> Those who keep the commandment keep their lives;
> those who disregard his ways will die. (Prov. 19:16)

According to this passage, the one who "will live" keeps "the commandment" (*mitswah*). In context, the verse probably refers to obeying the counsel of the wise, not specifically commandments of the Torah. Yet disobedience to proper authorities is contrary to God's will (Prov. 24:21). In fact, other texts specifically associate wisdom with keeping God's laws.

Scholars have detected a close connection between Israel's wisdom traditions and Deuteronomy (cf. Deut. 4:5–6).[9] At the end of the book of Deuteronomy, Moses exhorts Israel to keep the law, pleading with them to decide on life rather than death:

> *Choose life* so that you and your descendants may live, loving the Lord your God, obeying him, and clinging to him. For he is your life and he will lengthen your days, that you may live in the land that the Lord swore to give to your fathers, to Abraham, to Isaac, and to Jacob. (Deut. 30:19–20)

Moses calls to Israel to decide on the path to life—namely, obedience.

The glaring problem with all of this is that, in the end, even the righteous suffer and die. How is that the case? From where did death come? According to different biblical writers, even though the righteous die, death is still bound up with sin.

9. On Deuteronomy's use of wisdom traditions, see the classic study by Moshe Weinfeld, *Deuteronomy and the Deuteronomic School* (Oxford: Clarendon, 1972), as well as the critique and discussion in Reinhard Müller, "The Blinded Eyes of the Wise: Sapiential Tradition and Mosaic Covenant in Deut 16:19–20," in *Wisdom and Torah: The Reception of "Torah" in the Wisdom Literature in the Second Temple Period*, ed. Bernd U. Schipper and D. Andrew Teeter (Leiden: Brill, 2013), 9–33.

Righteousness Is Immortal

The pairing of life with righteousness, on the one hand, and sin with death, on the other, is especially pronounced in Wisdom of Solomon. The author is adamant that "God did not make death" (Wis. 1:13). Death, we are told, brings no pleasure to God. What brings death is "the work of your hands" (Wis. 1:12). But the author does not stop here.

Following this, we are told:

> For righteousness is immortal.
> But the impious called upon death by their hands and their deeds.
> Considering him a friend, they pined away
> and made a covenant with him,
> because they are worthy to belong to his company. (Wis. 1:15–16)

Here death is personified. The wicked not only view death as a "friend," they have "made a covenant with him" and "belong to his company." Conversely, righteousness is said to be "*immortal*." The author will go on to drive this point home in chapter 3, where he declares that "the souls of the righteous are in the hand of God, and no torment shall ever touch them" (Wis. 3:1).

In Wisdom, then, we have a clear affirmation of life after death. Those who die in righteousness will be glorified: "They will shine forth" (Wis. 3:7). The section climaxes by declaring that "the faithful ones will remain in love in him" (Wis. 3:9). The main point to emphasize here is that the author has now addressed a problem never explicitly treated in Israel's earlier wisdom books—the hope of the righteous beyond the grave. In Wisdom of Solomon, righteousness truly is "immortal."

Where, then, did death come from if God did not create it? According to the book of Wisdom, death entered the world through the devil:

> Through the devil's envy death came into the world,
> and those who are partners with him experience it. (Wis. 2:24)

According to Wisdom of Solomon, death is due not to God but to disobedience. Where does Wisdom locate the origins of sin? Scholars generally agree that the book seems to be drawing on Genesis traditions, though it is not clear if the passage has the story of Adam and Eve in mind or the story of the first death, Cain's murder of Abel.[10] Either way, the point for Wisdom of Solomon is that God did not cause death; its origins are associated with the devil.

The Disobedience of Adam and Eve and Death

There is certainly a strand of ancient Jewish interpretation that holds that sin and death entered the world due to Adam's failure. Consider the following statements from *2 Baruch* and *4 Ezra*, works that date to the late first century or early second century AD.

> Adam sinned first and has brought death upon all who were not in his own time, yet each of them who has been born from him has prepared for himself the coming torment. (*2 Baruch* 54:15; cf. 23:4)[11]

> And you laid upon him one commandment of yours; but he transgressed it, and immediately you appointed death for him and for his descendants. (*4 Ezra* 3:7)[12]

> O Adam, what have you done? For though it was you who sinned, the fall was not yours alone, but ours also who are your descendants. (*4 Ezra* 7:118)[13]

Jewish opinion would diverge on the precise effects of Adam's disobedience.[14] We see some of that disagreement in the texts quoted above. While *2 Baruch* insists that the ultimate fate of all will depend on their own actions, *4 Ezra* holds that all humans are "fallen" in Adam. It is important to examine the Genesis story to see how such interpretations could arise from its narrative.

We should note that contemporary biblical commentators often contest traditional Christian readings of Genesis 3. Like *4 Ezra*, Christian theology reads Genesis 3 as telling the story of humanity's "fall" in Adam's "transgression." It is often pointed out, however, that the Hebrew text of Genesis never explicitly uses this language in reference to the garden of Eden narrative. Does Christian tradition, then, misinterpret the story by using such terms?

10. See, e.g., David Winston, *The Wisdom of Solomon*, AB 43 (New York: Doubleday, 1979), 121; Roger A. Bullard and Howard A. Hatton, *A Handbook on the Wisdom of Solomon*, United Bible Societies' Handbooks (New York: United Bible Societies, 2004), 39–40.

11. *OTP* 1:640.

12. *OTP* 1:528.

13. *OTP* 1:541.

14. See Amy-Jill Levine and Marc Zvi Brettler, *The Bible with and without Jesus: How Jews and Christians Read the Same Stories Differently* (New York: HarperOne, 2020), 101–34.

One must be careful to avoid the "word-thing" fallacy—that is, the claim that an idea is not present because particular words fail to appear. In other words, though Genesis 3 never explicitly makes a reference to "sin" or "transgression," it would be obtuse to insist that such ideas are not implied in the narrative. In Genesis 2, we read:

> The LORD God commanded the man, "From every tree of the garden you may eat freely; but from the tree of the knowledge of good and evil you shall not eat, because in the day that you eat from it you shall certainly die." (Gen. 2:16–17)

Let us register two important observations. First, the instruction not to eat of the tree of the knowledge of good and evil is described as a "commandment." Mark S. Smith writes, "The choices given by God in Genesis 2–3 are not simply neutral options."[15] The word "sin" may not be used for Adam and Eve's decision, but it is not difficult to see why later interpreters used that terminology to describe the story.

Second, God states that the consequence of eating from the tree is *death*: "In the day that you eat from it [the tree of knowledge of good and evil] you shall certainly die" (Gen. 2:17). Yet when Adam and Eve do eat of the fruit, *they do not die*. The serpent adds further complexity to the narrative by directly contradicting what God announces. When Eve relays to the serpent what God has said would be the consequences of eating from the tree, the serpent is emphatic: "*You will not certainly die*" (Gen. 3:4). In no uncertain terms, the serpent explicitly insists that what God says will happen will not occur. When Adam and Eve eat of the fruit and do not die, the story seems to raise a critical question: Did the serpent, in the end, get it right?

One solution to the difficulty posed by Genesis 3—an ancient one, which goes back to Jewish rabbis—is to see mercy at work.[16] James Barr is a modern representative of this view. He argues that God is portrayed as simply having a change of heart: God promised to punish disobedience with death but ultimately decides to allow Adam and Eve to live.[17]

15. Mark S. Smith, *The Genesis of Good and Evil: The Fall(out) and Original Sin in the Bible* (Louisville: Westminster John Knox, 2019), 38. Smith goes on to explain that he prefers to see the story in terms of a "fallout" rather than a "fall."

16. See *Rabbah Genesis* 21:6; *Rabbah Leviticus* 29:1.

17. James Barr, "Is God a Liar? (Genesis 2–3)—and Related Matters," *JTS* 57 (2006): 1–22. See also Gerhard von Rad, *Genesis: A Commentary*, trans. John H. Marks, OTL (Philadelphia: Westminster, 1972), 95, who suggests that the narrator wanted to show that God "allowed grace to prevail."

It makes sense to see mercy at work in the story. Still, Barr's interpretation is not fully satisfactory. For one thing, contrary to his insistence, it is not simply toil that God mentions as Adam's punishment; physical death *is* part of the penalty. In the aftermath of their consuming the forbidden fruit, God is explicit: "To dust you shall return" (Gen. 3:19).

In addition, Barr ignores the stakes that have been established by the narrative; in the end, the serpent appears more trustworthy than God. To argue that the tension is resolved by recognizing that Adam and Eve *eventually* die is unconvincing given the shape of the narrative.[18] The natural reading of God's command—"In the day [*beyom*] that you eat from it you shall certainly die" (Gen. 2:17)—suggests immediate death. It is surely therefore significant that, not only do Adam and Eve survive, they also go on to live *extraordinarily* long lives; Adam lives a whopping 930 years (Gen. 5:5)! While we cannot delve into the question of how Genesis's fantastically long lifespans should be interpreted, the fundamental point is that the serpent appears correct and God appears to be wrong.[19] Derek Beattie even writes, "I cannot help but feel sorry for the poor old snake, condemned to crawl forever on his belly . . . just for telling the truth and exposing God's lie."[20] As much as I appreciate his honesty, I believe Beattie's reading is wholly untenable.

The supposition that the biblical writer is impugning God and revealing the serpent to be the real truth-teller is, quite simply, preposterous. The narrative has established that while God promised immediate death would follow upon eating the fruit, the serpent assured Eve that this would not happen. The account seems deliberately provocative. That should not surprise us. Israel's scriptures—especially the wisdom literature—*frequently* present the reader with the challenge of finding deeper meanings in texts (e.g., Prov. 1:6). Is there reason to think that Genesis 2–3 should be read in a way similar to thought-provoking wisdom literature? I believe so.

The tip-off may very well be Genesis's mention of the "tree of life." The term appears elsewhere in Israel's sapiential literature, where it is associated with wisdom and behavior linked to wisdom (Prov. 3:18; 11:30; 13:12; 15:4). This would suggest that there are hidden truths to be found in the Genesis

18. James Barr, *The Garden of Eden and the Hope of Immortality* (Minneapolis: Fortress, 1992), 10.

19. To insist that the tension in the narrative is merely due to the fact that Genesis is the end result of different sources hardly addresses the issue. Why would the final editor bring the sources together *in this way*?

20. See Derek Beattie, "What Is Genesis 2–3 About?," *ExpTim* 92 (1980): 8–10.

story if we are willing to pay close attention. Although it may at first seem that the serpent is correct, Adam and Eve do die a death upon eating the fruit. How? Todd Patterson suggests that the story can be interpreted as indicating that exile from the presence of God involves a kind of death.[21] This interpretation, however, can be recognized only if one notices clues that often escape the eye of the modern reader. To these we now turn.

Exile from God's Presence as Death

An ancient Jewish interpretive tradition speaks of the garden of Eden as "the holy of holies" (*Jubilees* 8:19). While this may seem unwarranted, once one reads the Genesis narrative carefully, that identification is not difficult to explain. The opening chapters of Genesis are chock-full of imagery that seems intentionally evocative of Israel's liturgical life.

Creation, Eden, and the Sanctuary

In Genesis 1:14 the sun, moon, and stars are described as "lights" or "lamps" (*me'orot*), translating a Hebrew word that everywhere else in the Pentateuch refers to the candelabra found in Israel's place of worship, the tabernacle (Exod. 25:6; 27:20; 35:8, 14, 28; 39:37; Lev. 24:2; Num. 4:9, 16). Moreover, Genesis 1:14 says that the lights were created for "appointed times" (*mo'adim*). Here Genesis uses the plural of the Hebrew word *mo'ed*, a word that is later used in connection with the tent of "meeting" (*mo'ed*)—that is, the place of sacrificial worship (e.g., Exod. 27:21; 28:43; 29:4, 10).[22] Because of such markers, scholars generally attribute the seven-day creation narrative in Genesis 1:1–2:3 to a priestly writer. Yet the liturgical echoes do not end after chapter 1. The material that follows in Genesis 2:4 is normally attributed to a different source than that of Genesis 1:1–2:3, but even here liturgical and priestly imagery abounds.

Take, for instance, Adam's duties in the garden as spelled out by God. Adam is put in the garden to "serve" (*'abad*) and to "keep" (*shamar*) it (Gen. 2:15). In Hebrew, the words that are used are the same terms used to describe the priest's duties in the sanctuary (e.g., Num. 3:7–8; 8:26; 18:5–6). Later, we

21. See Todd L. Patterson, *The Plot-Structure of Genesis*, BIS 160 (Leiden: Brill, 2018), 50–59.

22. See Walter Vogels, "The Cultic and Civil Calendars of the Fourth Day of Creation (Gen 1:14b)," *SJOT* 11, no. 2 (1997): 163–80.

read that God "walked" in the garden (Gen. 3:8). The Hebrew verb that appears here, *halak*, occurs later in reference to God's dwelling in the sanctuary (Lev. 26:12; Deut. 23:14 [23:15 MT]; 2 Sam. 7:6–7).

Tabernacle symbolism may also be detected in the mention that cherubim were placed at the east end of the garden to guard it (Gen. 3:24). The next time these creatures are mentioned in the Pentateuch is in the description of the tabernacle; images of cherubim are placed on the lid of the ark of the covenant (Exod. 25:18–22; cf. 37:7–9). They are also depicted on the curtains of the tabernacle (Exod. 26:1, 31; 36:8, 35). In other words, apart from the garden, cherubim are especially found in one place: the sanctuary. Many scholars recognize that the garden is depicted as a kind of sanctuary.[23]

We see a critical payoff of this liturgical imagery at the close of the book of Exodus. In the final chapter of the book, God comes to dwell in the tabernacle. Significantly, the completion and dedication of the sanctuary in Exodus's final chapters evoke the opening and closing of the creation narrative in Genesis.[24] Consider the following chart:

The Completion of Creation (Gen. 1–2)	**The Completion of the Tabernacle (Exod. 39–40)**
"And God saw everything that he had made, and behold, it was very good." (Gen. 1:31)	"And Moses saw all the work, and behold, they had done it." (Exod. 39:43)
"Thus the heavens and the earth were finished, and all the host of them." (Gen. 2:1)	"Thus all the work of the tabernacle of the tent of meeting was finished." (Exod. 39:32)
"God finished his work." (Gen. 2:2)	"So Moses finished the work." (Exod. 40:33)
"So God blessed the seventh day." (Gen. 2:3)	"And Moses blessed them." (Exod. 39:43)

The echoes are too striking not to be deliberate. When these texts are read together, then, the building of the tabernacle in Exodus seemingly provides the key to solve the problem set in motion in Genesis 3: How is "death" the punishment for eating the fruit in the garden? How did Adam and Eve "die" on the day they ate the fruit? They were expelled from God's presence in the primordial sanctuary. The tabernacle represents a kind of return to Eden—something of what was lost at Eden is restored in Israel's liturgical worship.

23. See, e.g., L. Michael Morales, *The Tabernacle Pre-Figured: Cosmic Mountain Ideology in Genesis and Exodus*, BTS 15 (Leuven: Peeters, 2012), 115–19; Gary A. Anderson, *The Genesis of Perfection: Adam and Eve in Jewish and Christian Imagination* (Louisville: Westminster John Knox, 2001), 46.

24. See Gary A. Anderson, *That I May Dwell among Them: Incarnation and Atonement in the Tabernacle Narrative* (Grand Rapids: Eerdmans, 2023), 19–48.

To be sure, we should not *overstate* this problem. Contact between God and humanity is not completely severed after Adam and Eve's disobedience. God continues to speak to human beings. This is evident in the immediate aftermath of Adam and Eve's banishment from the garden. After Adam and Eve leave paradise, their sons bring sacrificial offerings to the Lord (Gen. 4:3–4). In this context, God speaks directly to Cain (Gen. 4:6). In the following chapter, we read about righteous Enoch, who is said to have "walked with God" (Gen. 5:24). Furthermore, God continues to speak to people, including Noah (e.g., Gen. 6:13–21), Abraham (e.g., Gen. 12:1), Abimelech (Gen. 20:3–7), Rebekah (Gen. 25:23), Isaac (Gen. 26:2–5), and Jacob (Gen. 28:13–15). It is not as if the divine presence has left the world.

Yet we should also not discount the significance of God's presence in the tabernacle as if it were nothing special. Historically, we can detect different sources and traditions in the biblical texts, but we also need to make sense of its final form as a narrative. And in its canonical form, there is a tension in the biblical narrative that must not be erased: God is portrayed as present to people but also as dwelling with Israel in a unique way in the sanctuary. Significantly, then, this tabernacling presence of God is portrayed in the overall narrative as evocative of the garden, the place where God "walked" with humanity.[25]

Exile from the Divine Presence

A foreshadowing of Israel's worship at the sanctuary can also be detected in the Genesis narrative after the garden story. Cain and Abel are said to bring their offerings "to the LORD" (Gen. 4:3). But how do they do this? L. Michael Morales convincingly argues that, given the larger narrative, the natural reading of Genesis 4 would understand that the two brothers bring their offering to the entrance of the garden, the place portrayed as God's sanctuary in the story.[26] In this, Genesis seems to anticipate Israel's worship, where Israel assembles to sacrifice its offerings on an altar that is placed not in the holy place itself but at its entrance (Exod. 40:29; Lev. 1:3; etc.).

Strikingly, then, there is a discernible movement going eastward from the garden starting with humanity's eating of the forbidden fruit. First, in

25. Note that Enoch "walks" with God in Gen. 5:22, but God is not the subject of the verb in the same way as in the garden story (cf. Gen. 3:8).

26. Morales, *Tabernacle Pre-Figured*, 111.

Genesis 3 we learn that the entrance to the garden is "at the east" (Gen. 3:24), implying that Adam and Eve go out from it in an eastward direction. Second, after his sin, Cain is sent away from "the presence of the LORD" and settles in "the land of Nod, *east* of Eden" (Gen. 4:16). From this we see that "the presence of the LORD" appears to be primarily identified with the garden. Adam and Eve were sent outside of it, but Cain is driven further away.

As critical scholars often note, the motif of exile shapes the Pentateuch.[27] The stories of Adam and Eve being banished from the garden and Cain's punishment as a "wanderer" (Gen. 4:12) set up the exile motif. Indeed, ancient rabbinic interpretation connected the story of Genesis 3 with Israel's exile. In *Rabbah Genesis*, one rabbi speaking in the voice of God explains:

> Just as I led Adam into the garden of Eden, and commanded him and he transgressed my commandment, whereupon I punished him by dismissal and exile . . . so also did I bring his descendants into the land of Israel and command them, and they transgressed my commands, and I punished them by dismissal and exile.[28]

Israel's exile is likened to the expulsion of Eden. Sin equals banishment from God's presence.

Exile from God's Presence and Death

In the biblical literature, exile means being parted from God's holy presence, identified with the Jerusalem temple. For example, through the prophet Jeremiah, God warns the people of exile, saying, "I will surely lift you up and *send you away from my presence*" (Jer. 23:39). Later, the exile is described in similar terms: "The things that happened in Jerusalem and Judah so angered the LORD that *he cast them from his presence*" (Jer. 52:3). That God's presence is localized in a unique way in the Jerusalem temple is clear from numerous texts.

Similarly, in the opening lines of Psalm 42, the psalmist speaks of his longing to be with God: "My soul thirsts for God, for the living God. When

27. Richard H. Moye therefore highlights the "main" themes of "exile and return" in the Pentateuch. See Richard H. Moye, "In the Beginning: Myth and History in Genesis and Exodus," *JBL* 109 (1990): 577–98.

28. See *Rabbah Genesis* 19:9. Translation from Gary Anderson, *Christian Doctrine and the Old Testament: Theology in the Service of Biblical Exegesis* (Grand Rapids: Baker Academic, 2017), 59. Anderson goes on to discuss the connection between Gen. 3 and Israel's exile (70–71).

shall I go and see *the face of God*?" (Ps. 42:2). That the psalmist expects his yearning to see the "face of God" to be fulfilled by going to the sanctuary is made clear in the following lines:

> These things I remember,
> as I pour out my soul within me:
> how I walked with the multitudes,
> and led them in procession *to the house of God*. (Ps. 42:4)

The psalmist longs for the presence of the Lord as he pines to return to the liturgical processions that went up to "the house of God." The psalmist goes on to speak of his pining for the sanctuary. The language in the following lines speaks of flood waters overwhelming him: "All your waves and your breakers have swept over me" (Ps. 42:7). In other words, being deprived of God's presence in the sanctuary is not simply a matter of nostalgia; it is described as a matter of life and death.

Something similar can be detected in Psalm 84, where the psalmist declares:

> How lovely is your dwelling place,
> O Lord of hosts!
> My soul longs and wastes away
> for the courts of the Lord. (Ps. 84:1–2)

The psalmist describes how he "wastes away" because he is unable to be in the temple. Going on, the psalmist prays, "One day in your courts is better than a thousand elsewhere" (Ps. 84:10). Why is the temple to be desired? We are told, "The Lord God is a sun and shield" (Ps. 84:11)—light, warmth, protection, and so forth are thus associated with the Lord's sanctuary.

We can now turn back to the story of Cain and note that when he is said to be sent away from "the presence of the Lord," he complains, "*I shall be hidden from your face*; I shall be a fugitive and a wanderer on the earth, and *whoever finds me will kill me*" (Gen. 4:14). Notice that Cain does not simply speak of concern about being murdered. Cain's concern that he will lose his life is explicitly linked to being driven from God's presence and God's "face." Life is found in God's presence; outside of it one is exposed to death.

I would suggest that all of this helps us better understand the story of Adam and Eve. The Lord is not unreliable in assuring them that the day they eat of the fruit they shall die. Given the larger themes in Genesis and Israel's traditions elsewhere, we can see how being cast away from God's presence in the garden is tantamount to a kind of death. As Gordon Wenham writes, "Only life in the garden counts as life in the fullest sense."[29]

Christ as the New Adam and the Hope for the Oil of Mercy

In the previous chapter, we noted that oil was associated with Jewish eschatological hopes. Here we can turn to look at ways this is brought together with the New Testament's teaching that Christ comes to reverse the effects of Adam's sin.

Christ as the New Adam in Paul

Above we looked at Wisdom of Solomon, which explains that "through the devil's envy death came into the world" (Wis. 2:24). This may very well represent an early interpretation of the story of Adam and Eve, which we have seen brings together disobedience and death. It appears that at least some Jews held that Adam's sin had implications for all humanity. Paul brings these traditions together. Though Genesis does not explicitly describe Adam and Eve's eating of the fruit as a "sin," Paul is explicit about the sinful nature of Adam's deed. In 1 Corinthians 15, he explains that "all die in Adam" (1 Cor. 15:22). In his epistle to the Romans, he further elaborates.

In Romans, Paul says, "Sin came into the world through one man, and death through sin" (Rom. 5:12). Going on, he adds a phrase that has been much discussed: "and so death spread to all people with the result that [*eph' hō*] all have sinned" (Rom. 5:12). The core question is: What does the Greek phrase *eph' hō*—which I have translated "with the result that"—mean?[30] Latin translations rendered this expression as "in whom." In other words, Latin Bibles indicated that Paul spoke of how all have sinned "in Adam." This was understood to imply that all humanity is implicated in Adam's sin. It is often said that, on the basis of this erroneous reading, Augustine developed the doctrine of "original sin."[31] This doctrine holds that Adam's descendants are

29. Gordon Wenham, *Genesis 1–15*, WBC 1 (Nashville: Nelson, 1987), 83.

30. I borrow the translation from Joseph A. Fitzmyer, *Romans*, AB 33 (New York: Doubleday, 1993), 413–17.

31. See, e.g., Elaine Pagels, *Adam, Eve, and the Serpent: Sex and Politics in Early Christianity* (New York: Random House, 1989), 109.

born with a "fallen nature" and are therefore in need of salvation from their very birth. A few words on this are in order.

First, the doctrine of original sin is not simply or even primarily based on Romans 5:12. As one Augustinian scholar says of Augustine's theology of original sin, "The main influence was Romans 7 and 9 and 1 Corinthians 15, not the much-discussed Romans 5:12."[32] Other texts such as Psalm 51:5 ("I was born in iniquity, and in sin did my mother conceive me") also played an important role in the development of the doctrine.

Second, it must be clarified that the doctrine of original sin does not mean that all humans are necessarily damned from birth—that is, subject to eternal torment in hell. While it is true that Augustine taught that, without baptism, unbaptized infants are unable to enter heavenly beatitude and end up in hell, his understanding of what this entailed is far more nuanced and complex than is often appreciated. For one thing, he insisted that such individuals would find only the "gentlest" of punishments awaiting them.[33] Moreover, it should also be emphasized that Augustine's views were not universally adopted as part of the doctrine of original sin. Thomas Aquinas makes clear that no one can be sent to hell due to the sin of another and that damnation must be merited by one's own personal sins.[34]

Third, although Augustine had an important role to play in the development of the doctrine of original sin, he was hardly its originator.[35] More recent work in Origen has called into question previous readings of the Alexandrian's views about creation. While older approaches emphasized his debt to Platonism, there is a greater recognition that the biblical texts are the primary source for his theology.[36] Although it is often overlooked, Origen sometimes sounds remarkably similar to Augustine. Thomas Scheck observes that Origen "seems to allow the interpretation of Romans 5:12 as a relative clause, i.e., 'in whom,' namely in Adam."[37] Origen interprets Romans 5 not

32. Paul Rigby, "Original Sin," in *Augustine through the Ages: An Encyclopedia*, ed. Allan D. Fitzgerald (Grand Rapids: Eerdmans, 1999), 607.

33. Augustine, *Enchiridion on Faith, Hope, and Love* 23.93.

34. See, e.g., Thomas Aquinas, *Commentary on the Sentences*, II, d. 32, q. 2, a. 2, c. 2.

35. See the sources discussed in Carol Harrison, *Augustine: Christian Truth and Fractured Humanity*, CTC (Oxford: Oxford University Press, 2000), 89n18.

36. See, e.g., the discussions in Ronald E. Heine, *Origen: An Introduction to His Life and Thought* (Eugene, OR: Cascade Books, 2019), 95–107; John Behr, ed. and trans., *Origen: On First Principles*, vol. 1, OECT (Oxford: Oxford University Press, 2017), lvi–lxxxviii.

37. See Origen, *Commentary on the Epistle to the Romans, Books 1–5*, trans. Thomas Scheck, FC 103 (Washington, DC: Catholic University of America Press, 2001), 303n1.

only in light of 1 Corinthians 15:22, where all die "in Adam," but also in light of Hebrews, which speaks of the way Levi was in the loins of Abraham (Heb. 7:9–10). Origen says:

> *How much more were all men, those who are born and have been born in this world, in Adam's loins* when he was still in paradise. And all men who were with [Adam], or rather in him, were expelled from paradise when he was himself driven out from there; and through him the death which had come to him from the transgression consequently passed through to them as well, who were dwelling in his loins; and therefore the Apostle rightly says, "For as in Adam all die, so also in Christ all will be made alive" [1 Cor. 15:22].[38]

Although we have to rely on Rufinus's Latin translation of Origen's work, which abridges Origen's commentary and bears the former's fingerprints, there is no reason to doubt that Origen used 1 Corinthians 15:22, which speaks of all dying "in Adam," as a lens for interpreting Romans 5. The interpretation offered by this is hardly far-fetched. If Paul believes that all participate in death "in Adam" (1 Cor. 15:22), and Romans 5:12–19 indicates death is the result of sin, it makes sense to think that Paul held that all are also somehow implicated in Adam's sin. Such a reading is even more plausible since at least one strand of Jewish interpretation took this view.

Fourth, Paul may very well hold *two* ideas together—namely, that (1) all were somehow implicated in Adam's sin *and* that (2) Adam's sin is recapitulated in the lives of each believer, who are under the reign of sin not only because of Adam but due to their own transgressions as well. Either way, whatever one makes of Romans 5:12,[39] the rest of the section leaves no doubt that Paul teaches that Adam's sin is what brought death into the world.[40] About Adam, Paul writes:

- "By the trespass of one man the many died" (Rom. 5:15).
- "By the trespass of one man death reigned through that one man" (Rom. 5:17).

38. Origen, *Commentary on Romans* 5.1.14, in Origen, *Commentary on the Epistle to the Romans*, 311 (emphasis added).

39. For an intriguing alternative approach, see Matthew V. Novenson, *Paul and Judaism at the End of History* (Cambridge: Cambridge University Press, 2024), 201–2.

40. Remarkably, Augustine makes a similar point, acknowledging the different ways of reading Rom. 5:12. See Augustine, *Answer to the Two Letters of the Pelagians* 4.7.

- "Through the disobedience of one man the many were *made* [*katestathēsan*] *sinners*" (Rom. 5:19).

Paul maintains that death and sin are inextricably bound together and that both entered the world through Adam. In sum, death results from sin.

The reverse side of this for Paul, of course, is that where sin entered through Adam's disobedience, Christ's obedience has brought life and caused believers to become just: "Through one righteous act [*dikaiōmatos*] all people came to justification of life" (Rom. 5:18). Note here that "justification"—a term bound up with "righteousness"—is linked to "life." Whereas Adam's disobedience brought sin and death, Christ's obedience brought righteousness and life. These ideas are brought together in a fascinating work known as the *Life of Adam and Eve*. What makes this work especially relevant for our purposes is that here we find early evidence that the Christian use of oil was connected with the idea that what was lost in Adam is restored in Christ.

Adam and the Hope for the Oil of Mercy

The origins of the *Life of Adam and Eve* have long baffled scholars. Some suggest it is based on a pre-Christian Jewish work.[41] There are good reasons to think that Paul knew some form of it or at least was drawing on traditions that influenced it.[42] Elements of the narrative of the *Life of Adam and Eve* also appear to be known to the author of the *Protoevangelium of James*,[43] a work dated to the second century.[44] In its final form, however, the *Life of Adam and Eve* bears the mark of a Christian writer. The Greek version of the narrative, which is undoubtedly earlier than the Latin, is therefore probably best dated between the second and fourth centuries.[45] One of its most arresting features is its imaginative account of Adam's death.

41. See, e.g., Michael D. Eldridge, *Dying Adam with His Multiethnic Family*, SVTP 16 (Leiden: Brill, 2001).

42. John R. Levison, *The Greek Life of Adam and Eve*, CEJL (Berlin: De Gruyter, 2023), 141–45; Levison, "Adam and Eve in Romans 1.18–25 and the Greek *Life of Adam and Eve*," *NTS* 50 (2004): 519–34.

43. Compare, e.g., *Protoevangelium of James* 13:1 with *Greek Life of Adam and Eve (Apocalypse of Moses)* 7:1–2 and 17:1.

44. Bart Ehrman and Zlatko Pleše, *The Apocryphal Gospels* (Oxford: Oxford University Press, 2011), 31–35.

45. Marinus de Jonge and Johannes Tromp, *The Life of Adam and Eve and Related Literature* (Sheffield: Sheffield Academic, 1997), 77. The Greek version has often been known as the *Apocalypse of Moses*.

Realizing his end is near, Adam calls his sons together. In the Latin version, he is depicted as sick and in bed. Adam's children are perplexed by his condition. They do not understand what is happening to him. We read: "And all his sons said to him, 'What is it, Father, to be sick with pains?'" (*Life of Adam and Eve* 30:4).[46] The scene highlights the horror of physical death and suffering. The children of Adam have never witnessed a fatal illness. What they are seeing unfold before their eyes is profoundly distressing to them.

Adam makes known to his sons why he is deteriorating. God, he explains, announced that suffering would come upon him because of his faithlessness in the garden (*Life of Adam and Eve* 34:1–2).[47] The point is obvious: sin results in sickness and death. Yet Adam has one last hope for solace: *oil*.

Going on, Adam asks Eve and Seth to return to the garden and implore the Lord for a certain holy chrism that can be found in the garden:

> Rise and go with my son Seth to *the regions of Paradise* and put dust on your heads and prostrate yourselves to the ground and mourn in the sight of God. Perhaps he will have mercy and send his angel to the tree of his mercy, *from which flows the oil of life*, and will give you a little of it with which *to anoint me, that I might have rest from these pains by which I am wasting away*. (*Life of Adam and Eve* 36:1–2)[48]

In the earlier, Greek edition of the story, Adam asks for the "oil of mercy," which is a play on words in Greek (*to elaion tou eleou*). The holy oil of paradise, then, is portrayed as the remedy for that which ails Adam. The solution to his plight is the oil from the tree of life.

What is found in the story of the *Life of Adam and Eve* is strikingly similar to other ancient works. *Fourth Ezra*, a work that likely dates to the end of the first century AD, explains that in the future age the tree of life will be a source of perfume that will bring refreshment: "The tree of life shall give them fragrant perfume, and they shall neither toil nor become weary" (*4 Ezra* 2:12).[49] This passage also is evocative of what we find in *2 Enoch*, where supernatural oil is associated with a heavenly garden of Eden (cf. *2 Enoch* 8:5). Both books, which seem to have been important to Christian readers, bear witness to a tradition that links supernatural oil to Eden.

46. *OTP* 2:270.
47. *OTP* 2:272.
48. *OTP* 2:272 (emphasis added).
49. *OTP* 1:527.

In the *Life of Adam and Eve*, the story continues with Eve and Seth's trip back to the garden of Eden. Upon reaching it, Eve and Seth pray for "many hours," asking the Lord to "pity Adam in his pains and to send his angel to give them *the oil from the tree of mercy*" (*Life of Adam and Eve* 40:3; 41:1). At last, Michael appears and explains that they are not to be given the chrism. It will be available only "in the last days" (*Life of Adam and Eve* 42:1).[50]

In a few copies of the Latin version of the *Life of Adam and Eve*, the angel explicitly links the future gift of oil to the coming of Christ:

> The most beloved Christ, Son of God, shall come upon the earth to revive the body of Adam and with him the bodies of the dead. And when he, the Son of God, comes, he himself will be baptized in the river Jordan, and when he has come out of the water of the Jordan, then *he will anoint from the oil of mercy all who believe in him*. And *the oil of mercy shall be from generation to generation for those who are born again of water and the Holy Spirit into eternal life*. Then the most beloved Son of God, Christ, shall descend to the earth, and lead your father Adam to Paradise to the tree of mercy.[51]

Here we likely have a Christian expansion that seeks to make explicit what Michael means when he says the sacred oil will be made available in the "last days." The Armenian version of the text seems to preserve a more primitive version of the story. There Michael is portrayed as finally anointing Adam in the eschatological age.[52]

It is not hard to explain the reason for these expansions of the story. Later Christians likely revised the text to more clearly indicate that the hope for oil would be realized in Christ. For early Christians, Jesus's coming was understood to inaugurate the "messianic age." In the New Testament, Christ has ushered in the "last days" (Acts 2:16–17; Heb. 1:2; cf. 1 Cor. 10:11). Here the oil is especially connected with baptismal imagery ("born again of water and the Holy Spirit"); it is the baptized who receive this oil of healing. Still, it is incredibly difficult to establish that the oil reflects *only* baptismal practices and is in no way related to the ancient and widespread practice of anointing the sick with oil.

50. *OTP* 2:274 (emphasis added).

51. *OTP* 2:274n42a (emphasis added).

52. See Michael E. Stone, "The Angelic Prediction in the Primary Adam Books," in *Literature on Adam and Eve: Collected Essays*, ed. Gary A. Anderson, Michael E. Stone, and Johannes Tromp (Leiden: Brill, 2000), 118.

Christ as the Oil of Mercy

The story of the oil of mercy promised to Adam is further expanded upon in *The Legend of the Holy Rood Tree*, which purports to tell the story of the true cross. The work is likely dated to the late twelfth to early thirteenth century and enjoyed immense popularity throughout Europe in the Middle Ages. Notably, here the oil of mercy is explicitly identified as Christ himself. After Seth has a vision of a child at the top of the tree of life in Eden, he is told:

> The child you have just seen is the Son of God, who mourns the sins of your parents, whose sins he shall also erase when the fullness of time comes: *This one is the Oil of Mercy promised to your parents.*[a]

Jesus thus not only is the *dispenser* of the supernatural oil but *is* the oil of mercy itself.

a. Translation from Stephen C. E. Hopkins, "The Legend of the Holy Rood Tree: A New Translation and Introduction," in *New Testament Apocrypha: More Noncanonical Scriptures*, ed. Tony Burke (Grand Rapids: Eerdmans, 2020), 2:155.

There is also a parallel account in the *Gospel of Nicodemus*, which is difficult to date with confidence. The earliest known Greek manuscript of it dates to the twelfth century, but most acknowledge that it likely preserves textual traditions that go back to the fifth or sixth century.[53] Here we find a section known as *Christ's Descent into Hell*, which was likely originally an independent work that came to be added to the *Gospel of Nicodemus*. In this section, Adam's son Seth explains:

> An angel of the Lord came and asked me, . . . "Because of the sickness of your father do you desire the oil that raises up the sick, or the tree from which flows such oil? This cannot be found now. Therefore go and tell your father that . . . the only-begotten Son of God shall then become man and shall descend upon

53. See J. K. Elliott, *The Apocryphal New Testament: A Collection of Apocryphal Christian Literature in an English Translation* (Oxford: Oxford University Press, 1993), 164–66; Barbara Baert, *The Heritage of Holy Wood: The Legend of the True Cross in Text and Image* (Leiden: Brill, 2004), 316.

> the earth. And he shall anoint him with that oil." (*Christ's Descent into Hell* 3 [19].1)[54]

The reappearance of the legend about Adam longing to be healed and the notion that Christ would one day make the anointing he longed for possible suggests this tradition's popularity in Christian circles.[55] The apocryphal story brings together biblical traditions we have been exploring in this chapter: suffering, death, the effects of sin, and holy *oil*. Strikingly, what we find here is a conviction that the healing Adam longed for is realized through the anointing brought in *Christ*—the "Messiah," or "Anointed One." The imagery here seems even more reflective of the practice of anointing of the sick than baptism.

Oil in Early Christian Healing

Does the apocryphal story of Adam's longing for oil tell us anything about ancient Christian use of oil in ministering to the sick, or is the "anointing" in Christ merely spiritual and unrelated to any use of physical oil? We must avoid false dichotomies. The use of material oil in Christian practice certainly does not rule out a theological understanding of a corresponding *spiritual* anointing.[56] After all, the theology of a spiritual washing in Christ did not rule out for early Christians the importance of a rite of physical washing in baptism. We need not pit ritual against faith or theology as if ritual were *necessarily* "empty." As we have seen, James's instructions indicate that Christians used oil to minister to the sick and suffering—but they also prayed over the sick. The tradition that an ailing Adam longed for the oil that finally became available in Christ shows us that Christians were developing a theology of oil that would further illuminate its use.

Some might ask whether the oil is to be seen as merely medicinal or whether it is understood to work healing effects because of the work of God. This question, however, represents ignorance about James's ancient context. Medicine and beliefs about the gods were intertwined. As Manfred Horstmanshoff explains,

> Temple medicine is an integral part of ancient Greek medicine. . . . The story that Hippocrates copied out the *Iamata* [= texts describing miraculous healings]

54. Translation from Elliott, *Apocryphal New Testament*, 186–87.
55. See *Gospel of Nicodemus* 19 (*Christ's Descent into Hell* 3 [19].1).
56. In the apocryphal *Acts of Thomas* 67, an actual physical anointing takes place in connection with a prayer that speaks of spiritual anointing.

Origen on "Visible Anointing" and the Gift of the Spirit

Origen recognizes that a physical anointing is part of the baptismal rite of his day, which points to a spiritual reality—the gift of the Spirit:

> And although all of us may be baptized in those visible waters and in a *visible anointing,* in accordance with the form handed down to the churches, nevertheless, the one who has died to sin and is truly baptized into the death of Christ and is buried with him through baptism into death, he is the one who is truly baptized in the Holy Spirit and with the water from above.[a]

a. Origen, *Commentary on Romans* 5.8.3. Translation from Origen, *Commentary on the Epistle to the Romans, Books 1–5,* trans. Thomas P. Scheck, FC 103 (Washington, DC: Catholic University of America Press, 2001), 355.

> at the temple of Asclepius on Cos, the presence of the gods as witnesses to the "Hippocratic Oath," and the attendance of physicians at the temples all point to a symbiotic relationship.[57]

What is found here is also present in ancient Jewish sources, which—as we will see in more detail in the next chapter—attribute the efficacy of physicians' efforts to God.[58] In short, while modern readers may want to ask James whether he attributes the use of oil to medicinal effects or to divine intervention, such a dichotomy reflects a modern rather than ancient perspective.[59]

What is most important here, however, is to note that this passage from the *Life of Adam and Eve* shows unmistakably that the early Church connected the hope for healing with the coming of the Messiah—healing is found in Christ. These hopes are unmistakably rooted in the Genesis traditions that connect exile from God's presence with death. The *Life of Adam of Eve* makes explicit that these expectations are fulfilled in the New Testament traditions where Christ—the "Messiah"—is depicted as coming to bring healing through deliverance from sin and death.

57. Manfred Horstmanshoff, "Aelius Aristides: A Suitable Case for Treatment," in *Paideia: The World of the Second Sophistic*, ed. Barbara E. Borg (Berlin: De Gruyter, 2004), 289.

58. Sir. 38:6–9, 12–15; Philo, *Allegorical Interpretation* 3.178. These will be discussed below.

59. See Sophie Laws, *The Epistle of James*, BNTC (London: Adam & Charles Black, 1980), 227.

Do the appearances of oil in Mark and James have anything to do with the traditions about Adam and/or the coming of Christ we have looked at above? There are no obvious telltale signs that Mark knows the *Life of Adam and Eve*. In James, there is at least one interesting parallel; the letter describes God as "the Father of lights" (James 1:17), a title for God that also appears in the *Life of Adam and Eve* 36:3. But this is flimsy evidence for thinking James knows this particular Jewish work or that it has influenced his theology.

That said, since Paul seems to know traditions found in the *Life of Adam and Eve*, and given the fact that anointing is connected in Mark with the apostles' share in Jesus's *messianic* ministry, it is difficult to insist that James was completely unaware of emerging traditions that linked oil to eschatological hopes. As Allison writes, "It makes sense to see the oil as mediating divine power."[60] In addition, as we saw at the end of the previous chapter, James seems to draw upon expectations of Jesus's eschatological return (James 5:7), reinforcing the presence of eschatological themes. It seems likely, then, that James finds oil to be a fitting symbol for hopes that healing will occur through the invocation of the Messiah's name. And it is likely that he thought of the oil somehow *doing* what it symbolizes.

In the next chapter we will investigate the way Jesus's ministry of physical healing is connected to spiritual healing—that is, forgiveness of sins. This will put us in a better position to approach one of the key questions that has surrounded the practice of anointing the sick: In what way does the sacrament bring about healing? More specifically, what is the relationship between physical and spiritual healing?

60. Allison, *James*, 759, 761.

5

Healing and the Forgiveness of Sins

Salvation for the Sick

> And the prayer of faith will save the one who is sick, and the Lord will raise him up. And *if he has committed sins, he will be forgiven.*
>
> —James 5:15

> Given that bodily and spiritual health were scarcely distinct categories for early Christians, an exclusive emphasis upon the physical may assume a false dichotomy.
>
> —Dale C. Allison Jr.[1]

As we have seen, James 5 appears to associate physical healing with what might be called spiritual healing—that is, forgiveness of sins. In this chapter, we revisit questions we first raised in chapter 2:

- What is the relationship between sickness and sin?
- Does forgiveness of sins bring about a cure of physical ailments?

1. Dale C. Allison Jr., *James*, ICC (London: Bloomsbury, 2013), 766.

Once again, in this chapter we will discover that interpreting James properly requires us to see how his teaching is informed by the scriptures of Israel.

We should begin with an important observation: James does not insist that all who become ill do so simply because they have committed sin. Some biblical writers are adamant in rejecting the idea that sickness is the result of sin. James is clearly aware of such texts. The book of Job, for example, famously rejects the contention that sickness and infirmity are proof of personal guilt (Job 2:7–10).[2] James assumes his readers are familiar with Job's story: "You have heard of the patient endurance of Job" (James 5:11). This seems to rule out the possibility that James holds that sickness is *necessarily* the result of personal sin; he knows the righteous suffer.

Still, within the context of physical healing, James writes, "Confess your sins to one another and pray for one another, that you may be healed" (James 5:16). While James does not attribute *all* sickness to sin, this verse does seem to imply a connection between the two *can* exist. Such a view is well established in various biblical traditions.

It is important to make two general points up front. First, we should definitely reject approaches that portray Jewish attitudes toward the sick as somehow cold and heartless. For example, in his book on sacramental theology Bernard Häring begins his discussion of the sacrament of anointing of the sick by describing "the widespread conviction of the Semitic world" that "looked down upon the sick person as a sinner."[3] This view is not only shaded with troubling antisemitic tendencies, but it also fails to do justice to the nuanced understanding of sickness in ancient Judaism, expressed in books like Job. We must be on guard against approaches that seek to elevate the New Testament's teaching by disparaging the Jewish world out of which it came.[4] The better we appreciate the Jewish sources of the Letter of James, the better we will be able to interpret its teaching.

A second caution also bears repeating. The idea that infirmity can be caused by sin is often profoundly troubling to modern readers. Those who

2. For other examples, see Amy-Jill Levine and Ben Witherington III, *The Gospel of Luke*, NCBC (Cambridge: Cambridge University Press, 2018), 144.

3. Bernard Häring, *The Sacraments and Your Everyday Life* (Liguori, MO: Liguori Publications, 1976), 181.

4. For a helpful corrective that every Christian student of the New Testament should read and reread as an important reminder, see Amy-Jill Levine, "Bearing False Witness: Common Errors Made about Early Judaism," in *The Jewish Annotated New Testament*, ed. Amy-Jill Levine and Mark Zvi Brettler, 2nd ed. (Oxford: Oxford University Press, 2017), 759–63.

are sick may be led to wonder if some unknown personal sin is the cause of their affliction. Those who struggle with spiritual scrupulosity are especially prone to such thoughts. Yet one is hard-pressed to find biblical support that sickness results from sins of which a person is unaware.

In this chapter, then, we will first examine sources where sin and sickness are viewed as interrelated. While disease is sometimes presented as a punishment for a personal sin, individuals who repent are also sometimes portrayed as being healed by God. Second, we will turn to examine the relationship of sin and sickness in the New Testament's accounts of Jesus's ministry. Finally, we will return to James 5 and consider the implications of our analysis for understanding that important passage.

Sickness and Sin in Jewish Sources

As we have noted above, the book of Job famously rejects the notion that sickness and affliction are proof of personal guilt (Job 2:7–10). It is important to emphasize this point given the antisemitic trope that Jews all regarded the sick, weak, and disabled as somehow cursed and so mistreated and discarded them, which ignores what is found in various Jewish sources.[5] At the same time, without implying that it necessarily led to a cold neglect or abuse of the infirm, we can recognize that, as Bernd Kollmann writes, "interpreting sickness and death as divine punishment for sins is a common feature in Second Temple literature."[6] We should also hasten to add a further point: it was understood that those who are sick due to sin could be healed by Israel's God if they repented.

Sin and Sickness, Repentance and Restoration

In Exodus 15, God promises the following to Israel through Moses:

> If you will listen carefully to the voice of the Lord your God, and you do what is right in his sight, and if you pay attention to his commandments and keep all his precepts, then I will not bring upon you any of the diseases that I brought upon the Egyptians, for I am the Lord, your healer. (Exod. 15:26)

5. See Levine and Witherington, *Gospel of Luke*, 144–45.

6. See Bernd Kollmann, "Sickness and Disease," in *T&T Clark Encyclopedia of Second Temple Judaism*, ed. Daniel M. Gurtner and Loren T. Stuckenbruck, 2 vols. (London: Bloomsbury T&T Clark, 2020), 2:736.

According to this passage, health is inextricably bound up with obedience to the Lord. The divine warning is unmistakable in meaning: God will not bring diseases on Israel, but this is a contingent promise—the people will avoid the diseases suffered by the Egyptians *only if* they are obedient to the Lord's commandments. Said another way: if the Israelites fail to keep the Lord's laws, they can count on suffering as the Egyptians did. The reader of Exodus knows better than to see this as an empty threat. The Egyptians had opposed the God of Israel and so brought upon themselves the various plagues sent by the Lord through Moses (Exod. 7:14–12:32). The lesson Israel is to learn is simple: disobedience to the Lord will be punished with suffering. Exodus 15:26 spells out the specific kind of suffering Israel should expect sin to trigger: affliction with "diseases."

Nevertheless, the passage above from Exodus does not conclude on this point. God is also described to Israel as "your healer" (Exod. 15:26). This image for God is repeated later in the book of Exodus. In Exodus 23, the Lord declares, "You shall serve the Lord your God, and he will bless your bread and your water, and *I will take away sickness from among you*" (Exod. 23:25). Here we see that while infirmity is connected to sin, the Lord is also portrayed as capable of removing such sickness. In other words, if the people of Israel heed the Lord, they will be healed. This promise plays out in various ways in the historical books. Sin is connected with sickness; yet in some cases, health seems to be restored due to repentance.

A prominent example of the principles articulated above is found in the book of Numbers. In Numbers 12, Moses's sister Miriam participates in a rebellion against her brother. We read: "And the anger of the Lord was kindled against them" (Num. 12:9). Immediately after this, Miriam is struck with leprosy. Miriam's condition is best interpreted as a punishment from God. The text explicitly indicates that the leprosy is the result of sinfulness. Aaron implores Moses, "Please, my lord, *do not punish us for a sin* that we have foolishly committed" (Num. 12:11). In later rabbinic tradition, there is no doubt about the penal nature of the leprosy. The account of Miriam plays a prominent role in the discussion of leprosy as a divine punishment for slander (cf. *Babylonian Talmud Shabbat* 97a; *Rabbah Leviticus* 16:1). Even Rabbi Maimonides explains that the Sages have laid down "the established principle" that leprosy "is a punishment for slander."[7]

7. Moses Maimonides, *The Guide of the Perplexed* 3.47, trans. Shlomo Pines, 2 vols. (Chicago: University of Chicago Press, 1963), 2:596.

Yet the story does not end with Miriam in affliction. Moses intercedes for her, and she is healed. Sin leads to sickness; repentance, however, brings healing. This idea is underscored in other biblical texts.[8]

When King Jeroboam attempts to have a prophet who speaks against him arrested, the king's hand "withered so that he could not draw it back to himself" (1 Kings 13:4). Commentators recognize that the king is presented as incurring divine wrath for his action.[9] As in the case of Miriam above, in this episode the king's hand is restored after the king asks the prophet to pray on his behalf (1 Kings 13:6). In what appears to be an attempt to rectify his earlier response, the king even invites the prophet to dine at his house and promises to give him a gift (1 Kings 13:7). Though the prophet rejects the offer, announcing that he was told by the Lord to take no food or drink and to return home straightaway, the king's healing is nonetheless bound up with some sort of change of attitude on his part. The story also therefore suggests that infirmity can be reversed by repentance.[10]

Likewise, in the book of Daniel, King Nebuchadnezzar is told that a sickness will come upon him due to his arrogance. However, the prophet explains to him that his time of suffering can be minimized: "Redeem your sins by almsgiving and your iniquities by generosity to the poor" (Dan. 4:27).[11] In the end, he returns to his right state of mind and lives in prosperity, which, it seems, was due to his mitigating his punishment through following the prophet's advice.

In the Psalms, sickness is also understood to result from sin. Psalm 38 offers a classic expression of this. The psalmist begins by praying,

> O Lord, do not rebuke me in your anger
>   or discipline me in your wrath.
> For your arrows have pierced me,
>   and your hand has pressed down on me.
> There is no soundness in my flesh
>   because of your indignation;

8. For this understanding in nonbiblical Jewish texts, see Rebecca Raphael, "Sickness and Disease," in *The Eerdmans Dictionary of Early Judaism*, ed. John J. Collins and Daniel C. Harlow (Grand Rapids: Eerdmans, 2010), 1228–30.

9. See, e.g., Mordechai Cogan, *I Kings*, AB 10 (New York: Doubleday, 2001), 368.

10. A similar story is found in 2 Kings 1 involving King Ahaziah. See also the story of Antiochus in 1 Macc. 6, who attributes his sickness to his evil deeds (1 Macc. 6:12).

11. Translation taken from Gary A. Anderson, *Sin: A History* (New Haven: Yale University Press, 2009), 142 (for a defense, see 135–51).

Cyril of Jerusalem and the Healing Power of Repentance

In his *Catechetical Lectures,* which are dated to sometime in the middle of the 300s, Cyril of Jerusalem highlights King Hezekiah as a model of repentance, explaining that the king was able to avert sickness by turning away from sin. According to Isaiah 38, after the king falls sick, he is told by the prophet Isaiah that he will not recover from his illness (Isa. 38:1). Hezekiah's response is to turn to the LORD and beseech him with tears (Isa. 38:2–3). The LORD hears the king's prayers and promises to add fifteen years to his life (Isa. 38:5). Cyril writes:

> Do you want to know what kind of power repentance has? Do you want to know what a strong weapon of salvation it is and learn what the force of confession is? . . . [Hezekiah] by repentance obtained the recall of a divine sentence that had already been pronounced. . . . Hezekiah did not desist from repentance. Instead, he remembered what is written, "When you shall turn and lament, then you shall be saved" [Isa. 30:15].[a]

a. Cyril of Jerusalem, *Catechetical Lectures* 2.15; translation from Joel C. Elowsky, *We Believe in the Holy Spirit*, ACD 4 (Downers Grove, IL: IVP Academic, 2009), 55.

there is no health in my bones
  because of my sin. (Ps. 38:1–3)

Here guilt and infirmity are inseparable. The psalmist goes on to describe his physical ailments. His wounds "grow foul and fester" (Ps. 38:5), his "loins are filled with burning" (Ps. 38:7), and his "pain is always with me" (Ps. 38:17). Writing on these verses, the famous Psalms scholar Mitchell Dahood explains that the passage reflects the "common belief that illness was a punishment for sin."[12]

How can the afflicted one find relief? The answer seems to be a confession of sin: "I confess my guilt; / I am sorry for my sin" (Ps. 38:18). Some commentators suggest there is a tension between this admission and the next line, in which the psalmist complains that his enemies hate him without cause

12. Mitchell Dahood, *Psalms I:1–50*, AB 16 (Garden City, NY: Doubleday, 1965), 234.

(Ps. 38:19). Yet there is no necessary conflict here. The psalmist could be oppressed by others wrongfully but also know of sins that are not necessarily directed against his persecutors.[13] The bottom line is that the psalmist seems to attribute his suffering to the guilt of sin. The psalm's ending then asks the Lord to be "my salvation" (Ps. 38:22). In this, once again repentance of sin is linked with the hope of salvation.

Sin, Healing, and Physicians

Sirach is an especially fascinating text in that it not only deals with the connection of sin, sickness, forgiveness, and healing but also discusses the role of physicians. Consider a passage from Sirach 38:

> My child, when you are sick, do not be neglectful,
> but pray to the Lord, and he will heal you.
> Turn away from your trespasses and direct your hands rightly,
> and cleanse your heart from all sin. (Sir. 38:9–10)

In this passage, healing is closely bound up with forgiveness of sin. This, of course, suggests that the sin is in some way a cause of the sickness. Healing is tied to cleansing one's "heart" from sin.

Yet the passage goes on to speak of the work of physicians:

> And give the physician his place, for the Lord created him.
> Let him not leave you, for he is necessary.
> There may come a time when recovery is in the hands of physicians,
> for they too will pray to the Lord
> that he grant them success in diagnosis,[14]
> and in healing, for the preservation of life.
> The one who sins against his Maker
> will be defiant towards the physician.[15] (Sir. 38:12–15)

This passage underscores that while healing comes from God, this does not dispense one from the need of physicians. The sinner sets himself up not only against God but also against the physician.

13. John Goldingay, *Psalms*, 3 vols., BCOT (Grand Rapids: Baker Academic, 2006–7), 1:549.
14. I here follow the Greek text. The Hebrew reads "rest" instead of "diagnosis."
15. I here follow the Hebrew text. The Greek version has "may he fall into the hands of the physician."

In the West, people commonly distinguish between medicine and miracle, or natural and supernatural healing. A look at ancient Jewish works reveals that such distinctions were not common in the Second Temple period. For example, in the book of Sirach, written between 185 and 175 BC, we are told that physicians' ability to heal "is from the Most High" (Sir. 38:2). We read:

> And [God] gave skill to humans
> that he might be glorified in his wonderful deeds.
> By them the physician heals and removes pain,
> the pharmacist makes a mixture of them.
> God's works will never cease,
> and from him health spreads over all the earth.
> My child, do not delay when you are sick,
> but pray to the Lord, and he will heal you. (Sir. 38:6–9)

Healings, even when through human physicians, are said to be God's "wonderful deeds." The physician's success is not simply due to medical knowledge but is attributed to God-given skills. Eric Eve summarizes Sirach's understanding this way: "God generally chooses to exercise his healing power through the ministrations of a physician."[16] Philo, the first-century Alexandrian Jew, takes a similar view of healing as is found in Sirach. According to him, health comes through medical knowledge and physicians because God lets "both knowledge and practitioner enjoy the credit of healing, though it is God himself that heals by these means and without them."[17]

Healing and Forgiveness of Sins in Jesus's Ministry

There are passages in the canonical Gospels in which Jesus warns against attributing illness, infirmity, or suffering to sin. In John 9, Jesus's disciples see a man blind from birth and ask: "Rabbi, who sinned that he was born blind, this man or his parents?" (John 9:2). Jesus responds, "Neither this man nor his parents sinned. But it happened so that the works of God might be revealed in him" (John 9:3). Likewise, in Luke 13:1–5, Jesus insists that people who

16. Eric Eve, *The Jewish Context of Jesus' Miracles*, JSNTSup 231 (London: Sheffield Academic, 2002), 107–8.

17. Philo, *Allegorical Interpretation* 3.178; slightly adapted from Philo, *On the Creation; Allegorical Interpretation of Genesis 2 and 3*, trans. F. H. Colson and G. H. Whitaker, LCL 226 (Cambridge, MA: Harvard University Press, 1929), 421.

die tragically do not necessarily do so because of their sins. Nevertheless, the Jewish association between sin and sickness is not absent from the biblical Gospels. Even when they are portrayed as distinct realities, sin and sickness are interrelated.

Healing and Forgiveness of Sins in the Speech at Nazareth

In the Gospel of Luke, Jesus's public ministry commences with a speech in a synagogue at Nazareth. This episode is widely viewed as a programmatic scene that sets the stage for what follows in Luke's narrative.[18] Because of its importance, we will return to it frequently in chapters to come. Here Jesus reads a passage from Scripture, announcing its fulfillment in his ministry.

> The scroll of the prophet Isaiah was given to him, and when he had unrolled the scroll, he found the place where it was written,
>
> "The Spirit of the Lord is upon me,
> because he has anointed me
> to announce good news to the poor.
> He has sent me to proclaim *release to the captives*,
> *recovery of sight to the blind*,
> to let the oppressed go free,
> and to proclaim *the year of the Lord's favor* [Isa. 61:1–2]."
>
> Rolling up the scroll, he gave it to the attendant and sat down. And the eyes of everyone in the synagogue were fixed on him. He began to say to them, "Today, this scripture is fulfilled in your hearing." (Luke 4:17–21)

The figure of Isaiah 61 is said to be *anointed* by the Spirit. We will return to this in chapter 7 and consider more carefully what this means for Jesus's identity as the "Messiah"—that is, the "Anointed One." For now, let us focus on what Isaiah 61 says the coming anointed figure will do.

In Isaiah 61, the anointed one is repeatedly said to *announce* or *proclaim*. First, he is said to "announce good news to the poor." The Greek word translated "announce good news" (*euangelisasthai*; Luke 4:18; cf. Isa. 61:1 LXX) is the verbal form of the Greek word that is often rendered "gospel"

18. See, e.g., Alexander Phillip Thompson, *Recognition and the Resurrection Appearances of Luke 24*, BZNW 225 (Berlin: De Gruyter, 2023), 169.

(*euangelion*). Therefore, translating this word literally, we might say that the figure of Isaiah 61 comes to "gospelize." Going on, he is twice said to "proclaim." The Greek in these instances is *kēryxai* (Luke 4:18, 19), the verbal form of another Greek word that becomes important in Christian tradition: *kērygma*. Other New Testament writers use *kērygma* to refer to the saving message of Jesus (see 1 Cor. 2:4; 15:14; 2 Tim. 4:17; Titus 1:3). The word *kērygma* is therefore often used in Christian tradition as a shorthand description of the gospel message.

What is the gospel message? According to the passage from Isaiah, the gospel that is preached is not a general or nebulous message about salvation in the abstract. Rather, it is twofold: (1) "release to the captives" and (2) "recovery of sight to the blind." The essential gospel proclamation involves two fundamental ideas that are inextricably bound up together: "release" and miraculous healing.

The Greek term translated "release" is *aphesis*. Strikingly, outside of Luke 4, every time this term occurs in the Gospel of Luke it refers to "forgiveness" of sin.[19] In other words, one is "forgiven" of sin by being "released" from it. It may be helpful to put both words—"forgiveness" and "release"—together in translating certain passages so that this dual meaning is heard in English. For example, in Luke 1, John the Baptist's father speaks of how his son will one day "give knowledge of salvation to [God's] people by the *forgiveness of / release from* [*aphesis*] *their sins*" (Luke 1:77). Likewise, the evangelist describes how John preaches "a baptism of repentance for the *forgiveness of / release from* [*aphesis*] sins" (Luke 3:3).[20]

The verbal form of *aphesis*—*aphiēmi*—is also used with the sense of forgiveness in Luke. When Jesus announces to the paralytic that his sins have been "forgiven," *aphiēmi* is the term Jesus uses (Luke 5:20, 21, 23, 24).[21] The same verb occurs again in the story of the sinful woman who anoints Jesus when he says that her sins are "forgiven" (Luke 7:47). In addition, when Jesus teaches his disciples to pray the Lord's Prayer, he uses the same

19. See Barbara Reid and Shelly Matthews, *Luke*, Wisdom Commentary 43A–B, 2 vols. (Collegeville, MN: Liturgical Press, 2021), 140.

20. Here and below I will simply use the lexical form of the word rather than the inflected form that appears in context so that readers not familiar with Greek can more easily catch the term.

21. Notably, in the ancient Greek translation of the Old Testament the verb *aphiēmi* (as well as the noun form *aphesis*) carries both the dual connotations of "release" (e.g., Lev. 25:10; Isa. 61:1; Jer. 34:8, 15, 17 [41:8, 15, 17 LXX]) and "forgive" (e.g., Lev. 16:26; Isa. 55:7; see also Josephus, *Jewish War* 1.481).

verb in the petition involving forgiveness: "*Forgive* [*aphiēmi*] us our sins, for we ourselves *forgive* [*aphiēmi*] everyone indebted to us" (Luke 11:4). It may strike us as odd to think of being "released" from sin instead of merely "forgiven" of it, but that reflects our own conceptions. Notice that in the Lord's Prayer sin is described as a debt. Since one is "forgiven" of a debt by being "released" from it, the language makes sense. This is an essential conceptual framework through which forgiveness of sins is understood in biblical literature.[22]

Finally, it is also worth mentioning that the passage from Isaiah 61 highlights one other important dimension of the "good news" or "gospel": "to let the oppressed go free" (Luke 4:18). As the narrative of the Gospel of Luke unfolds, this idea is especially related to Jesus's exorcisms. It is also related to Jesus's healing ministry since Jewish sources understood that sickness could be the result of demonic activity.[23] The oppressors of God's people in Luke, then, are not merely political figures but spiritual ones; they are demons. In Acts, which is presented as the sequel to the Gospel of Luke, this is underscored when Peter describes how Jesus went around "healing all those *oppressed by the devil*" (Acts 10:38).

Immediately following Jesus's announcement that he has come to fulfill Isaiah 61, we read about the beginnings of Jesus's ministry in Galilee. His work begins with an exorcism: Jesus casts a demon out of a man in the synagogue at Capernaum (Luke 4:31–37). Here Jesus's mission to free those oppressed by spiritual powers commences.

Yet Jesus's work of healing is inextricably bound up with his work of "release." After the exorcism in the synagogue, Jesus next heals Peter's mother-in-law. This is described in an odd way; Jesus heals her by "rebuking the fever" (Luke 4:39). Here Jesus seems to speak to the sickness as if it were a person. This might suggest that the illness was due to a demon, though this is far from clear. Either way, the work of exorcism and healing go together. Immediately after the healing of Peter's mother-in-law, we read about Jesus doing both things, healing the sick *and* casting out demons (Luke 4:40–41). Whether or not the healing of Peter's wife's mother is meant to be read as

22. See Anderson, *Sin*; Nathan Eubank, *Wages of Cross-Bearing and Debt of Sin* (Berlin: De Gruyter, 2013).

23. See, e.g., various Dead Sea Scrolls (*4Qpap Damascus Document*[b] [4Q273], fragment 4, 2:1–11; *1QGenesis Apocryphon* 2:16–17), *Jubilees* 10:1–6; Pseudo-Philo, *Biblical Antiquities* 60.

an exorcism, we see that these ideas are all bound up tightly together. Jesus comes to proclaim "release"—from sin, from demons, and from sickness.[24]

What is especially worth highlighting is that the term used for the healing of Peter's mother-in-law's condition is, once again, a form of the verb *aphiēmi*, the term that elsewhere refers to "forgiveness" or "release": "[Jesus] stood over her and rebuked the fever, and *it left her* [*aphiēmi*]" (Luke 4:39). In all of this, Jesus is fulfilling the mission to proclaim the "forgiveness" and "release" described in Isaiah 61. This aspect of Jesus's ministry is given special attention in the book of Acts, in which Jesus's work is repeatedly tied to the forgiveness of sins (Acts 2:38; 3:18–19; 5:31; 10:38–43; 13:38).

Healing and Forgiveness in Jesus's Ministry in Luke

After the events in Luke 4, Luke 5 spotlights Jesus's work of overcoming sin and its effects. Jesus's power of overcoming sin is especially on display in the healing of the paralytic (Luke 5:17–26). Although we have already discussed the parallel accounts of this story in Matthew and Mark above, it is necessary to make a few more observations about Luke's version of the story. First, Jesus pronounces that the man's sins are forgiven *prior* to healing him. This indicates that the man's paralysis is not contingent on his sinful state; a *separate* speech act is required from Jesus to raise him to his feet. In other words, the scene suggests that "sin and sickness are distinct."[25] This means that forgiveness of sins does not necessarily result in a physical healing. Second, Jesus's act of healing is meant as a physical sign of the man's healing. Put another way, the miracle makes manifest that the invisible change he has announced—his forgiveness of sin—has occurred. As Jesus says, he performs the miracle "so that you may know that the Son of Man has authority on earth to forgive sins" (Luke 5:24).

The story of the healing of the paralytic gives way to the scene of the calling of the tax collector Levi and Jesus's meal with him (Luke 5:27–32). Although Levi is not explicitly identified as a "sinner," Luke elsewhere uses the term for publicans (cf. Luke 18:13). Here in Luke 5 the Pharisees are appalled that Jesus dines with "tax collectors and sinners" (Luke 5:30). Jesus explains his actions with a statement that metaphorically describes sinners as the "sick": "Those

24. Note that in Luke 13:12 Jesus uses the language of being "freed" (*apolelysai*) to describe the woman who has been bent over for eighteen years: "Be freed from your infirmity."

25. Slawomir Szkredka, *Sinners and Sinfulness in Luke: A Study of Direct and Indirect References in the Initial Episodes of Jesus' Activity*, WUNT 2/434 (Tübingen: Mohr Siebeck, 2017), 85.

who are healthy have no need for a physician, but those who are sick do. I have come to call not the righteous but sinners to repentance" (Luke 5:31–32). Jesus comes to heal the "sick"—namely, sinners. He does this not simply by accepting them as they are but by calling them to *repentance*.[26] Implied here is that Jesus is the divine physician—he has come to cure the "sick," not only physically but spiritually. To repent of sin and be released from it is therefore to become spiritually "healthy" (*hygiainontes*; Luke 5:31). Here we see in even sharper terms why Jesus performs *physical* healings: in performing such acts, Jesus demonstrates his identity as the physician who can also perform *spiritual* healing.

That healing is a sign of "release" is emphasized later in Luke 13. There we read about a woman who is healed "from a spirit of infirmity" (Luke 13:11)—language that seems to imply a demonic presence—which causes her to be bent over. Jesus heals her by announcing, "Woman, you are freed [*apolelysai*] from your sickness" (Luke 13:12). In this episode, healing and demonic oppression are interconnected. We should add, however, that there is no indication that the woman is herself "bound" because of sin. Nevertheless, the woman's healing is bound up with Luke's overall message: Jesus brings "release."

Given that Jesus speaks of spiritual health, it is worth pointing out that the language of Jesus's "saving" work is specifically linked to *both* his physical healings and his ministry of forgiving sins. Jesus's identity as the Savior is underscored in Luke's birth narrative. When the angels tell the shepherds about Jesus's birth, they explain that a "savior" (*sōtēr*) has been born "who is Christ" (Luke 2:11). For Luke, the Messiah comes to "save"—but this can refer to restoring health and delivering from death.[27] Jesus's physical healings are spoken of in terms of salvation. When Jesus heals the woman with the flow of blood, he says, "Daughter, your faith *has saved* [*sesōken*] you" (Luke 8:48). Here the language of "salvation" is especially connected to restoration of physical health.

At the same time, there can be no doubt that Jesus's work of salvation also involves a spiritual component—namely, the forgiveness of sins. This is evident in Luke 7. Jesus tells a sinful woman who has received forgiveness, "Your faith *has saved* [*sesōken*] you" (Luke 7:50). Here Jesus uses the same word he uses to describe the woman healed from a flow of blood. Yet here there is no indication that physical restoration is in view.

26. Elsewhere Jesus makes clear that forgiveness for the disciples is somehow contingent on their act of forgiving others (Luke 6:37; 11:4).

27. See also the passion narrative, where Jesus's detractors use the language of being "saved" from death (Luke 23:35, 37, 39).

Freedom from Affliction and Sin in the Liturgy of Anointing of the Sick

In the rite of anointing of the sick, the connection between "freedom from sickness" and "freedom from sin" is clearly present. First, the priest offers the following prayer over the oil:

> May the prayer of faith and the anointing with oil *free them from every affliction*.[a]

Later, the priest anoints the hands of the sick person, praying:

> May the Lord who *frees you from sin save you* and raise you up.[b]

The prayers thus emphasize that Jesus sets his people free, connecting his work of release from physical affliction to his gift of forgiveness from sin. Even if the faithful are not immediately granted physical healing in the sacrament, it is understood that the fullness of health will be enjoyed in the resurrection of the dead, which is emphasized in the eucharistic prayer used in connection with the rite of anointing of the sick, which speaks of how Christ's "rising" involves the "promise of a *new and glorious world, where no bodily pain will afflict us*."[c]

a. Taken from the revised rite approved by the National Conference of Catholic Bishops of America, published in *Pastoral Care of the Sick: Rites of Anointing and Viaticum* (Totowa, NJ: Catholic Book Publishing, 1983), 116 (emphasis added).
b. Taken from the revised rite approved by the National Conference of Catholic Bishops of America, published in *Pastoral Care of the Sick*, 116 (emphasis added).
c. Taken from the revised rite approved by the National Conference of Catholic Bishops of America, published in *Pastoral Care of the Sick*, 120 (emphasis added).

The language of "salvation" also appears in the story of the tax collector Zacchaeus, where it appears in the sense of deliverance from sin.[28] As we have seen, tax collectors are associated with sinners. Zacchaeus repents of his ways, pledging to make restitution for his unjust actions (Luke 19:8). Jesus responds: "Today *salvation* [*sōtēria*] has come to this house" (Luke 19:9). The scene concludes with Jesus announcing that he has come to "*save* [*sōsai*] *the lost* [*to apolōlos*]" (Luke 19:10). The language of lostness is reminiscent of the

28. We might also add that salvation can refer to escape from God's wrath and from eschatological judgment due to sin (Luke 13:23) and to entering into God's kingdom (Luke 18:26–27).

story of the prodigal son, whose father says he "was *lost* [*apolōlōs*] and has been found" (Luke 15:32). Zacchaeus is "saved" from being lost by turning from sin, a process that involves Jesus—the Savior—taking the initiative and coming to Zacchaeus's house (Luke 19:5).

Not only is the language of being "saved" associated with physical health and forgiveness, but it is also bound up with the imagery of oppression; Jesus comes to fulfill the hope of Zechariah that God will grant his people "salvation [*sōtērian*] . . . from all who hate us" (Luke 1:71). As we have seen, this oppression likely includes the idea of demonic subjugation. Jesus's physical healings, then, make manifest the "release" he comes to realize for his people—they are freed from sin and the power of the evil one. Rather than being under the subjugation of evil, they can enter into the realm of God's reign, the kingdom of God.

Jesus's Healing Ministry and the Suffering Servant in Matthew

As in Luke, after Jesus heals Peter's mother-in-law, Matthew tells us about Jesus healing the crowds:

> When it was evening, they brought to him many who were possessed by demons. And he cast out the spirits with a word and healed all who were sick, so that what was spoken through Isaiah the prophet might be fulfilled,
>
> > "He took our infirmities,
> > and carried our diseases." (Matt. 8:16–17, quoting Isa. 53:4)

Rather than connect Jesus's ministry to a passage that speaks of miraculous healing, Matthew instead interprets it through the lens of the Suffering Servant passage. It is important to consider carefully the logic at work here, which seems to involve a surprising theological assertion.

Matthew affirms that Isaiah announced the Servant would take away infirmities and diseases. What we find here differs from the Greek Old Testament and seems to represent Matthew's own translation.[29] While the more well-known Greek translation says that the Servant took away "our sins [*hamartias*]" (Isa. 53:4 LXX), Matthew translates Isaiah's passage as indicating that

29. See W. D. Davies and D. C. Allison, *A Critical and Exegetical Commentary on the Gospel according to Saint Matthew*, 3 vols., ICC (London: T&T Clark, 1988–97), 2:37–38.

the Servant "took our *infirmities* [*astheneias*]." Matthew is certainly not denying that Jesus has come to deliver his people from sin. In Matthew 1, Joseph is told that Jesus "will save his people from their sins" (Matt. 1:21). What is more, elsewhere in Matthew we see Jesus demonstrate his power to forgive sins (Matt. 9:2–8). So why does Matthew seemingly bypass the Septuagint's translation of the passage? Does he deny that Jesus dies vicariously for sin?

It is difficult to believe that Matthew rejects the idea that Jesus's suffering benefits others. In Matthew 20:28, Jesus announces, "The Son of Man came not to be served but to serve, and to give his life as a ransom for many." Despite claims to the contrary, it seems likely that this passage is shaped by the Suffering Servant passage of Isaiah 53.[30] As W. D. Davies and Dale Allison show, there are multiple points of contact between Matthew's text and the Greek version of Isaiah's oracle.[31] First, Jesus's statement that he will serve as a ransom for "many" evokes Isaiah 53, which uses the same term (Isa. 53:11–12 LXX). Second, the expression in Greek for "give his life as a ransom" is strikingly similar to Isaiah 53:10 LXX ("you make his life a guilt offering") and Isaiah 53:12 LXX ("he poured out his life to death"). Third, Jesus identifies himself as one who "serves" (*diakonēsai*), which matches up nicely conceptually with the description of the figure as the "servant" (*douleuonta*; Isa. 53:11 LXX).

That Matthew presents Jesus's suffering as serving a role in the forgiveness of sins is also supported by Jesus's words over the cup at the Last Supper: "For this is my blood of the covenant, which is poured out for many for the forgiveness [*aphesis*] of sins" (Matt. 26:28). Earlier in the narrative, Matthew makes it clear that Jesus has the authority to forgive sins. Yet somehow this ability is linked also to his death—Jesus's blood is ultimately "poured out" to effect this forgiveness. The saying here is most likely shaped by the Suffering Servant passage,[32] which makes the likelihood of a reference to it in Matthew 20:28 even more difficult to dismiss.

Matthew's use of Isaiah 53 demonstrates the interrelation of sin and sickness. In Matthew 8, Jesus is the Servant inasmuch as he removes *diseases*. Yet elsewhere in the Gospel, Jesus's fulfillment of the Suffering Servant passage is

30. The scholarship on this passage is voluminous. See especially J. Christopher Edwards, *The Ransom Logion in Mark and Matthew: Its Reception and Its Significance for the Study of the Gospels*, WUNT 2/327 (Tübingen: Mohr Siebeck, 2012).

31. Davies and Allison, *Matthew*, 3:95–97.

32. Matthias Konradt, *The Gospel according to Matthew: A Commentary*, trans. M. Eugene Boring (Waco: Baylor University Press, 2020), 306; Davies and Allison, *Matthew*, 3:474.

connected to the forgiveness of sins (Matt. 26:28). Jesus fulfills his mission to "save his people from their sins" (Matt. 1:21) through his ministry, in which he forgives sins, and the authority to do so is demonstrated in physical healing (Matt. 9:2–8).

Why does the Gospel of Matthew use the Suffering Servant passage to highlight Jesus's work of *healing*? The evangelist connects Jesus's passion to his role as the Suffering Servant. The idea, then, seems to be that Jesus's work of healing and forgiveness of sins finds its climax in his passion, death, and resurrection. Jesus's healing of the paralytic is a sign of his authority to forgive sins (Matt. 9:2–8). Yet, as we have seen, the forgiveness of sins is also bound up with the shedding of his blood, which is signified by his words over the cup at the Last Supper (Matt. 26:28). The cross and resurrection, then, are the ultimate expressions of God's work of healing and restoration.

Sin and Sickness in the Gospel of John

Let us turn briefly to the Fourth Gospel. There we also see the connection between sin and sickness. In John 5, Jesus heals a paralyzed man on the sabbath. After doing so, Jesus explains: "Behold, you have become well. Sin no longer *that nothing worse happens to you*" (John 5:14). With this, Jesus seems to suggest that the man's previous infirmity was due to personal sin.[33] As we have shown, the conviction that sin is the cause of physical maladies is attested in numerous scriptural texts and Jewish sources. Here, then, we have a parallel to those passages as well as with James's teaching, which likewise suggests that a connection between personal sin and sickness may exist.

Finally, we should note that Jesus's authority to forgive sins is assumed in John in that Jesus imparts the power to forgive sins to others—namely, the disciples. He says to them, "As the Father has sent me, so I also send you. . . . Receive the Holy Spirit. If you forgive the sins of any, they are forgiven them; if you retain the sins of any, they are retained" (John 20:21–23). Jesus sends out the disciples on a mission, anchoring said mission in his own identity as one who is "sent" by the Father. By giving the disciples the authority to forgive sins, Jesus is portrayed as giving them a participation in his ministry.

33. Adam Kubiś recognizes that this is the view of the majority of commentators ("The Current Debate on the Relationship between Sin and Sickness in John 5:14," *Biblical Annals* 12, no. 2 [2022]: 205). Though Kubiś offers an alternative explanation, this interpretation has a long history because it is the most natural reading. See, e.g., John Chrysostom, *Homilies on John* 38; *Homilies on Matthew* 43.5; Fourth Lateran Council of 1215, Canon 22.

The "Salvation" of the Sick in James 5

James's instructions for ministering to the sick combines healing and forgiveness of sins. This is a natural connection for a Jewish writer to make. As we have seen, sin and sickness often went together in Jewish sources. The two ideas are also intertwined in the accounts of Jesus's ministry in the Gospels. Turning back to James 5, we can ask the two questions we began this chapter with: (1) What is the relationship between sickness and sin?; and (2) Does forgiveness of sins bring about a cure of physical ailments?

"Saved" from Sickness and Sin

That James 5 brings together the hope of being delivered from sickness and sin coheres beautifully with what is found in the scriptures of Israel and Jewish beliefs broadly. To sum up what we have seen above: sickness is often understood in Jewish works as a *result* of sin. It is sometimes even portrayed as a punishment for sin. Sinfulness is depicted as the inverse of "health." Leprosy in particular is connected with sin. Healing physical ailments, then, is naturally associated with spiritual healing.

This does not mean that James believes all who are sick are suffering as a punishment for personal sin. James knows the story of Job, the righteous sufferer. Moreover, he is aware that Jesus suffered and died; it is impossible to imagine that James holds Jesus suffered because he was being punished for his personal sin. Nevertheless, James probably also thinks that *some* people who are sick are experiencing affliction because of sin. He explicitly asserts that sin leads to death: "Desire, when it has conceived, gives birth to sin, and sin, when it is fully grown, gives birth to *death*" (James 1:15). There is no indication that James is thinking only of spiritual death. Sin and death are intertwined.

It only makes sense, then, that James would connect healing with forgiveness of sins. James ties healing to "salvation." He says that those who are sick should call for the elders, who will both pray for and anoint them. We are then promised: "The prayer of faith will *save* [*sōsei*] the one who is sick, and the Lord will *raise him up* [*egerei*]" (James 5:15). The language is evocative. As we have seen, those who are healed of physical ailments by Jesus in the Gospels are said to be "saved" (*sōzō*; e.g., Matt. 9:22//Mark 5:34//Luke 8:48; Mark 10:52; Luke 17:19). Yet the word is also used with respect to deliverance from sin (e.g., Matt. 1:21; Luke 7:50) or eschatological deliverance (e.g., Luke 13:23; 19:10; John 3:17; 10:9). The multivalent meaning of the term is not at all difficult to understand since sin and sickness were closely interrelated. As we saw earlier, in Luke-Acts the work of physical healing is of one piece with Jesus's mission of "release," understood as a fulfillment of Isaiah 61. In Matthew, Jesus's work of healing relates also to his overall mission as the Suffering Servant and his broader mission to "save his people from their sins" (Matt. 1:21). We should be careful about ignoring the diverse ways the different New Testament authors speak of Christ's mission (and, more broadly, neglecting their distinctive theological messages),[34] yet here there is profound continuity between Matthew and Luke-Acts: Jesus's works of healing and forgiveness of sins are interrelated in his role as Savior.

Moreover, James knows that death cannot be avoided forever. Earlier in the letter, he writes of the fleeting nature of human life: "You are like a mist that appears for a little time and then disappears" (James 4:14). Although James does not mention it, he likely does not believe that physical death can be put off forever by calling the elders and repeatedly having them perform their ministry.

It is noteworthy, therefore, that James equates being "saved" with the promise that the Lord will "raise up" the sick. Again, the most natural reading of this would seem to be that the sick person will recover from physical sickness. The verb for being "raised up," *egeirō*, is also used in the Gospels in connection with physical healing. Nevertheless, one can hardly forget that the term for "rising" also evokes resurrection hopes (cf. Mark 12:26//Luke 20:37). For example, in all three Synoptic Gospels, the term is used in the story of Jesus raising the ruler's daughter from the dead. In Mark and Luke, Jesus takes the dead girl's hand and says to her, "Rise up" (*egeire*; Mark 5:41; Luke 8:54). Matthew simply says that she "arose" (*ēgerthē*; Matt. 9:25).[35] The term also appears in contexts where Jesus is thought to be John the Baptist "raised" from the dead (Matt. 14:2//Mark 6:14//Luke 9:7). It is also used recurrently to describe Jesus's resurrection in the Gospels (e.g., Matt. 16:21//Luke 9:22; Matt. 17:9, 23; 20:19; 26:32; Mark 14:28; 16:6; Luke 24:6–7; John 2:22; 21:14)

34. For a treatment of the diversity and unity in the theological perspectives of the New Testament writers, see Frank J. Matera, *New Testament Theology: Exploring Diversity and Unity* (Louisville: Westminster John Knox, 2007).

35. The verb *egeirō* is also used in reference to Jesus's work of raising the dead to life in Matt. 11:5//Luke 7:22; Luke 7:14; John 12:1, 9, 17.

and in other New Testament works.[36] James's instructions, then, likely have further meaning beyond physical restoration. If the sick person is not immediately restored to life, he or she can look with confidence to a future hope, resurrection from the dead.

For our purposes, it is worth noting that the verb translated "raised up" is used in a story to which we have continued to return, the healing of the paralytic; Jesus tells the paralyzed man whose sins have been forgiven to "rise up" (*egeire*; Mark 2:9//Luke 5:23; cf. Matt. 9:6). The man's physical action of "rising up" makes visible the invisible reality that has already occurred in him: his sins have been forgiven. I am not suggesting that this story is somehow echoed in James's instructions. I mention it, however, to point out that since physical healing and forgiveness of sins often go together in Jewish sources, it is natural that James moves from a discussion of physical healing to the idea of sins being forgiven. Physical healing could be seen as a sign pointing beyond itself to spiritual restoration; James seems to be building on such perspectives.

So, while the text's interest in bodily concerns should not be questioned, one should not somehow imagine that this necessarily rules out a spiritual dimension. As Allison observes, "Given that bodily and spiritual health were scarcely distinct categories for early Christians, an exclusive emphasis upon the physical may assume a false dichotomy."[37] Indeed, there is every reason to think that James has both physical and spiritual concerns in mind here.

Restoration through Forgiveness of Sins

James may believe that some are sick *precisely due to personal sin.* (The sick person's desire to be anointed "in the name of the Lord" might signify a desire to return to God.) As we have seen, various biblical and nonbiblical Jewish texts affirm the possibility that sickness *may* be a punishment for sin. These same sources, however, also often indicate that repentance can lead to restoration of health. It seems that James has this idea in mind when he writes, "*If he has committed sins, he will be forgiven.* Therefore, confess your sins to one another and pray for one another, *that you may be healed*" (James 5:15–16). "If" one has committed sins, one will be forgiven. The next line naturally follows: If you are sick, you should "therefore" confess sins

36. See, e.g., Acts 3:15; 4:10; 5:30; 10:40; 13:30, 37; 26:8; Rom. 4:24–25; 6:4, 9; 7:4; 8:11, 34; 10:9; 1 Cor. 6:14; 15:4, 12–17, 20; 2 Cor. 5:15; Gal. 1:1; Eph. 1:20; Col. 2:12; 1 Thess. 1:10; 2 Tim. 2:8; Heb. 11:19; 1 Pet. 1:21.

37. Allison, *James*, 766.

"that you may be healed." Here it would seem that one confesses and prays *precisely to experience healing*. This is different from the story of the paralytic, where Jesus's action of forgiving the man's sins requires a separate act. James's directives seem to suggest a closer association between physical and spiritual healing. Here anointing seems, in some way, connected to healing infirmities related to personal sin.[38] That said, to claim that James thinks healing takes place *only* in instances where infirmity is due to sin would be to go beyond the text.

The fact that forgiveness of sins is mentioned at all, however, is striking in light of the Gospel accounts of Jesus's healing of the man who was paralyzed. In these stories, the bystanders are stunned that Jesus possesses the ability to forgive sins. Yet in James 5 it seems somehow that the elders are able to participate in the ministry of forgiveness of sins. In context, it is clear that "Confess your sins to one another and pray for one another" refers especially to the sick person confessing his sins to the elder and the elder praying over the sick. James says "pray for one another" that you may be healed, but the core idea is that the *elders* are to pray over the sick so that *the sick* may be healed. When James says that the "prayer of the righteous has great power in its effects" (James 5:16), he is especially (though not exclusively) referring to the *elders*. This naturally raises questions: Who are these elders? Why must elders be called to anoint the sick? We will consider these questions in the next chapter.

38. Thomas Aquinas, *Summa Theologiae*, Supplement, q. 32, art. 4.

6

The Elders and the Continuation of Jesus's Ministry

Christ's Work and the Ministers of Anointing

> Is anyone among you sick? He should call for the elders of the church.
>
> —James 5:14

> We read in the Gospel that the apostles also did this. And now the custom of the Church holds that those who are sick be anointed with consecrated oil by the presbyters.
>
> —Bede the Venerable (d. 735)[1]

James makes it very clear that the sick should call the "elders" to come, anoint them, and pray over them. But who are these individuals? The Greek term used by James is the noun *presbyteros*. Translators sometimes render this word into English with the word "presbyter." But why is it necessary to

1. Bede, *Commentary on James* at 5:14, in Bede the Venerable, *Commentary on the Seven Catholic Epistles*, trans. Dom David Hurst (Kalamazoo, MI: Cistercian Publications, 1985), 61.

call *these* individuals? Why not simply have a family member pray over and anoint the sick? This chapter is focused on the identity of the individuals mentioned by James.

Ancient Greco-Roman works frequently use the term "elders" to describe members of voluntary councils, civic leaders, and temple officials.[2] In the Greek translation of the scriptures of Israel, the term *presbyteros* is used to refer not merely to those of advanced biological age but to those who have roles of civic leadership in the community (Gen. 50:7; Deut. 31:28; Judg. 11:8–11; Ruth 4:2; Jdt. 8:10; 10:6; Isa. 24:23; 1 Macc. 7:33; 11:23; 2 Macc. 13:13; 14:37). Within the Second Temple Jewish period, the term could refer to teachers and honored members of the community.[3]

In the Gospels and Acts, the term "elders" is applied to members of the Jerusalem Sanhedrin.[4] This coheres well with other Jewish traditions. In the Mishnah, a second-century collection of rabbinic traditions, the concept of the "seventy elders" is connected with the Sanhedrin, which is said to have seventy members plus the high priest.[5] The Mishnah indicates that the rationale for having *seventy* members in the Sanhedrin came from Numbers 11, where Moses is told to appoint seventy elders to help him judge Israel (cf. Num. 11:16–25). We will have more to say about this passage later, in chapter 7 (see p. 139). For now, it is worth mentioning that the symbolism of seventy elders appears even earlier in the Torah; in Exodus, the God of Israel has Moses invite seventy elders up to Mount Sinai: "Then [the Lord] said to Moses, 'Go up to the Lord, you and Aaron, Nadab and Abihu, and *seventy of the elders of Israel*, and you shall worship from a distance'" (Exod. 24:1). This group participates in a meal in God's presence at Sinai (Exod. 24:9–11).[6] The book of Ezekiel also mentions a group of seventy elders (Ezek. 8:11).

2. R. Alastair Campbell, *The Elders: Seniority within Earliest Christianity* (Edinburgh: T&T Clark, 1994), 67–98.

3. See, e.g., Matt. 15:2; 16:21; 21:23; 26:3, 47, 57; 27:1, 3, 12, 20, 41; 28:12; Mark 7:5; 8:31; 11:27; 14:43; 15:1; Luke 7:3; 9:22; 15:25; 20:1; 22:52; John 8:9; Acts 2:17.

4. See, e.g., Matt. 26:3, 57; 27:1; Mark 14:43, 53; Luke 22:66; Acts 22:5.

5. *Mishnah Sanhedrin* 1:6. The historical reliability of the Mishnah's description of the Sanhedrin is contested. See Kenneth D. Litwak, "Sanhedrin," in *T&T Clark Encyclopedia of Second Temple Judaism*, ed. Daniel M. Gurtner and Loren T. Stuckenbruck, 2 vols. (London: Bloomsbury T&T Clark, 2020), 2:708; E. P. Sanders, *Judaism: Practice and Belief, 63 BCE–66 CE* (Philadelphia: Trinity Press International, 1992), 472–88.

6. That the elders are appointed later in Num. 11 raises redactional questions that we cannot enter into here. See, e.g., Nahum M. Sarna, *Exodus*, JPS Torah Commentary (Philadelphia: Jewish Publication Society, 1991), 97–98.

Given James's Jewish outlook, it is important to note that synagogue communities also had elders.[7] It is now recognized that older scholarship overemphasized the function of elders in synagogues, downplaying the role of priestly authorities.[8] Still, synagogue communities knew of figures identified as "elders." In what way this aspect of synagogue life shaped Christian practice, however, is difficult to say.

This chapter will do four things. First, we will analyze the word "elder" in the New Testament. The term is frequently used to describe those who are recognized as leaders and teachers in the Church. Second, we will look at the way the Gospels present Jesus as establishing his disciples as leaders of the eschatological community. Third, we will consider ways the book of Acts presents the disciples as continuing Jesus's ministry. Finally, we will explore the implications of these considerations for interpreting James's directives for anointing the sick.

The Elders as Church Leaders

The reference to "elders" in James does not come *ex nihilo*. There is clear evidence that there were recognized leaders in the early Church. Here we will look at the data, specifically examining the role of elders in our earliest sources.

Elders in the Pauline Epistles

The earliest New Testament writer is Paul. In some of the letters that bear his name, elders are described as having leadership roles. The problem, however, is that none of the apostle's undisputed letters contain references to such figures. That is not to say that Paul is silent about the role of leaders in the churches to whom he writes. The Letter to the Philippians is addressed to "the saints in Christ Jesus who are in Philippi, with the *bishops* and *deacons*" (Phil. 1:1). The noun translated "bishop," *episkopos*—also rendered more literally as "overseer"—was used by other Greek writers to

7. See, e.g., Philo, *Hypothetica* 7.11–14; Pseudo-Philo, *Biblical Antiquities* 11:8; J. B. Frey, ed., *Corpus Inscriptionum Judaicarum*, 2 vols. (Rome: Pontificio Istituto di Archeologia Cristiana, 1936, 1952), 2:1404.

8. See Campbell, *Elders*, 44–54; Daniel R. Schwartz, "Introduction: Was 70 C.E. a Watershed in Jewish History? Three Stages of Modern Scholarship, and a Renewed Effort," in *Was 70 C.E. a Watershed in Jewish History? On Jews and Judaism before and after the Destruction of the Second Temple*, ed. Daniel R. Schwartz, Zeev Weiss, and Ruth A. Clements (Leiden: Brill, 2012), 15.

refer to various kinds of officials, including financial supervisors and temple officials.[9] The term is used throughout Jewish sources to describe leaders.[10] Strikingly, the Dead Sea Scrolls use a Hebrew equivalent, *mebaqqer*, as the title for the superior of their community,[11] who is also identified as a "father" and "shepherd" figure.[12] In Philippians, Paul clearly uses the term *episkopos* to refer to community leaders. A reference to these individuals may also be found in 1 Thessalonians 5:12, where Paul speaks of "those who are *over you*" (*proistamenous hymōn*). Craig Keener is correct when he writes, "There can be no question that Pauline churches included people in leadership roles, whatever their 'titles' (1 Cor. 16:15–16; Phil. 1:1; 1 Thess. 5:12)."[13] It seems likely that in the earliest period, "bishops" and "elders" were essentially synonymous terms for heads of the community.[14]

Mention of "bishops" is found in 1 Timothy, but here there seems to be some more development since in this letter the bishops appear to be a group of leaders distinct from the "elders." First Timothy 3 lays out the qualifications for the one who "aspires to the office of bishop [*episkopēs*]," which is described as a "good work" (1 Tim. 3:1). The letter is also aware of "deacons" (1 Tim. 3:8, 12) and "elders" (1 Tim. 4:14). Timothy is told: "Do not neglect the gift which is in you. It was given to you through prophecy with the laying on of hands [*epitheseōs*] by the *council of elders* [*presbyteriou*]" (1 Tim. 4:14).[15] The spiritual gift bestowed upon Timothy is said to be communicated through the council of elders' act of laying hands on him.[16] Laying

9. See Aeschylus, *Eumenides* 740; Aristophanes, *Birds* 1022–23; Plato, *Laws* 6.762D; 9.872E.

10. It is used this way throughout the Septuagint: Num. 31:14; 4 Kgdm. [2 Kings] 11:15, 18; 12:12 [12:11 Eng.]; 2 Chron. 34:12, 17; 2 Esd. 21:9, 14, 22 [Neh. 11:9, 14, 22 Eng.]; 1 Macc. 1:51; Isa. 60:17.

11. *1QRule of the Community* (1QS) 6:12, 20; *Damascus Document* (CD-A) 9:18, 19, 22; 13:6, 7, 13, 16; 14:8, 11, 13; 15:8, 11, 14.

12. *Damascus Document* (CD-A) 13:9. However, it is unlikely that the role of bishops in the Church was directly influenced by the Qumran community. See John H. Elliott, "Elders as Shared Household Heads and Not Holders of 'Office' in Earliest Christianity," *BTB* 33, no. 2 (2003): 80.

13. Craig S. Keener, *Acts: An Exegetical Commentary*, 4 vols. (Grand Rapids: Baker Academic, 2012–15), 3:3004–5.

14. See Campbell, *Elders*, 162.

15. There is a textual issue here with some manuscripts indicating that the laying on of hands was done not by a council of elders but by a single elder. These, however, are heavily outweighed by other witnesses. See Luke Timothy Johnson, *The First and Second Letters to Timothy*, AB 35A (New York: Doubleday, 2001), 253.

16. The Greek could be read as describing Timothy as being assimilated into the group of elders rather than as receiving a laying on of hands *by* them. This, however, seems unlikely. See Raymond F. Collins, *1 & 2 Timothy and Titus*, NTL (Louisville: Westminster John Knox, 2002), 131.

on of hands is used in Israel's scriptural traditions with the sense of investing another with authority (Num. 27:23; Deut. 34:9). All of this suggests that elders possess authority, which they can then pass on to others.

The imagery in 1 Timothy 4 is also reminiscent of what is found in the book of Acts. There Peter and John are sent to Samaria to communicate the Spirit to believers who had been baptized but who had not yet received the Spirit (Acts 8:15–16). We are told: "[Peter and John] laid their hands on them, and they received the Holy Spirit" (Acts 8:17). Likewise, in Acts 19, a similar story is found involving Paul. After disciples are baptized, we read: "When Paul had laid his hands on them, the Holy Spirit came upon them, and they spoke in tongues and prophesied" (Acts 19:6). As in 1 Timothy, laying on of hands is associated with prophecy.

In addition, in 1 Timothy 5, we read: "The elders who lead well are to be considered worthy of a double honor, especially those who labor in speaking and teaching" (1 Tim. 5:17). The figures here are not to be confused with the "older man" described in 1 Timothy 5:1.[17] Elders are a distinct group, not merely those who are older men. Indeed, although Timothy himself is never said to be an "elder," it is obvious that he performs the tasks associated with that role. For example, like the elders, he lays his hands on others (1 Tim. 4:14; 5:22). Likewise, as the elders in 1 Timothy 5:17 are teachers, Timothy also is a teacher (1 Tim. 4:11). Yet Timothy is not an older man but a "youth" (1 Tim. 4:12). Elders were thus not necessarily men of advanced age.

The elders in 1 Timothy 5:17 are those who have leadership roles (they "lead," *proestōtes*) and teaching responsibilities. The passage goes on to offer instructions on how to deal with accusations made against an elder. The letter insists that accusations against them must be backed up by two or three witnesses (1 Tim. 5:19).

Finally, there is a relevant passage found in the Letter to Titus. In the first chapter, Paul is depicted as telling Titus:

> For this reason I left you behind in Crete, in order that you might put in order what remains to be done and appoint elders in every town, as I directed you: someone who is blameless, the husband of one wife, having children who are faithful, not accused of debauchery or rebellious. (Titus 1:5–6)

17. Collins, *1 & 2 Timothy and Titus*, 144.

The letter goes on in the following verse to describe the qualifications of a bishop (*episkopos*), likely indicating that elders and bishops are seen as distinct roles.

It is often claimed that the undisputed Pauline letters bear witness to an earlier period in which leadership roles in the churches were underdefined. It is said that churches Paul himself wrote to were charismatic and were not likely characterized by the more developed leadership structures described in the Pastoral Epistles (1–2 Timothy and Titus). The description of a hierarchy of bishops, elders, and deacons in these latter epistles is taken, therefore, to betray a later period. For this and other reasons, the Pastorals are typically viewed as "inauthentic" letters of Paul.[18] Here we cannot discuss all of the issues involved. Nevertheless, as we have seen, Paul does mention both "bishops" and "deacons" in Philippians 1:1, an undisputed letter. In addition, the claim that a charismatic community would necessarily have little church structure is questionable.[19] That local churches developed leadership structures over the course of Paul's lifetime is eminently possible. At the very least, the Pastorals attest to the presence of "elders" who came to be known as serving important leadership roles in the various churches.

Elders in the Book of Acts

Acts also constitutes strong evidence that the role of "elders" was recognized in the early Church and that they were seen as authoritative figures. Even if leaders were not spoken of as "elders" in the earlier period of Paul, Keener is correct when he says, "We dare not begrudge Luke the freedom to communicate in the language familiar to his audience."[20] In Acts, after the apostles themselves, the elders serve as the primary leaders in the community.

When the controversy over gentile inclusion in the church emerges, Paul and Barnabas are selected with others to go to Jerusalem "to the apostles and *elders* concerning this question" (Acts 15:2). We read that they "met together to consider this matter" (Acts 15:6). Keener notes the irony: in the previous chapter, Paul was *appointing* elders (Acts 14:23); now he is forced to report

18. See, e.g., Margaret Y. MacDonald, *The Pauline Churches: A Socio-Historical Study of Institutionalization in the Pauline and Deutero-Pauline Writings*, SNTSMS 60 (Cambridge: Cambridge University Press, 1988), 159–258.

19. For this and other responses to the arguments against the authenticity of the Pastorals on the basis of church organization, see Johnson, *First and Second Letters to Timothy*, 74–76.

20. Keener, *Acts*, 3:3003.

to the elders in Jerusalem. In the end, Paul's work is vindicated. After the Jerusalem Council reaches its decision that gentiles need not be circumcised, we are told: "Then the apostles and elders, together with the whole church, decided to choose men from among them and to send them to Antioch with Paul and Barnabas" (Acts 15:22). In all of this, we see that the elders play more than an informal honorary role but, with the consent of the whole community, share with the apostles in a leadership role.

After the Jerusalem Council, we read that, as Paul and Timothy traveled from town to town, "they handed on [*paredidosan*] to [believers] for observance the decisions [*dogmata*] that had been made by the apostles and elders who were in Jerusalem" (Acts 16:4). The "handing on" language evokes the notion of "tradition" (*paradosis*). Here what is traditioned is nothing less than "decisions" (*dogmata*) determined by the "apostles and elders," which are understood to have a binding nature on the churches. Once again, the "elders" share in the apostles' authority.

Two final mentions of "elders" are worth including here. In Acts 20:17, Paul calls the Ephesian elders to meet with him. In an address to them, Paul tells them, "The Holy Spirit has made you *overseers* [*episkopous*], to shepherd the church of God" (Acts 20:28). The Greek term translated "overseer" is the same word that is usually elsewhere translated "bishops." We find a cognate term in the scene where a successor is chosen for the apostle Judas, Jesus's betrayer. Specifically, it appears in a translation of Psalm 109, which is cited to explain the role of Judas: "Let another take his *office* [*episkopēn*]" (Ps. 109:8 [108:8 LXX]; cf. Acts 1:20). The passage, therefore, makes the point that the role Judas had—the responsibility of *overseer*—must be taken by another now that he has died. In this, the apostolic office is associated with the language of "bishops." In a sense, the Twelve serve as the first bishops. It is therefore no wonder that the "elders" serve a prominent role in Acts alongside the apostles. Moreover, in his address in Acts 20, Paul also calls the Ephesian overseers "pastors"—that is, "shepherds." In Acts, then, elders are essentially equivalent with "overseers" (bishops) and "pastors." One of the earliest Christian works outside the New Testament, 1 Clement, uses the terms "elders" and "bishops" interchangeably (cf. *1 Clement* 44).[21] Papias (AD 80–130), a very early Christian writer who personally interacted with some of those who had followed Jesus

21. Campbell (*Elders*, 192) writes: "Elders and overseers, we may feel, did not need to be reconciled; they could simply be equated, seen to be a merely verbal distinction without a difference."

during his public ministry, even identifies the original apostles and disciples of Jesus as "elders."[22]

Finally, in Acts 21, Paul visits Jerusalem. There we read he went to "visit James, and all the elders were present" (Acts 21:18). James is undoubtedly to be viewed as the head of the Jerusalem church. Here he is said to be accompanied by "elders," who appear to share a leadership role with him.

Elders in the Catholic Epistles

The term *presbyteros* also shows up in the Catholic Epistles. In 1 Peter, the apostle uses the term in reference to himself: "So I exhort the elders [*presbyterous*] among you, as *a fellow elder* [*sympresbyteros*]" (1 Pet. 5:1). We cannot enter into the question of the authorship of this letter here.[23] What is most significant for our purposes is that Peter is himself portrayed as an "elder." This coheres well with what we have seen in Acts. As we saw above, the apostolic office Judas vacates is associated with "overseer" terminology (Acts 1:20). Moreover, "elders" are identified as "overseers" (Acts 20:28). If "elders" are "overseers," and a member of the Twelve can be identified as an "overseer," it is no surprise that Peter is able to be identified as an elder. The title here seems to signify an authoritative role in the community.

Finally, in 2 John and 3 John we find other letters in which the author describes himself as "the elder" (2 John 1; 3 John 1). We do not have the space to weigh the arguments in favor of the different views of the authorship of these letters. What is noteworthy is that, as in 1 Peter, "elder" is used in the singular. This points away from the idea that "elders" simply served as part of an informal honorary group and were not recognized in any way as holders of singular authority.[24]

That the community of believers in Christ would have their own specific authoritative "elders" coheres well with what we also see in the Gospels, which

22. Eusebius, *Ecclesiastical History* 3.39.4.

23. For differing perspectives, see the important treatments in Travis B. Williams and David G. Horrell, *1 Peter*, 2 vols., ICC (London: Bloomsbury T&T Clark, 2023), 1:116–62; Craig S. Keener, *1 Peter: A Commentary* (Grand Rapids: Baker Academic, 2021), 8–25; John H. Elliott, *First Peter*, AB 37B (New York: Doubleday, 2000), 118–30.

24. See Euan Marley, review of *The Elders: Seniority within Earliest Christianity*, by R. Alastair Campbell, *New Blackfriars* 78, no. 914 (1997): 203. On the difficulty of using the language of "office" for this period, see Elliott, "Elders as Shared Household Heads," 80. Much depends on how one defines the term. If one uses it with simply the connotation of a leadership position, it is difficult to contest that the term reflects the first-century Church. Obviously, the more one insists on narrowing the meaning of the word, the less applicable it is to earlier periods.

indicate that Jesus himself would establish leaders from among the ranks of his disciples. Indeed, the Synoptic Gospels indicate that the elders in Jerusalem understood that Jesus spoke against *them*, indicating that he would set up individuals in their place. We now turn to this evidence.

Jesus's Intention to Install New Leaders over God's People

That the early community would have leaders is hardly surprising. Moreover, that this community's leaders would involve figures *not previously* recognized as authority figures is also not difficult to explain.[25] The Gospels bear witness to the fact that Jesus intended to install *new* leaders in the eschatological age. This is perhaps most especially evident in the parable of the wicked tenants. Here we will carefully examine this important story told by Jesus.

The Parable of the Wicked Tenants and the Coming of New Leaders

All three Synoptic evangelists include an account of Jesus telling the parable of the wicked tenants (Matt. 21:33–43//Mark 12:1–12//Luke 20:9–18). Here I will focus on the Markan version of the story. I have treated this parable elsewhere in greater detail; here I will offer only a brief treatment. The story begins with an account of a man who builds a vineyard. The details are especially evocative of the Song of the Vineyard in Isaiah 5:

Jesus's Parable of the Wicked Tenants (Mark 12:1)	Isaiah's Song of the Vineyard (Isa. 5:2 LXX)
"A man . . . put a hedge around it [*periethēken phragmon*]."	"I put a hedge around it [*phragmon periethēka*]."
"He dug a pit for a winepress [*ōryxen hypolēnion*]."	"I dug a vat before a winepress [*prolēnion ōryxa en autō*]."
"He built a tower [*ōkodomēsen pyrgon*]."	"I built a tower [*ōkodomēsa pyrgon*]."

Given the striking parallels, the consensus view is that the parable includes an allusion to the Isaianic oracle. In Isaiah, the Song of the Vineyard serves as a judgment oracle against Jerusalem and Judea. The passage describes how God will allow defeat and destruction to come because—rather than

25. What follows here is a summary of conclusions drawn in Michael Patrick Barber, *The Historical Jesus and the Temple: Memory, Methodology, and the Gospel of Matthew* (Cambridge: Cambridge University Press, 2023), especially 157–233.

doing good works (bringing forth "good grapes")—the people are guilty of injustice (Isa. 5:7). God will therefore let his "vineyard" be "trampled down" (Isa. 5:5). Judgment is also the theme in Jesus's parable, though this must be carefully understood.

The rest of Jesus's story is well known, but I will summarize it here briefly. The owner of the vineyard—the "lord" (*kyrios*; Mark 12:9)—leases out his vineyard to tenant farmers before going off to a distant land (Mark 12:1). At harvest time, the owner sends a servant to collect the fruits of the vineyard, but the tenant farmers attack the servant and send him away empty-handed (Mark 12:2–3). The owner sends others who are also either beaten or killed (Mark 12:4–5). Finally, he sends his "beloved son," thinking that the tenant farmers will certainly respect him (Mark 12:6). Instead, the tenant farmers murder the owner's son (Mark 12:8). Jesus concludes that the owner will therefore come and execute the tenants and lease it out to others (Mark 12:9). There is little debate about the significance of the parable's basic features: the owner is the Lord; the servants are the Old Testament prophets, who were rejected by their contemporaries (Mark 6:4; cf. Matt. 13:57//Luke 4:24; see also Matt. 23:29–35//Luke 11:47–51; Matt. 23:37//Luke 13:34); and the "beloved son" is obviously Jesus (Mark 1:11; cf. Matt. 3:17//Luke 3:22; see also Matt. 17:5//Mark 9:7//Luke 9:35).

Yet contrary to some who have interpreted the parable as a story indicating God's rejection of *Israel*, it must be pointed out that the vineyard itself is not destroyed. Rather, it is the *tenants* who are the subjects of judgment and who are replaced with others: the owner "will come and destroy *the tenants* and give the vineyard *to others*" (Mark 12:9). Who are the tenants meant to symbolize? The evangelist tells us. In Mark, the context of the parable involves a setting in which Jesus has just been confronted by "the chief priests and the scribes and the elders" (Mark 11:27). When Jesus finishes the parable, we are told: "Then they sought to arrest him because they knew that he had spoken the parable against them, but they were afraid of the crowd" (Mark 12:12). The tenants then would seem to represent the Jerusalem leaders—namely, the chief priests, scribes, and elders. Not only, then, does Jesus announce that judgment is coming upon them, but the story indicates that *they will be replaced*.

Before moving on, it is important to emphasize that the entire episode of Jesus telling the parable of the wicked tenants is shot through with temple connections. First, the imagery from the Isaianic passage Jesus draws on is associated with the temple in Jewish sources.[26] Second, in all three accounts, Jesus finishes the parable with an allusion to the "stone rejected by the builders" in Psalm 118 (Ps. 118:22), a passage that describes a temple-building project (cf. Ps. 118:26: "We bless you from the house of the LORD"). Finally, what especially reinforces the likelihood that temple themes are intended is this: in all three New Testament Gospels, Jesus tells the parable *in the temple* (Matt. 21:23//Mark 11:27//Luke 20:1).

The temple backdrop is important since it helps illuminate the *kind* of leaders Jesus seems to envision establishing. As we have seen, in Mark the parable is directly said to be told against the "chief priests." Jesus, then, is replacing not merely "elders" but *temple* officials. Put simply, Jesus seems to envision not new *elders* but new *priests*. Who might Jesus have in mind as replacements for the current leadership? The answer seems clear: the Twelve.

The Twelve as Israel's Future Priestly Leaders

That Jesus viewed the Twelve as future authorities over God's people is uncontestable. Jesus explicitly connects the role of the Twelve to "judging" Israel. When Peter comes to Jesus asking what he and the Twelve should expect, Jesus responds:

> Amen, I say to you, in the renewed creation, when the Son of Man sits upon his throne of glory, you who have followed me will also *sit upon twelve thrones, judging the twelve tribes of Israel*. And everyone who has left houses or brothers or sisters or father or mother or children or lands, for my name's sake, will receive a hundredfold, and inherit eternal life. (Matt. 19:28–29)

This passage is remarkable for two significant reasons. First, Jesus identifies the Twelve as *judges* in the eschatological age. Second, Jesus appears to describe the apostles as having a role like the Levites.

First, the fact that Jesus identifies the apostles as *judges* is remarkable; Israel already had judges. The scriptures of Israel do speak of the laity serving in judicial roles (e.g., Exod. 18:25–26; Deut. 1:15–16). Yet, by Jesus's day, the concept of lay judges had largely faded and, from the evidence we have, the task of judging was apparently especially understood as priestly in nature.

26. See *4QBenediction* (4Q500); *1 Enoch* 89:56, 66–67, 73; *Tosefta Me'ilah* 1:16; *Tosefta Sukkah* 3:15. See also Klyne Snodgrass, *Stories with Intent: A Comprehensive Guide to the Parables of Jesus*, 2nd ed. (Grand Rapids: Eerdmans, 2018), 288.

When the first-century Jewish historian Josephus speaks of Israel's judges, he mentions only the priests,[27] leaving out references found in the Torah to non-priestly juridical figures.[28] Daniel Grossberg writes, "In Hellenistic times the high priest replaced the king as the principal judge (2 Chr. 19:8)."[29] It was also understood that the president of the ruling council, the Sanhedrin, was the high priest.[30] Not surprisingly, then, when Jesus is condemned to death, the "chief priests" have an outsized role in the narrative of Jesus's condemnation (Matt. 26:57–65; Mark 14:43, 53–64; Luke 22:54, 66; John 18:13, 24).

In passages describing the future age of redemption, judging is especially connected to the priesthood. According to the book of Ezekiel, it will be *priests* who will judge the people in the eschatological age: "In a dispute, they shall act as judges, and *they shall judge it according to my judgments*" (Ezek. 44:24). Strikingly, the prophet makes no provision for lay judges. Likewise, in the Dead Sea Scrolls, the leadership of the eschatological community is also understood to be priestly. For example, the *Damascus Document* refers to "the priest who governs [ov]er the Many."[31] In another Dead Sea Scroll text we learn that even the Messiah will defer to priests in legal matters: "According to what [the priests] teach [the Messiah], he will judge, and upon their authority."[32] To describe the apostles as *judges* in the eschatological age, then, would seem to assign to them a *priestly* role.

Second, as Dale Allison has shown, Jesus's response to Peter's question regarding what the apostles can expect to receive in the future age—"And everyone who has left houses or *brothers or sisters or father or mother or children or lands*, for my name's sake, will receive a hundredfold, and *inherit eternal life*" (Matt. 19:29)—mirrors statements in the Old Testament about the Levites. The Levites receive the priesthood in Exodus 32 after executing those who have worshiped the golden calf. In fact, Moses makes the point that the Levites are ordained to the priesthood because they have willingly

27. Josephus, *Jewish Antiquities* 2.165; 4.304.

28. See Sanders, *Judaism*, 171.

29. Daniel Grossberg, "Judge," in *Eerdmans Dictionary of the Bible*, ed. David N. Freedman, Allen C. Myers, and Astrid B. Beck (Grand Rapids: Eerdmans, 2000), 752.

30. Acts 5:17; Josephus, *Against Apion* 2.194; *Jewish Antiquities* 20.200, 251; Graham H. Twelftree, "Sanhedrin," in *Dictionary of Jesus and the Gospels*, ed. Joel B. Green, Scot McKnight, and I. Howard Marshall (Downers Grove, IL: InterVarsity, 1992), 730.

31. *DSSSE* 1:597. See *4QDamascus Document[a]* (4Q266), fragment 11:8; cf. *4QDamascus Document[a]* (4Q266), fragment 9:8; *4QDamascus Document[e]* (4Q270) fragment 7, 1:16; *4QBlessings[d]* (4Q289) 1:4.

32. *4QIsaiah Pesher[a]* (4QpIsa[a]) fragments 8–10, 24–25.

renounced family. Deuteronomy will go on to explain that the Levites also have forfeited land. Consider the following texts, which both refer to the Levites' opposition to those who worshiped the golden calf:

> Today you have ordained yourselves for the service of the LORD, each at the cost of his son and of his brother, bringing on yourselves a blessing this day. (Exod. 32:29)

> The one who says to his father and his mother, "I have not seen you," even his brother he did not acknowledge, and his children he disowned. (Deut. 33:9 LXX)

Jesus's assurance that the Twelve will "*inherit* eternal life" due to their renunciation of "lands" (*agrous*; Matt. 19:29) reinforces the connection to these Old Testament texts. Moses reveals that, rather than receiving *land* of their own, the Levites will receive a greater "*inheritance*"—the LORD (Num. 18:20, 23; Deut. 10:9).[33] Like the Levites, then, the Twelve have renounced "brothers," "father," "mother," and "lands" in order to receive a special "inheritance."

As I have shown elsewhere, other passages point to the priestly role of the apostles; we do not have time to engage them all here.[34] But let us return to the parable of the wicked tenants. For our purposes here, the key point to make is this: the Gospel writers indicate that the priests and elders understood that Jesus told the story against *them*. In Matthew, Mark, and Luke, then, Jesus teaches that they will be replaced as the leaders of Israel. Who would they be replaced by? The portrait that emerges from the Gospel accounts is that Jesus will appoint from his own disciples the future leaders of God's people.

Jesus and the Seventy(-Two)

Before moving on, we can also note that Jesus appoints not only "twelve" but, in the Gospel of Luke, another group of "seventy": "The Lord appointed seventy others, and he sent them out ahead of him two by two into every town and place where he intended to go" (Luke 10:1). There is a textual issue here. Some manuscripts indicate Jesus appointed "seventy-two" rather than "seventy." The disparity, however, is not difficult to explain.

33. See Dale C. Allison Jr., *The Intertextual Jesus: Scripture in Q* (Harrisburg, PA: Trinity Press International, 2000), 63–64.

34. See Barber, *Historical Jesus and the Temple*, especially 157–71, 214–16, 222–33.

Bede on the Twelve and the Seventy-Two as the First Bishops and Priests

Bede explains that the appointment of the Twelve and seventy-two signifies the distinction of roles between bishops and priests:

> For just as the number of the twelve apostles marked the beginning of the episcopal rank, it is apparent that the seventy-two disciples, who were also sent out by the Lord to preach the word, signify in their selection the lesser rank of the priesthood which is now called the presbyterate.[a]

a. Bede, *On the Tabernacle* 28.35. Translation from Bede the Venerable, *On the Tabernacle*, trans. Arthur G. Holder (Liverpool: Liverpool University Press, 1994), 128–29.

Luke appears to be evoking the story from Numbers 11 of Moses's appointment of seventy with whom he shares the Spirit given to him. In the Numbers account, however, two others also receive the Spirit, bringing the total of Spirit-appointed leaders to seventy-two. Both numbers—"seventy" or "seventy-two"—therefore evoke the Old Testament story. The key idea is that, as with the Twelve, Jesus is appointing new leaders in Israel. This impression is further strengthened if the leadership of the Sanhedrin was linked to the story of Moses appointing seventy elders, as the Mishnah suggests; perhaps the seventy disciples are being compared to the members of the Sanhedrin, serving as successors to the seventy appointed by Moses.[35] Again, however, the reliability of the Mishnah's account is disputed, so caution is needed here.

Either way, Jesus's appointment of seventy fits the larger motif we have been examining: Jesus is appointing his disciples for key leadership roles. Luke's terminology that Jesus "appointed" (*anadeiknymi*) the seventy is significant. As Amy-Jill Levine and Ben Witherington observe, the Greek verb "refers to an official commissioning."[36]

35. *Mishnah Sanhedrin* 1:6.

36. Amy-Jill Levine and Ben Witherington III, *The Gospel of Luke*, NCBC (Cambridge: Cambridge University Press, 2018), 277.

Jesus's Ministry through the Church in Acts

The unity of Jesus's ministry with that of his apostles is underscored in the introduction of the book of Acts, which begins, "In the first book, Theophilus, I wrote about all that Jesus *began* [*ērxato*] to do and teach" (Acts 1:1). The implication is that Acts, building on the Gospel of Luke, discusses what Jesus *continues* to do and teach.[37] Or, to borrow language from Paul, we might say that what Jesus formerly did in his personal body he now does in his ecclesial body.

Jesus's Work in Peter and the Apostles

Acts begins with Jesus promising to send the Spirit to the disciples, who enables them to serve as Jesus's authorized representatives: "You will receive power when the Holy Spirit has come upon you, and you will be my witnesses in Jerusalem, in all Judea and Samaria, and to the ends of the earth" (Acts 1:8). As David Moessner puts it, "The ones 'sent' continue to 'act and teach' (Acts 1:1) for the one *who continues to be present as the one who acts and speaks*."[38]

Not surprisingly, then, the book of Acts appears to carefully mirror the Gospel of Luke—the life of Jesus is mirrored in that of the early Church. To discuss all of the ways this is evident would require an entire monograph.[39] Here let us simply mention a few.

In the Gospel of Luke, Jesus's earthly life begins at the annunciation. The angel Gabriel explains to Mary how Jesus will be conceived: "*The Holy Spirit will come upon you*, and the power of the Most High will overshadow you" (Luke 1:35). Jesus's human story begins with the coming of the Spirit on Mary. Likewise, Jesus's earthly ministry begins with another appearance of the Spirit: at his baptism, the Spirit descends upon him (Luke 3:22). Similarly, in the book of Acts, the Church's life and ministry commences with the coming of the Spirit on the apostles at Pentecost. Note the parallels between Jesus's baptism in Luke and the story of Pentecost in Acts:

37. See Richard A. Burridge, "The Genre of Acts—Revisited," in *Reading Acts Today: Essays in Honour of Loveday C. A. Alexander*, ed. Steve Walton, Thomas E. Phillips, Lloyd K. Pietersen, and F. Scott Spencer, LNTS 427 (London: T&T Clark, 2011), 28.

38. David P. Moessner, *Luke the Historian of Israel's Legacy, Theologian of Israel's "Christ": A New Reading of the "Gospel Acts" of Luke*, BZNW 182 (Berlin: De Gruyter, 2016), 192.

39. See, e.g., the classic study in Charles H. Talbert, *Literary Patterns, Theological Themes and the Genre of Luke-Acts*, SBLMS 20 (Missoula, MT: Scholars Press, 1974).

Jesus's Baptism (Luke 3)	**The "Baptism" of the Spirit at Pentecost (Acts 2)**
Jesus is baptized and "was *praying* [*proseuchomenou*]." (3:21)	The disciples receive the Spirit after "devoting themselves to *prayer* [*proseuchē*]." (Acts 1:14)
The Spirit descends after "the heavens were opened" and a voice from heaven is heard. (3:21–22)	The coming of the Spirit is accompanied by a sound of mighty wind "from heaven." (2:2)
The Spirit comes upon Jesus "in bodily form, like a dove." (3:22)	The Spirit's coming occurs with a visible manifestation of "tongues of fire." (2:3)
Luke says that after his baptism Jesus was "full [*plērēs*] of the Holy Spirit." (Luke 4:1)	The disciples are "filled with [*eplēsthēsan*] the Holy Spirit." (2:4)

Jesus's public ministry begins with the descent of the Spirit upon him at his baptism in the Jordan (Luke 3:22), an event that takes place as he "was praying" (Luke 3:21). In addition, Luke tells us that the Spirit came upon Jesus "in bodily form like a dove" (Luke 3:22). After this event, Luke describes Jesus as being "full of the Holy Spirit" (Luke 4:1). Likewise, the apostles' public ministry in Acts commences after the Spirit descends in visible form ("tongues of fire") upon them at Pentecost (Acts 2:1–13). This occurs after we read that the disciples have been "devoting themselves to *prayer*" (Acts 1:14). The parallels are intentional. This is evident from another observation; when Jesus foretells the coming of the Spirit on the Twelve, he refers to this specific event as a "baptism": "You will be *baptized* with the Holy Spirit" (Acts 1:5).

The parallels continue after the baptism and the description of Pentecost. At the beginning of his public ministry, Jesus goes to the synagogue at Nazareth and delivers a speech in which he announces that he has come to bring fulfillment to the scriptures of Israel (Luke 4:16–21). The apostles' public ministry kicks off with a speech delivered by Peter in the temple in Jerusalem, which highlights Jesus's fulfillment of the scriptures (Acts 2:14–36).

We should also note that the disciples perform miracles reminiscent of Jesus's. One of Jesus's first miracles in the Gospel of Luke involves the healing of a paralyzed man (Luke 5:17–26). We have already examined the way this story underscores Jesus's ability to forgive sins. Here it is worth noting the way it foreshadows the ministry of the apostles in Acts. Specifically, Peter's first miracle takes place when he also heals a man who is unable to walk (Acts 3:2–10). Even though different Greek words appear, the two accounts are remarkably similar:

Jesus's Healing of the Paralyzed Man (Luke 5)	Peter's Healing of the Lame Man (Acts 3)
"Some men came *carrying* [*pherontes*] a man who was *paralyzed* [*paralelymenos*] on a mat." (5:18)	"And a certain man who was *lame* [*chōlos*] from birth *was being carried* [*ebastazeto*]." (3:2)
"They were trying to bring him in and *lay* [*theinai*] him in front of him." (5:18)	". . . whom they *laid* [*etithoun*] every day at that gate of the temple." (3:2)
"When Jesus *saw* [*idōn*] their faith . . ." (5:20)	"Peter *looked intently* [*atenisas*] at him . . ." (3:4)
"[Jesus] said to the man who was paralyzed, 'I say to you, *rise up* [*egeire*], take up your pallet, and go to your home.'" (5:24)	"Peter said . . . , 'In the name of Jesus Christ of Nazareth, *rise up* [*egeire*][40] and walk around.' And he took him by the right hand and *raised him up* [*ēgeiren*]." (3:6–7)
"*At once* [*parachrēma*] he *stood up* [*anastas*] before them . . ." (5:25)	"*At once* [*parachrēma*] . . . he *stood* [*estē*] and began walking around." (3:7–8)
"They were all seized with *amazement* [*ekstasis*] . . . and *were filled with* [*eplēsthēsan*] fear [*phobou*]." (5:26)	"And they *were filled with* [*eplēsthēsan*] *wonder* [*thambous*] and *amazement* [*ekstaseōs*]." (3:10)

It seems uncontestable that Peter's miracle is meant to call to mind the miracle worked by Jesus in the Gospel of Luke. By the invocation of Jesus's name, Jesus is present and working through Peter.[41]

Moreover, we should note another parallel between Jesus and Peter. In the Gospel of Luke, healing is mediated through Jesus's clothing. In Luke 8, a woman with a hemorrhage is healed after touching the tassel on Jesus's garment (Luke 8:44). Likewise, in Acts healing is effected through Peter's shadow: "They even carried the sick into the streets and laid them on cots and mats so that when Peter came by at least his shadow might fall on some of them" (Acts 5:15).[42]

Jesus and Stephen

Jesus's disciples are also conformed to Christ in their suffering. This is most evident in the case of Stephen. Again, consider the parallels:

40. Some manuscripts (ℵ, B, D) omit "rise up" here, but many include it (A, C, E, Ψ, 095, 33, 36, 81, etc.).

41. For more on the way the name of Jesus serves as a sign of Jesus's ongoing presence in the community in Acts, see Moessner, *Luke the Historian*, 193–98.

42. On the connection between the two stories, see Samson Uytanlet, *Luke-Acts and Jewish Historiography: A Study on the Theology, Literature, and Ideology of Luke-Acts*, WUNT 2/366 (Tübingen: Mohr Siebeck, 2014), 151.

Jesus's Death on the Cross (Luke 22–23)	Stephen's Martyrdom (Acts 6–7)
Jesus withdraws to pray, going "about a *stone's throw* [*lithou bolēn*] and, *falling to his knees* [*kai theis ta gonata*], he began to pray [*prosēucheto*]." (22:41)	Stephen is dragged out of the city, where "they began to *stone him* [*elithoboloun*], . . . and *falling to his knees* [*theis de ta gonata*]," Stephen prayed to Jesus. (7:58, 60; cf. 7:59)
Jesus is arrested, taken before the Sanhedrin, and questioned by the high priest. (22:54, 66)	Stephen is arrested, taken before the Sanhedrin, and questioned by the high priest. (6:12–7:1)
The Sanhedrin hands Jesus over to be killed after he calls himself "the Son of Man." (22:69)	Stephen is taken out to be killed after having a vision of Jesus as "the Son of Man." (7:56)
Jesus prays, "*crying out with a loud voice* [*phōnēsas phōnē megalē*]." (23:46)	Stephen "*cried out with a loud voice* [*ekraxen phōnē megalē*]." (7:60)
Jesus prays for his enemies: "Father, forgive them, for they know not what they do." (23:34)	Stephen prays for his enemies: "Lord, do not hold this sin against them." (7:60)
Jesus says, "Father, into your hands I commit *my spirit*." (23:46)	Stephen prays, "Lord Jesus, receive *my spirit*." (7:59)

The first parallel, Jesus going about a "stone's throw" and "kneeling" to pray and Stephen's kneeling in prayer while being stoned, is rarely caught by readers but is difficult to dismiss as unintentional given the other similarities between the two stories.[43] In describing Stephen's death in terms so evocative of Jesus's, it seems evident that Stephen is a Christlike figure. Jesus's work continues in believers—not merely his miraculous work but his obediential suffering. John Chrysostom noted these parallels, saying, "Just what they did in Christ's case, the same they do here also [to Stephen]. For as he said, 'You shall see the Son of Man sitting on the right hand of God' (Matt 26:64), . . . just so was it here."[44]

After Stephen's death, Saul—better known as Paul—encounters the risen Lord on the Damascus road. The scene once again underscores the unity between Jesus and the Church. The persecutor of the Church hears these words: "Saul, Saul, *why do you persecute me*?" (Acts 9:4). To this question, Saul responds, "Who are you, Lord?" (Acts 9:5). The life-changing response he receives is, "I am Jesus, whom you are persecuting" (Acts 9:5). To this revelation, Saul does not protest; he does not say, "Well, actually, I am persecuting your followers, not *you* personally, Jesus." Such a protest would be pointless.

43. Pablo T. Gadenz, *The Gospel of Luke*, CCSS (Grand Rapids: Baker Academic, 2018), 264.
44. John Chrysostom, *Homilies on Acts* 18, adapted from *NPNF*[1] 11:112.

Paul seems to understand the message: by persecuting the Church, he is persecuting *Jesus* because Jesus is inseparably united to believers. Augustine would see in this verse the doctrine of the Church as the "whole Christ," writing: "Were it not for the body's linkage with its Head through the bond of charity, so close a link that Head and body speak as one, he could not have rebuked a certain persecutor from heaven with the question, 'Saul, Saul, why are you persecuting me?' (Acts 9:4)."[45]

Jesus's Work in Paul's Ministry

Finally, we should mention that Paul is also portrayed as similar to Jesus in Acts. Again, an in-depth treatment cannot be offered here. The following parallels will, however, suffice to make the point.

Jesus's Public Ministry in Luke	The Church's Ministry in Acts
Jesus "set his face to go to Jerusalem." (9:51)	Paul "resolved . . . to go on to Jerusalem." (19:21)
Jesus arrives in Jerusalem and is well received; people praise God for his works. (19:37)	Paul arrives in Jerusalem and is well received by believers, who praise God for his work. (21:17–20)
Jesus celebrates a meal where he takes bread, gives thanks, and breaks it. (22:19)	Paul celebrates a meal in which he takes bread, gives thanks, and breaks it. (27:35)
A crowd arrests Jesus. (22:47, 54)	A crowd arrests Paul. (21:27, 30)
Jesus is tried four times: the Sanhedrin, Pilate, Herod, and Pilate. (22:66; 23:1, 8, 13)	Paul is tried four times: the Sanhedrin, Felix, Festus, and Herod Agrippa. (Acts 23, 24, 25, 26)
Pilate says Jesus is innocent three times. (23:4, 14, 22)	Paul is said to be innocent by three men: Lysias, Festus, and Agrippa. (23:29; 25:25; 26:31)
The crowd cries about Jesus: "Away [*Aire*] with this man." (23:18)	The crowd cries about Paul: "Away [*Aire*] with him." (21:36)
A centurion expresses faith in Jesus. (23:47)	A centurion is won over by Paul. (27:3, 43)

What Jesus did in Peter, Jesus also does in Paul. This, of course, includes multiple healings. Acts, then, essentially narrates the teaching of Paul in Galatians: "For he who worked through Peter to make him an apostle to the circumcised also worked through me for the gentiles" (Gal. 2:8).

45. Augustine, *Expositions of the Psalms 1–32*, ed. John E. Rotelle, trans. Maria Boulding, WSA III/15 (Hyde Park, NY: New City Press, 2000), 323.

In fact, healing is mediated through items associated with Paul just as healing is effected through touching Jesus's garment in Luke 8:44 and Peter's shadow in Acts 5:15. Acts tells us: "God was doing miracles and extraordinary things through the hands of Paul, so that even when the handkerchiefs or workman's aprons that had touched his skin were brought to the sick, their diseases left them, and the evil spirits came out of them" (Acts 19:11–12).

As we saw at the beginning of this chapter, in Acts the apostles are portrayed as sharing their leadership responsibilities over the Church with others, especially the "elders." The first indication that such figures had a role in the early community is found in Acts 11, where proceeds are sent to elders in Jerusalem to help bring relief during a famine. The money is sent through Barnabas and Paul (Acts 11:30). We are not told how these figures came to be recognized—one wonders if some of them had belonged to the group of the seventy(-two) appointed by Jesus (Luke 10:1)[46]—but we do see such figures are appointed: Paul and Barnabas are said to have "appointed elders for [the believers] in each church" (Acts 14:23). The Greek term translated "appointed" (*cheirotoneō*) is used in the sense of appointing or installing officials.[47]

Jesus, then, continues to work through the Church in Acts. Among other things, he does this by continuing his work in the apostles, whom Jesus has promised would be the leaders of God's people. Luke tells us what Jesus says at the Last Supper to the Twelve: "You will sit on thrones judging the twelve tribes of Israel" (Luke 22:30). In Acts 4–6 we begin to see the apostles fulfilling their role as God's future leaders as they "rule over" the community. Moreover, they share their authority with others, particularly "elders." As we have seen, in 1 Peter, the apostle himself is described as an "elder." With all of this, let us return to consider the significance of the elders in James 5.

46. The third- or fourth-century work by Adamantius, *De recta in Deum fide* (On Right Faith in God), includes Mark and Luke as members, though this appears to be based in imagination and not tradition. Likewise, Epiphanius (late third to early fourth century) includes Mark among the seventy(-two). See C. Clifton Black, *Mark: Images of an Apostolic Interpreter* (1994; repr., Minneapolis: Fortress, 2001), 149–52, 163.

47. See, e.g., Josephus, *Jewish Antiquities* 6.39, 43; Philo, *On Joseph* 248; *On the Life of Moses* 2.142; Joseph A. Fitzmyer, *The Acts of the Apostles*, AB 31 (New Haven: Yale University Press, 2008), 535.

The Elders in James

James insists that the sick person ought to "call for the elders of the church" in order to be anointed by them (James 5:14). Is this merely a reference to people of advanced biological age? If not, who might these people be? It is now time to tackle this question.

The Elders as Church Leaders

Whom does James likely have in mind when he speaks of the "elders"? One might think this simply refers to older individuals, but this is unlikely since James more fully describes them as "elders of the church [*ekklēsias*]." Since the term translated "church," *ekklēsia*, was used for synagogue assemblies,[48] it might be tempting to think that James is not referring specifically to figures in the Christian community. Some have argued that the audience of the epistle is not specifically Christian but broadly Jewish.[49] Yet this view is held by relatively few commentators. Although this position has much to commend it, three observations weigh against it.

First, the salutation specifically identifies the author as "James, a slave of God and of the Lord Jesus Christ" (James 1:1). It would be rather odd to begin a letter addressed to people who did not believe Jesus was either "Lord" or "Christ" by asserting that he was both. Indeed, some ancient commentators even thought that introduction indicates Jesus's equality to God.[50] Whatever one makes of that reading, one thing seems difficult to deny: such a greeting is hardly expected from a writer who is attempting to downplay or mute his Christian commitments.

Second, a non-Christian Jewish audience is also undermined by what is said in James 2: "Brothers, do not show partiality while holding your faith in our Lord Jesus Christ, the glorious" (James 2:1). This seems to identify the letter's readers as believers in Jesus. One must insist that the appearance of "Jesus Christ" in James 2:1 is the result of later textual corruption

48. See, e.g., Josephus, *Jewish War* 7.412; Philo, *Special Laws* 1.324–25; Ralph Korner, *The Origin and Meaning of Ekklēsia in the Early Jesus Movement*, AGJU 98 (Leiden: Brill, 2017), 123–26; Anders Runesson, Donald Binder, and Birger Olsson, *The Ancient Synagogue from Its Origins to 200 C.E.: A Source Book*, AJEC 72 (Leiden: Brill, 2008), 11–12.

49. The most comprehensive and compelling argument for this view is found in Dale C. Allison Jr., *James*, ICC (London: Bloomsbury T&T Clark, 2013), 32–50.

50. See also Pseudo-Oecumenius, *Commentary on James* (PG 119:456A), and Theophylact, *Commentary on the Catholic Epistle of St. James* (PG 125:1133D–1136A).

if one wishes to maintain that the audience was not specifically Christian. Yet the manuscript evidence overwhelmingly favors the authenticity of the use of Jesus's name.[51] There are other expressions in the book that seem to assume knowledge of Christian tradition, such as the parallels with Mark 13 in James 5:7–9 mentioned above, in chapter 3 (see pp. 48–51). So, while James has less material that is explicitly distinct in Christian formulation, the argument that it is not primarily written to believers in Jesus is not compelling.

Third, we must not forget the Jewish character of the early Church. As we have already emphasized in chapter 3 (see pp. 43–44), the early Jewish believers did not view themselves as *former* Jews (e.g., Acts 24:5, 14; Rom. 11:1; Gal. 2:15). The Jewish Christ-followers were identified as a Jewish "sect" (*hairesis*; Acts 24:5, 14), the same term Jewish sources use for groups like the Pharisees and Sadducees.[52] The supposed lack of "distinctly" Christian themes is, therefore, in the final analysis little more than an argument from silence. The letter begins with a reference to Jesus as "Lord" and "Messiah." To insist that Jewish believers in Jesus would necessarily engage in further explicit Christian signaling underestimates the way Jewish faith bound the community together.

For all of these reasons, then, it seems unlikely that James's reference to the "elders of the *ekklēsia*" involves a reference to non-Christian individuals. While it is certainly possible to imagine non-Christian Jews speaking of "elders of the *ekklēsia*," given that the letter begins with an affirmation of Jesus's identity as "Lord" and "Christ" and in light of the fact that Church leaders were already known as "elders"—Acts even uses the precise phrase James uses for them, "elders of the church" (Acts 20:17)—the most natural reading of the passage is that these refer to such individuals. To envision these figures as merely charismatic healers with no recognized role in the Church seems like special pleading in light of the fact that Christian "elders" were known as leaders in the community in other early sources.

51. The argument against authenticity depends upon the grammatical oddity of the phrase in Greek (*tēn pistin tou kyriou hēmōn Iēsou Christou tēs doxēs*; James 2:1), specifically, the positioning of the final two words. It has been argued that the most natural reading is to assume that the original text simply read "the Lord of Glory" and that a later copyist added "Jesus Christ" into the phrase (see Allison, *James*, 382–84). Yet (1) "Jesus Christ" is part of the letter's salutation; and (2) as elegant as James's Greek is, his phrasing elsewhere is also awkward (see, e.g., Allison, *James*, 470, on James 2:18).

52. Acts 15:5; Josephus, *Life* 10; 12; 191; *Jewish Antiquities* 13.171; 20.199.

Ignatius of Antioch on Submission to the Bishops and Presbyters

For the early Christian writer Ignatius of Antioch, who wrote in the early part of the second century, submission to the Church's leaders—especially the bishop and the *presbyterion* (that is, the presbyters)—is an essential mark of faithful disciples:

> For *when you are subject to the bishop as to Jesus Christ*, it is evident to me that you are living not in accordance with human standards but in accordance with Jesus Christ. . . . It is essential, therefore, that you continue your current practice and *do nothing without the bishop*, but *be subject also to the council of presbyters as to the apostles of Jesus Christ*.[a]

Obedience to the bishop and presbyters is thus equated with obedience to Jesus Christ and to the apostles.

a. Ignatius, *To the Trallians* 2:1–2, in Michael W. Holmes, *The Apostolic Fathers: Greek Texts and English Translations*, 3rd ed. (Grand Rapids: Baker Academic, 2007), 215–17 (emphasis added).

The Liturgical Role of the Elders

Allison points out that James's description of the elders is especially evocative of Old Testament texts in which the elders of Israel are "called."[53] For example, in Exodus we read, "[Moses] *called* [*ekalesen*] the *elders* of the people [*tous presbyterous*]" (Exod. 19:7). Notably, in this scene the elders have a liturgical role. To see this, however, it is necessary to look carefully at the way the Sinai story appears as paradigmatic for Israel's worship.

In Exodus, the encounter of the people with the Lord at Sinai involves three parts: (1) the people witness the sacrifices made at the foot of the mountain (Exod. 24:4); (2) Moses and the leaders of the people—among them, "the seventy elders" (Exod. 24:1, 9)—ascend partway up the mountain to eat a sacred meal in God's presence (Exod. 24:9–11); (3) Moses alone is permitted to enter the top of the mountain into God's presence (Exod. 24:2). All of this

53. Allison (*James*, 755) cites Exod. 12:21; 19:7; Lev. 9:1; 1 Kings 20:7 [3 Kgdm. 21:7 LXX]; Jdt. 6:16; 13:12; Joel 1:14.

seems to foreshadow Israel's worship at the tabernacle, which likewise has a three-part structure: (1) the people bring their sacrifices in the "outer court," which is outside the inner sanctuary (Exod. 40:6); (2) the priests alone are allowed into the holy place inside the tabernacle, where they eat the sacred food (Exod. 26:35); (3) the high priest alone is given access to the inner sanctum, the place of God's presence, the holy of holies (Lev. 16:12–13, 17).[54] We can visualize this as follows:

Mount Sinai	The Tabernacle
Foot of the Mountain Altar of sacrifice (Exod. 24:4)	**Outer Court** Altar of sacrifice (Exod. 40:6)
Partway Up the Mountain Elders eat a meal in God's presence (Exod. 24:11)	**Holy Place (Outer Sanctum)** Table of the bread of the presence with the lampstand (Exod. 26:35)
Summit of the Mountain Moses enters the glory-cloud (Exod. 24:2)	**Holy of Holies (Inner Sanctum)** High priest enters on the Day of Atonement (Lev. 16:12–13, 17)

Against this backdrop, the "elders" in Exodus have a quasi-priestly role. This is not nearly as surprising as it may first appear since it is only *after* Exodus 32 that the priesthood is reserved for the Levites. The elders of Israel, then, are portrayed as performing a priestly function.

When James speaks of the need to summon the "elders of the church," he does not seem to refer merely to members of the community that are advanced in age. The language he uses evokes other passages in early Christian writings where "elders" are described as having leadership roles in the community. Moreover, from a perspective that recognizes the canon as the proper context for theological reflection, the Church can see in the elders the very figures anticipated in the parable of the wicked tenants—that is, the eschatological priestly leaders of the people of God. Warrant for this priestly role of the "elders" is found in the opening chapter of Acts.

In Acts 1, the "office" Judas had vacated is filled through lot-casting (Acts 1:20, 26). It would be wrong to dismiss the mention of lot-casting as an inconsequential detail. While pagans like the soldiers at Golgotha cast lots as a game of chance (Mark 15:24, etc.), in Israel's traditions lot-casting is a

54. See Mary Douglas, *Leviticus as Literature* (Oxford: Oxford University Press, 1999), 59–64; Gary Larsson, *Bound for Freedom: The Book of Exodus in Jewish and Christian Traditions* (Peabody, MA: Hendrickson, 1999), 134.

sacred rite. Priestly duties are determined by lot-casting (see, e.g., 1 Chron. 24:5, 7, 31; 25:8, 9; Neh. 10:34). Luke is indisputably aware of the Jewish connection made between lot-casting and priesthood. He observes that John the Baptist's father was serving in the temple because "according to the custom of the priesthood it fell to him by lot" (Luke 1:9). Given the parallel structure of Luke and Acts, it is extremely difficult to insist that it is unimportant that both Luke 1 and Acts 1 open with a scene of lot-casting. The most reasonable explanation of the parallel is that the lot-casting in Acts 1 involves priestly imagery like that found in Luke 1. It is hard to believe Jewish readers would have not made the connection. The selection of Judas's successor by lot, then, would seem to confirm what has been proposed above—that is, that the leaders of the church were seen as *priestly* leaders. Since the apostles' authority merges in many ways with that of the elders in Acts, it is difficult to avoid the conclusion that the elders in Acts are priestly. Notably, in Titus 1:5, Titus is told to "appoint" (*kathistēmi*) elders, using a Greek verb associated with the installation of priests (cf. 1 Macc. 10:20; 2 Macc. 14:13).

Within such a framework, the figures mentioned by James can be viewed as priestly much like the elders in Exodus 24. Like the apostles in Acts, these figures represent those through whom Jesus's ministry is continued in the life of the Church. And as healing occurred through the apostles in Acts by being anointed by oil (Mark 6:13) and was mediated to others through other physical objects such as handkerchiefs and workman's aprons, so too healing is mediated to the sick through anointing and prayer in James's instructions.

Yet the very fact that the sick in James are not merely touched by handkerchiefs as in Acts is worth considering more closely. Why is anointing significant? Indeed, sacral anointing has profound meaning in the scriptures. In the following chapters, we will consider this more closely. I believe that in doing so we can come to a better understanding of the way the Church's tradition has developed its understanding of the sacrament of anointing of the sick.

7

Kings, Priests, and Prophets as Anointed Ones

The Power of Sacral Anointing

> Those anointed to be high priests, and kings, and prophets, were reckoned more holy.
>
> —Clement of Alexandria[1]

> Oil, properly applied, confers divinely sanctioned power.
>
> —Matthew Novenson[2]

In his *Lives of the Caesars*, the Roman writer Suetonius tells us that Jews were expelled from Rome under the emperor Claudius because of disturbances that took place "at the instigation of Chrestus" (*Claudius* 25.4). There are good reasons to think that Suetonius is confused here. The controversy he writes about may not have involved a man named "Chrestus"—which was a common Roman name—but, instead, it may have been over claims concerning Jesus "Christ." Other sources indicate that non-Jews misheard "Christ" as

1. Clement of Alexandria, *Stromata* 4.25 (*ANF* 2:438).

2. Matthew V. Novenson, *The Grammar of Messianism: An Ancient Jewish Political Idiom and Its Users* (Oxford: Oxford University Press, 2017), 47, referring specifically to Ps. 45:6–7.

"Chrestus." For example, Codex Sinaiticus, one of the most important ancient copies of the Bible, misspells the Greek word for "Christian" as *Chrestionos*.[3] Why did non-Jews have difficulty with the word "Christ"? It was an unfamiliar name to them. In fact, they would have been altogether unacquainted with the Jewish traditions that shaped a central aspect of the early Church's message: Jesus is the "Christ."

When the Hebrew scriptures were translated into Greek, the Greek term *christos* was used to translate the Hebrew noun *mashiakh*, the word from which we get the English term "messiah." The Hebrew word *mashiakh* simply means "anointed one." The noun is related to the Hebrew verb that means "to anoint," *mashakh*. Similarly, the Greek verb *chriō* means "to anoint." To proclaim Jesus as the "Christ" or "Messiah" is to affirm that he is the "Anointed One" par excellence. This terminology, however, would have been obscure to non-Jewish audiences. So instead of hearing *Christos*—"Christ" or "Messiah"—some apparently mistakenly thought believers in Jesus were simply talking about a man with a common Roman name, *Chrestus*.

Israel's scriptures—as well as nonbiblical Jewish sources—depict various figures as recipients of solemn anointings, often involving oil. As we have seen, oil was commonly used in ancient Israel. Yet, in addition to everyday applications, such as medicinal use, anointing also had sacral significance in ancient Israel. In particular, three types of individuals were connected to sacral anointing: kings, priests, and prophets. As the next chapters will demonstrate, these traditions stand in the backdrop of Jesus's identity as "Christ" in the New Testament. Here we will first offer a careful analysis of these types of anointing in Israel's scriptures.

Kings as Anointed Ones

Outside of ancient Israel, we have no evidence that anointing served as part of royal installation ceremonies.[4] An intriguing use of oil, however, is found in ancient Egypt. From what we can tell, pharaohs themselves were not anointed, yet it seems that the rulers who served under the king of Egypt were. Evidence for this is found in the Amarna letters, a group of clay tablets that date back

3. Acts 11:26; 26:28; 1 Pet. 4:16. See A. Andrew Das, *Solving the Romans Debate* (Minneapolis: Fortress, 2007), 150.

4. For what follows, see Giovanni Garbini, *History and Ideology in Ancient Israel*, trans. John Bowden (New York: Crossroad, 1988), 68.

to the fourteenth century BC. Letter 51 reports that Pharaoh Thutmose III (d. 1425 BC) anointed the author's ancestor as a king. The letter is damaged, but here is how the extant text reads:

> When . . . the king of Egypt, your ancestor, made [T]a[ku], my ancestor, a *king* in Nuhasse, *he put oil on his head* and [s]poke as follows: "Whom the king of Egypt has made a king, [and on whose head] he has put [oil]."[5]

While it is incomplete, what we possess of this letter confirms that client-kings under Pharaoh were anointed. This is significant because it shows us that *the anointing of the ruler served to identify a figure as one invested with Pharaoh's own authority*. The Egyptian custom sheds light on the meaning of royal anointings in ancient Israel: the anointing of the human king serves to designate him as the authorized representative and instrument of the true King, God.

The Divine King's Anointed One

Various scriptures attest to the idea that God is King. The identification is especially dominant in the Psalter.[6] Consider, for example, Psalm 29:

> The LORD sits enthroned over the flood;
> *the LORD sits enthroned as king forever.* (Ps. 29:10)

The description here evokes what is said about God after Israel is delivered from the Egyptian armies through the waters of the Red Sea: "The LORD will *reign* forever and ever" (Exod. 15:18). The line underscores the message of Exodus: Israel's true king is to be not Pharaoh but the LORD.

In some texts, human kingship is portrayed as in tension with God's kingship. A parade example can be found in the book of Judges' account of Gideon, an unlikely hero who leads Israel to victory over their enemies through God's help. After Gideon's success, the Israelites decide to make him and his children after him king. Gideon, however, renounces the offer, explaining, "I

5. Slightly adapted from William L. Moran, *The Amarna Letters* (Baltimore: Johns Hopkins University Press, 1992), 122 (emphasis added).

6. See, e.g., Pss. 24:10; 44:4; 47:2, 6–8; 48:2; 68:24; 74:12; 84:3; 95:3; 98:6; 99:4; 145:1; 149:2. See also Sir. 50:15; 51:1; Isa. 6:5; 8:21; 33:22; 41:21; 43:15; 44:6; Jer. 8:19; 10:7, 10; 46:18; 48:15; 51:57; Ezek. 17:16; 20:33; Dan. 2:37; 4:37; Zeph. 3:15; Zech. 14:16–17; Mal. 1:14.

will not rule over you, and my son will not rule over you; *the Lord will rule over you*" (Judg. 8:23). The idea of a human king seems to be an affront to Gideon's conviction that God is Israel's king. As the story unfolds, matters become more complicated.

Gideon later has a son, whom he names Abimelech (Judg. 8:31), which literally translates as "My father is king." It seems, then, that Gideon fails to wholly detach himself from royal aspirations. This has disastrous consequences. Abimelech attempts to make himself king, massacring his own brothers. His actions are condemned by the prophet Jotham, who notably describes the situation with the metaphor of trees seeking to "*anoint* a king over themselves" (Judg. 9:8). Anointing is thus linked to kingship. Abimelech's short reign comes to an end when a woman throws a millstone down upon him, crushing his head (Judg. 9:53). God is therefore said to have repaid him in this for his wicked deeds (Judg. 9:56). Abimelech's reign lacks divine approval and ultimately fails.

The case is quite different when we get to the story of Saul, who is anointed king in 1 Samuel. The people go to Samuel the prophet and demand that he appoint for them a king "like other nations" (1 Sam. 8:5). God acknowledges that the people "have *rejected me from being king* over them" (1 Sam. 8:7). Instructing Samuel to warn the people about the dangers of having a human king, the Lord has Samuel anoint a man named Saul as king over the people.

It is important to observe that God is not portrayed as simply permitting Saul's kingship. Rather, God is said to *empower* Saul to be king through royal anointing. Samuel explains to the king-to-be that royal anointing will bestow upon him the gift of the Spirit: "Then the Spirit of the Lord will come upon you in power, and you will prophesy along with [prophets], and will turn into a different person, . . . for God is with you" (1 Sam. 10:6, 7). All of this comes to pass when Saul is anointed. We read that "God changed his heart" (1 Sam. 10:9). The anointing, therefore, involves more than oil. It signifies the coming of the Spirit of God, which involves reception of "the vital force of the deity" and "the invigorating power of God."[7] Implicitly, anointing demonstrates that God remains, in some sense, the true King. The human is empowered to serve as king at God's approval.

Saul, however, ends up disobeying the Lord. Samuel is therefore sent by God to anoint a new king—namely, David. Samuel is sent to the family of a

7. P. Kyle McCarter Jr., *I Samuel*, AYB 8 (New Haven: Yale University Press, 2008), 182.

man named Jesse. Once again, the royal anointing is connected to the coming of the Spirit of God: "Then Samuel took the horn of oil, and anointed him in the presence of his brothers; and the Spirit of the LORD came upon David in power from that day forward" (1 Sam. 16:13). As with Saul, the Spirit comes upon David at his anointing. After this, David is shown to have a special closeness to the LORD, which is painfully evident even to Saul, who recognizes that "the LORD is with him [= David]" (1 Sam. 16:18). Moreover, after his anointing, David even displays exorcistic abilities (1 Sam. 16:23).

In addition, as with Saul, David's status as "anointed one" is associated with the charism of prophecy. In 2 Samuel 23, we encounter the last words of David, which are presented as a song of thanksgiving to God. It begins:

> Now these are the last words of David:
> *The oracle of David*, son of Jesse,
>   *the oracle of the man* God raised on high,
> *the anointed of the God of Jacob*. (2 Sam. 23:1)

In these lines David is portrayed as delivering an "oracle" (*ne'um*), a term connected with *prophetic* utterance (e.g., Num. 24:3, 15). Later sources make explicit what is implicit in these texts by speaking of David as a "prophet" (Acts 2:30).[8] We must reiterate, however, that David's prophetic charism is tied explicitly to his identity as "the anointed one."

In his discussion of royal anointing in Scripture, P. Kyle McCarter uses the terminology of a "sacramental act" to describe how the action is understood by the biblical author:

> The practice [of anointing] involved a symbolic transfer of sanctity from the deity to an object or person and thus was *essentially a sacramental act*. . . . The divine virtue, believed to be especially present in living things, was directly transferred to the sanctified individual. . . . The ceremony was believed to impart something of the sanctity of the national god to the king.[9]

The royal anointing was seen as anything but an empty ritual. As Matthew Novenson puts it, in the ancient mindset, "oil, properly applied, confers

8. *11QPsalms*[a] (11Q5) 27:11; Pseudo-Philo, *Biblical Antiquities* 59; Josephus, *Jewish Antiquities* 6.166; see also *Targum on 2 Samuel* 22:1; 23:1.

9. McCarter, *I Samuel*, 178 (emphasis added).

divinely sanctioned power."[10] In the use of the sacred oil, the anointing itself was understood as bestowing on the king God's own Spirit. This Spirit empowered the king to act as the divinely chosen king. Therefore, even after being anointed himself, David vigorously protests taking any action against Saul, "the Lord's anointed" (e.g., 1 Sam. 24:6, 10).

Anointing and Divine Approval

It is not the case that every king undergoes a royal anointing. Scenes of royal anointings are typically limited to individuals whose claims to the throne are not established on grounds of dynastic succession.[11] The Jerusalem Talmud recognizes, therefore, "They anoint kings only on account of controversy" (*Jerusalem Talmud Horayot* 3:2).[12]

Saul requires a public anointing since he is the first king to reign with God's approval. For the same reason, David is anointed multiple times. In the first instance, he is anointed in the company of his family (1 Sam. 16:13). This is necessary since another king, Saul, is presently reigning. David is then anointed again after Saul's death by the members of the tribe of Judah (2 Sam. 2:4, 7). This act makes manifest that the tribe acknowledges David as the true king rather than accepting someone from Saul's line. After Saul's death, those aligned with the former king make his son Ishbaal king (2 Sam. 2:8–10). In Ishbaal's case, no public anointing occurs; dynastic succession is simply assumed as the basis of his kingship. David is anointed a third time in 2 Samuel 5, after the death of Ishbaal. The anointing helps to signify that the northern tribes have transferred their allegiance from the house of Saul to David.

Absalom, who attempts to wrest the kingdom from his father as part of a coup, is anointed by the people (2 Sam. 19:10). While Ishbaal did not need to be anointed since he was the obvious successor to his father, Saul, who had died, Absalom is anointed precisely because he is seeking to usurp his father, who is still alive. The precise identity of Absalom's anointers is never given. This seems significant. Unlike Saul and David, Absalom is not anointed by a duly recognized prophet or priest. Confirmation of God's approval of his kingship is thus lacking.

10. Novenson, *Grammar of Messianism*, 47.
11. For what follows in this section, see Novenson, *Grammar of Messianism*, 104–8.
12. Translation from Novenson, *Grammar of Messianism*, 108.

David has his son Solomon anointed king by both the priest Zadok and the prophet Nathan. Again, the public act appears in a context of controversy—another son of David, Adonijah, has "exalted himself, saying, 'I will be king'" (1 Kings 1:5). That Solomon is anointed by both the recognized priest and prophet is crucial here as they serve to authenticate divine approval of Solomon's coronation (1 Kings 1:38–39).

Likewise, when the northern tribes split from the Davidic kingdom during the reign of Rehoboam, royal anointing in the Northern Kingdom occurs when a new king emerges from a different dynastic line. Jehu is anointed by the prophet Elijah, marking a break from the line of Omri (1 Kings 19:16). Similarly, in the Davidic kingdom, after Solomon, the next Davidic king said to be anointed is Joash (2 Kings 11:12), whose rise spells the end of wicked Queen Athaliah's rule.

Before moving on, it is also worth mentioning an especially surprising case of a figure said to be "anointed" by God: the Persian king Cyrus II. In the book of Isaiah, this gentile king is explicitly called God's "anointed one" (Isa. 45:1). This is the only instance in Jewish Scripture where a gentile is described as the Lord's "anointed" or "messiah." That a pagan king is identified with this label would have surely been surprising to ancient Jewish readers of Isaiah. It raised questions for later rabbis (e.g., *Babylonian Talmud Megillah* 12a). The message in Isaiah, however, is not that there is only one future deliverer and that Cyrus is the fulfillment of these hopes. Again, in Hebrew, "messiah" simply means "anointed one." The prophet speaks of Cyrus as the Lord's "anointed one" to explain that, as shocking as it might have seemed, God is working through a gentile king to accomplish his plans.[13]

Royal Anointing and the Sacred Oil

As we have seen, different kinds of oil are spoken of in the scriptures. A special type of oil is reserved for liturgical use, which the book of Exodus calls "the sacred anointing oil" (Exod. 30:25). Leviticus explains the purpose of this oil: Moses uses it to "consecrate" the tabernacle (Lev. 8:10). In other words, this type of anointing oil makes things "holy" (Exod. 40:9). Remarkably, it is this very oil that is used in royal anointings.

13. See Shalom M. Paul, *Isaiah 40–66: Translation and Commentary*, ECC (Grand Rapids: Eerdmans, 2012), 251–52.

In 1 Kings, we read about the anointing of Solomon. There we are told that the king is anointed by the priest Zadok: "Zadok the priest took *the horn of oil from the tent* and anointed Solomon" (1 Kings 1:39). Although the text is not explicit about the meaning of the "tent" here, commentators generally agree that it refers to the liturgical tent David built for the ark of the covenant (2 Sam. 6:17).[14] The oil poured over Solomon, then, is almost certainly to be understood as the sacred liturgical oil.

That royal figures are to be anointed with the sacred liturgical oil is also attested in the book of Zechariah. In chapter 4, Zechariah has a vision of a golden "lampstand" and "two olive trees" (Zech. 4:2–3). The lampstand is undoubtedly a menorah—that is, the lampstand in the sanctuary (Exod. 25:31–40; 37:17–24). We are told that the two olive trees represent "the two anointed ones" (Zech. 4:14)—that is, two "messiahs." One of the figures is Zerubbabel, a man from the royal line of David (1 Chron. 3:10–19).[15] Though he was never technically a king, he became governor during the Persian period. The second olive tree seems to be a symbol of the high priest Joshua, whose divine investiture is described in the previous chapter (cf. Zech. 3:1–10).[16] As we will see in greater detail below, the high priest is also anointed (e.g., Lev. 8:12; 21:12), so it is nearly certain that Joshua is the other leader in the prophet's vision. In fact, other texts speak of the dual leadership of Zerubbabel and Joshua (cf. Hag. 1:12). Both figures, then—the royal Zerubbabel *and* the high priest Joshua—are anointed in connection with the holy oil linked to the sanctuary's lampstand.

Finally, we should mention the meaning of the symbolism of the vision. Zechariah is told: "'Not by might, nor by power, but by my Spirit,' says the Lord of hosts" (Zech. 4:6). Once again, then, to be divinely anointed is understood as being invested with the Spirit of God.

Passages describing the anointing of a king do not always specify that the oil involved is that from Israel's liturgical rites. Nor is it explicitly stated that royal anointings effect "consecration." Still, the evidence suggests that royal anointings indicate the human king serves as God's designated and Spirit-empowered co-ruler.

14. See, e.g., Mordechai Cogan, *I Kings*, AB 10 (New York: Doubleday, 2001), 162.

15. See Novenson, *Grammar of Messianism*, 69–72.

16. Carol L. Meyers and Eric M. Meyers, *Haggai, Zechariah 1–8*, AYB 25B (New Haven: Yale University Press, 2008), 239: "The vision contains two trees which, according to the identity of verse 14, must represent the figures of two community leaders, notably high priest and governor."

The Davidic Anointed Figure as Divine Son and Divine Representative

In the scriptures, not all divinely sanctioned royal anointings are presented in the same way. Both ancient rabbis and contemporary biblical scholars, for example, note that while Saul and Jehu are anointed with oil taken from a "vial" (*pak*; cf. 1 Sam. 10:1; 2 Kings 9:3), David and Solomon are anointed with oil from a "horn" (1 Sam. 16:13; 1 Kings 1:39), a common symbol of royal power (e.g., 2 Sam. 22:3; Pss. 89:24; 132:17). It has been suggested, then, that Saul and Jehu's anointings are presented as having a transient character, lacking the stability of the Davidic dynasty.[17] Whatever we make of the vial/horn symbolism, however, there can be little doubt that the Davidic line is often presented as uniquely privileged by God.

That the Davidic ruler serves as God's special representative is emphasized in the Psalms. Psalm 2, which many have thought played a role in the installation ceremony of the king,[18] begins:

> Why do the nations rage,
>   and the peoples plot in vain?
> The kings of the earth set themselves,
>   and the rulers take counsel together,
> against *the* Lord *and his anointed*. (Ps. 2:1–2)

To conspire against the "anointed one" is portrayed as futile. The psalmist goes on to explain why: the king has been established by none other than the Lord:

> "I have installed my king on Zion, my holy hill."
>   I will declare the decree of the Lord:
> He said to me, "You are my son,
>   today I have begotten you."
> Ask of me, and I will make the nations your inheritance,
>   and the ends of the earth your possession. (Ps. 2:6–8)

The Davidic king has been chosen by God; God will defeat those who think to usurp him.

17. *Babylonian Talmud Megillah* 14a. See, e.g., Diana Vikander Edelman, *King Saul in the Historiography of Judah* (Sheffield: JSOT Press, 1991), 51.

18. See, e.g., S. E. Gillingham, "The Messiah in the Psalms," *King and Messiah in Israel and the Ancient Near East*, ed. John Day, LHBOTS 270 (1998; repr., London: Bloomsbury T&T Clark, 2013), 212–13.

Moreover, Psalm 2 says that the Davidic king reigns from the LORD's "holy hill" (Ps. 2:6), a reference to Zion as the location of God's temple. Appropriately, the Davidic king's palace stands on Zion, adjacent to the house of God, on property owned by the king (2 Chron. 3:1; cf. Ezek. 43:7–9). The idea that the king sits at the LORD's "right hand," as Psalm 110:1 puts it, was thus expressed architecturally. The connection between Zion and the Davidic king is also underscored in Psalm 78, where the LORD's appointment of David is bound up with God's decision to build his sanctuary on Mount Zion (Ps. 78:68–70).

It is also significant that in Psalm 2 the king's status as the anointed one and as the one "installed" by God is further emphasized by his identity as God's *son*. Divine sonship is pointedly not associated with other kings, such as Abimelech, Saul, or kings of the Northern Kingdom. Instead, in the biblical narrative, it is uniquely associated with the royal line of David. It is important to note that the promise of divine sonship to the Davidic king is closely bound up with temple traditions. After David announces his plan to build a "house" for the LORD—that is, a temple—the prophet Nathan is sent to David to declare to the king that the LORD has other plans. The story is found in both 2 Samuel and 1 Chronicles. In both places, a pun appears: God promises to build a "house" for David (namely, a line of dynastic successors) and that it will be the son of David who will build the LORD a "house" (namely, a temple).

> When your days are full and you lie down with your fathers, I will raise up your offspring after you, who will come forth from your body, and I will establish his kingdom. *He shall build a house for my name*, and I will establish the throne of his kingdom forever. *I will be his father, and he will be my son*. (2 Sam. 7:12–14; cf. 1 Chron. 17:11–13; 22:7–10)

David's son's status as "son of God" is closely bound up with his identity as temple builder.

The Davidic king's connection to Israel's temple worship is underscored in other surprising ways. Perhaps most astonishing is that though the Torah specifies that the legitimate priests are to come solely from Aaron's line, David and his royal sons do things that only the Levitical priests are permitted to do: David offers sacrifices (2 Sam. 6:17; 1 Chron. 16:2; cf. Num. 3:6–8, 14–38; 4:47; 6:16–17; 8:14–26), wears the priestly garments (2 Sam. 6:14; 1 Chron. 15:27; cf. Exod. 28:4), builds the tabernacle where the ark of the covenant is placed (2 Sam. 6:17; 1 Chron. 15:1; 16:1; cf. Num. 1:51; 4:1–33), and blesses the people (2 Sam. 6:18; cf. Num. 6:22–27). David's sons are even explicitly called "priests" (*kohanim*; 2 Sam. 8:18).[19]

The relationship between the Davidic king and the temple underscores the king's sacral status; the LORD reigns through him. In 1 Chronicles 29:20, then, we read that after Solomon is enthroned the people of Israel "worshiped the LORD and the king."[20] Solomon is not an idol; he is not competing for the worship due to God. Rather, Solomon is a kind of icon or visible sign of the LORD himself. Because of this it even makes sense to say that the king sits on "the throne of the LORD" (1 Chron. 29:23). Here the idea is that Solomon sits on God's own throne.

This close identification of the human king with God is at the heart of the anointing ceremony. This is made especially evident in Psalm 45:

> Your throne, *O God*, endures forever.
> The scepter of your kingdom is a scepter of justice;
> you love righteousness and hate wickedness.
> Therefore God, your God, *has anointed you*
> with the oil of gladness above your companions. (Ps. 45:6–7 [7–8 MT])

The first line speaks of the human king as divine—"Your throne, O God"—before the psalm goes on to speak of how "God, your God, has anointed you." As Novenson writes: "Anointing a person with oil can effectively make him an embodiment of a god."[21] In other words, through his anointing, the Davidic king becomes the visible representative of Israel's God.

Priests as Anointed Ones

In the scriptures of Israel, references to "the LORD's anointed" are usually best assumed as descriptions of kings.[22] Nonetheless, biblical traditions indicate

19. For further discussion, see C. E. Armerding, "Were David's Sons Really Priests?," in *Current Issues in Biblical and Patristic Interpretation*, ed. Gerald F. Hawthorne (Grand Rapids: Eerdmans, 1975), 84. Psalm 110 refers to the Davidic king as "a priest forever according to the order of Melchizedek" (Ps. 110:4).

20. English translations sometimes obscure the clear meaning intended by the Hebrew. See, e.g., the RSV, which reads "[the people] worshiped the LORD, and did obeisance to the king." In contrast to this translation, in the Hebrew, God and the king are the objects of one and the same verb.

21. Novenson, *Grammar of Messianism*, 46–47.

22. See, e.g., Lam. 4:20, where the anointed figure is understood to be Zedekiah. For a discussion, see Delbert R. Hillers, *Lamentations*, AB 7A (New York: Doubleday, 1992), 151–52. An

that priests and prophets were also anointed. Above we saw that Zechariah describes "the two anointed ones" (Zech. 4:14), including both a royal figure (Zerubbabel) and a priestly one (Joshua). This is not the only place where priests are portrayed as anointed.

The Anointing of Priests as Extending the Sanctuary's Holiness

While the term "anointed one" is used in connection with the king, there is another complex of traditions that associate anointing with the priesthood. Throughout the laws for sacrifices in Leviticus 1–7, we read again and again of the "anointed priest" (e.g., Lev. 4:3, 5, 16). Although the precise term "high priest" is not used in the original Hebrew, the Greek translation of the Old Testament confirms that this was the meaning understood by ancient readers. The Greek version translates "anointed priest" as "high priest" (Lev. 4:3 LXX).

In various places, the purpose of priestly anointing is explicitly stated: "[Moses] poured some of the anointing oil on Aaron's head and anointed him, *to consecrate him*" (Lev. 8:12). The anointing thus serves as a means of consecration, which is necessary for the priest to be able to stand before the LORD (see also Exod. 28:41; 30:30; 40:13, 15; Lev. 16:32). In 2 Maccabees, the high priest Aristobulus is identified as being of the "family of anointed priests" (2 Macc. 1:10).

Interestingly, later rabbinic tradition holds that the sacred anointing oil was lost in the time of King Josiah.[23] Given that the oil is explicitly needed to "consecrate" the priest, the rabbis feel the need to explain how later priests could be consecrated. Their solution is that priests could also be consecrated by their vestments. The Mishnah therefore distinguishes between the priests "anointed with the oil of unction" (high priests in the pre-Josiah period) and those "dedicated by the many garments" (later high priests).[24] All of this underscores the important function of oil in making the priests fit for service.

exception to this rule is Dan. 9:25, which most scholars view as a reference to a priestly figure. See John J. Collins, *Daniel*, Hermeneia (Minneapolis: Fortress, 1993), 356–57.

23. See *Tosefta Sotah* 13:1; *Jerusalem Talmud Sheqalim* 6:1; *Jerusalem Talmud Sotah* 8:3; *Babylonian Talmud Horayot* 12a; *Babylonian Talmud Yoma* 52b; *Babylonian Talmud Kerithot* 5b.

24. See *Mishnah Horayot* 3:4.

Heavenly Priestly Anointings

Later Jewish texts depict heavenly priestly anointings. One occurrence of such anointing is in the *Testament of Levi*, a work that has pre-Christian origins, as evidenced from findings among the Dead Sea Scrolls (cf. 1Q21). It was later expanded by Christian redactors. The final form of the text quoted below is dated to around the year 200.[25] In one scene, the patriarch Levi recounts a vision he had involving an angelic priestly ordination ceremony:

> And I saw seven men in white clothing, who were saying to me, "Arise, put on the vestments of the priesthood, the crown of righteousness, the oracle of understanding, the robe of truth, the breastplate of faith, the miter for the head, and the apron for prophetic power." Each carried one of these and put them on me and said, "From now on be a priest, you and all your posterity." *The first anointed me with holy oil* and gave me a staff. (*Testament of Levi* 8:1–4)[26]

The seven men in white clothing are clearly angels who are sent to invest Levi with priestly authority. Significantly, the first step in the ordination ritual involves being anointed by an angel "with holy oil." The details are taken from the descriptions of Aaron's garments in Exodus 28:3–43. It also bears similarities to the portrait of Simon the high priest in Sirach 45:8–12 and the portrayal of Jacob's bestowal of the priestly garments on Levi in the book of *Jubilees* (*Jubilees* 32:3).

Another relevant passage for our discussion is found in *2 Enoch*. We cited this passage in chapter 3, but it is worth returning to it here, this time to note the way it depicts Enoch being invested with heavenly garments:

> And the Lord said to Michael, "Go, and extract Enoch from his earthly clothing. And anoint him with my delightful oil, and put him into the clothes of my glory." And so Michael did, just as the Lord had said to him. *He anointed me and he clothed me.* And the appearance of that oil is greater than the greatest light, and its ointment is like sweet dew, and its fragrance myrrh; and it is like the rays of the glittering sun. And I looked at myself, and *I had become like one of his glorious ones, and there was no observable difference.* (*2 Enoch* 22:8–10)[27]

25. See Eric Mason, *"You Are a Priest Forever": Second Temple Jewish Messianism and the Priestly Christology of the Epistle to the Hebrews*, STDJ 74 (Leiden: Brill, 2008), 127–28.
26. *OTP* 1:791 (emphasis added).
27. *OTP* 1:138 (emphasis added).

This scene is strikingly similar to that found in the passage from *Testament of Levi* quoted above. The imagery is inescapably priestly. As Martha Himmelfarb explains, the combination of clothing and anointing in *2 Enoch* 22 is a "heavenly version of a priestly investiture."[28] The text is likely influenced by the priestly imagery found in Zechariah 3–4, where an angel removes the high priest's dirty garments and clothes him with the high priest's vestments (Zech. 3:1–5).[29] The use of priestly imagery for Enoch makes sense since Enoch is portrayed as a priestly figure in other Jewish sources.[30]

The scenes of a heavenly priestly anointing are rooted in the understanding that the earthly sanctuary corresponds to a heavenly one. In the book of Wisdom, we read: "You commanded me to build a temple on your holy mountain, / and an altar in the city that is your dwelling place, / *a copy of the holy tent which you prepared from the beginning*" (Wis. 9:8).[31] The source of this tradition is undoubtedly the book of Exodus, which explains that Moses built the tabernacle after a "pattern" (*tabnit*) revealed to him on Sinai (Exod. 25:9, 40; cf. 26:30; 27:8; Num. 8:4). According to the Chronicler, David was also given a pattern for the temple (1 Chron. 28:19). Later, in chapter 8 (see pp. 152–54), we will explore how the New Testament letter to the Hebrews picks up this tradition, rooting it in the book of Exodus (Heb. 8:5; citing Exod. 25:9).

The Transformation of the Anointed Priest

Yet the passage from *2 Enoch* above goes further than merely envisioning priestly investiture; Enoch's anointing is also associated with heavenly *transformation*. Enoch says, "I had become like one of his glorious ones" (*2 Enoch* 22:10). This is consistent with other priestly traditions.

Some Jewish texts bear witness to an understanding that the priests underwent a quasi-metaphysical transformation when they served in the sanctuary. This interpretation is based on the description of the high priest's entrance into

28. Martha Himmelfarb, *Ascent to Heaven in Jewish and Christian Apocalypses* (Oxford: Oxford University Press, 1993), 40.

29. See Crispin H. T. Fletcher-Louis, *All the Glory of Adam: Liturgical Anthropology in the Dead Sea Scrolls*, STDJ 42 (Leiden: Brill, 2002), 23–24.

30. *Jubilees* 4:25; *1 Enoch* 14:8–23. See Himmelfarb, *Ascent to Heaven*, 23–25, 30.

31. In addition, see *Targum on 2 Chronicles* 6:2; *Targum Yerushalmi I* on Exod. 15:17; *Rabbah Numbers* 4:13; 12:12; *Midrash on the Psalms* 30:1; *Tanhuma* on Exod. 11:1–2; *2 Baruch* 4:5; Philo, *On the Life of Moses* 2.74–76; Pseudo-Philo, *Biblical Antiquities* 11:15. See G. K. Beale, *The Temple and the Church's Mission: A Biblical Theology of the Dwelling Place of God* (Downers Grove, IL: IVP Academic, 2004), 31–32.

the holy of holies in Leviticus: "There *shall be no man in the tent of meeting* when [Aaron] enters" (Lev. 16:17). Jewish readers concluded that if there is no *man* in the holies of holies when the high priest enters it, this must mean that the high priest becomes something *more* than human while performing his duties. This is especially clear in *Rabbah Leviticus* 28:12—a work that long postdates the New Testament—which explains that the high priest became suprahuman when he enters the holy of holies. Similar views, however, can be traced back to Second Temple Jewish writers. In two separate places, Philo expresses this idea:

> To tell the truth, the high priest is *a being whose nature is midway between man and God, less than God, superior to man.* "For when the high priest enters the Holy of Holies he shall not be a man" [Lev. 16:17]. Who then, if he is not a man? A God? I will not say so, for this name is a prerogative, assigned to the chief prophet, Moses, while he was still in Egypt, where he is entitled the God of Pharaoh [Exod. 7:1]. *Yet not a man either, which form, as it were, one his head, the other his feet.* (Philo, *On Dreams* 2.188–89)[32]

> Similar to this is the oracle given about the high priest: "When he enters," it says, "into the Holy of Holies, *he will not be a man until he comes out*" [Lev. 16:17]. And *if he then becomes no man, clearly neither is he God, but God's minister,* through the mortal in him in affinity with creation, through the immortal with the uncreated, and *he retains this midway place until he comes out again to the realm of body and flesh.* (Philo, *On Dreams* 2.231–32)[33]

Certain passages in the Dead Sea Scrolls may imply something similar about priestly transformation. Take, for instance, *4QSongs of the Sage*[b] (4Q511) 35:3–5:

> God makes some holy for himself like an everlasting sanctuary, and there will be purity amongst those purified. And *they shall be priests,* his just people, his army and servants, *the angels of his glory.* They shall praise him with fantastic marvels.[34]

To serve in the sanctuary is to enter into heavenly realities—and to do that is transformative.

32. Translation from Philo, *On Flight and Finding; On the Change of Names; On Dreams*, trans. F. H. Colson and G. H. Whitaker, LCL 275 (Cambridge, MA: Harvard University Press, 1934), 529 (emphasis added with slight formatting changes).

33. Translation from Philo, *On Flight and Finding*, 547 (emphasis added with slight formatting changes).

34. *DSSSE* 2:1033 (emphasis added with formatting changes).

Prophets as Anointed Ones

Prophets were also associated with anointing, though the evidence for physical anointing ceremonies for such figures is rather meager. Nevertheless, such figures are identified as, in some sense, recipients of an "anointing." Here we briefly consider the data.

Anointing and Spiritual Prophetic Succession

In 1 Kings, the prophet Elijah receives the following instructions from the Lord: "Anoint Jehu son of Nimshi as king over Israel. And *you shall anoint Elisha son of Shaphat of Abel-meholah as prophet in your place*" (1 Kings 19:16). Here prophetic anointing is connected with royal anointing. We have already mentioned that the anointing of Jehu represents a break in dynastic succession; Jehu supplants Joram, the son of the wicked Ahab. The anointing of Jehu, then, identifies him as the rightful ruler even though he may not be viewed as the obvious heir to the throne. Similarly, Elisha is to be anointed. The reason, in context, is clear: the anointing signifies him as the *prophetic* successor to Elijah. This explains why in Sirach, Elijah is told that he "anointed kings to inflict retribution, and *prophets to succeed you*" (Sir. 48:8). It is worth noting that Elijah does *not* end up anointing Jehu. It is Elisha, the "new Elijah," who carries this out (2 Kings 9:6).

Despite the fact that Elijah is told to anoint them, we never read of an anointing ceremony involving Hazael or Elisha. Some have suggested, therefore, that anointing can simply be a way of describing "making holy" or "consecrating" another.[35] Was Hazael anointed "off-screen"? Perhaps, but that cannot be assumed. What we can say with confidence is that spiritual anointing is certainly associated with prophets.

In Psalm 105, the psalmist speaks in the voice of God. Referring to the patriarchs, he says: "Do not touch my *anointed ones*, / do my *prophets* no harm" (Ps. 105:15). As far as biblical traditions go, Abraham, Isaac, and Jacob are not literally anointed with oil. Nonetheless, here they are identified as "anointed ones." Why? It seems to be understood that their status as prophets involves a spiritual anointing of sorts. This is evident in the story of Elisha's succession of Elijah.

35. J. Roy Porter, "Oil in the Old Testament," in *Oil of Gladness: Anointing in the Christian Tradition*, ed. Martin Dudley and Geoffrey Rowell (London: SPCK, 1993), 39.

Justin Martyr on the Significance of Anointing

In his dialogue with the Jew Trypho, written somewhere between AD 155 and 167, Justin Martyr says the following: "Indeed, even your kings were appointed and anointed by the Spirit in these prophets."[a] For Justin, the "Spirit" is said to be "in [the] prophets." Here we seem to have the idea that prophets are different from kings and priests; prophets have the Spirit in such a way that they can become a source of the Spirit to others. Moreover, by ceremonially anointing kings, the prophets therefore "establish" kings. It seems here that the anointing confers on royal figures their legitimacy.

a. Justin, *Dialogue with Trypho* 52.3. Translation from Justin Martyr, *Dialogue with Trypho*, trans. Thomas B. Falls, rev. Thomas P. Halton, FC 3 (Washington, DC: Catholic University of America Press, 2003), 79 (slightly adapted).

Elisha's commissioning as a prophet—which we might associate with his "anointing" since no other scene of anointing is found in the story—corresponds with his reception of Elijah's "spirit." In 2 Kings 2, a group of prophets reveals to Elisha that Elijah will be taken up by the Lord. Not wanting to be separated from his teacher, Elisha insists on joining Elijah in journeying to the river Jordan. Once they arrive there, Elijah parts the waters with his mantle in Moses-like fashion (2 Kings 2:8; cf. Exod. 14:21–22). After they cross over to the other side, Elisha makes a request of his master: he asks to "inherit a double share of your spirit" (2 Kings 2:9). The language here evokes the inheritance given to a firstborn son (Deut. 21:17). Elisha is essentially wishing to identify himself as Elijah's spiritual son. When Elijah is taken up in a chariot of fire, then, the young prophet calls out to Elijah, saying, "Father, father!" (2 Kings 2:12). That the gift Elisha has asked for is bestowed upon him is evident in that he picks up the mantle of Elijah and parts the water as his master has done with it (2 Kings 2:14).

But what does it mean that Elisha has received a "double share" of Elijah's "spirit"? Mordechai Cogan and Hayim Tadmor write: "The source of Elijah's spirit is YHWH; it is not some inherent personal quality. In this regard, Elijah, like Moses, enjoyed a special relationship with YHWH, described in terms of spirit transferable to others (cf. Num. 11:16–17, 24–26)."[36] The connection to Moses's work in Numbers 11 is important for understanding what is portrayed in the Elijah-Elisha narrative. The narrator of 1–2 Kings seems to deliberately present Elijah as a "new Moses" figure. Similarities between Moses and Elijah abound.[37] The following chart highlights a few of them.

Moses	Elijah
Moses fasts for "forty days and forty nights" in the wilderness (Exod. 34:28).	Elijah fasts for "forty days and forty nights" in the wilderness (1 Kings 19:8).
God provides "quail" and "manna" each evening and morning for Israel in the wilderness through Moses (Exod. 16:1–36; Num. 11:4–33).	Elijah is miraculously provided "bread" and "meat" in the morning and in the evening in the wilderness (1 Kings 17:6).
Moses parts the waters of the Red Sea so that the Israelites cross through it "on the dry ground" (Exod. 14:22).	Elijah parts the waters of the Jordan so that he and Elisha cross through it "on the dry land" (2 Kings 2:8).

Given that Elijah is presented as a new Moses, the story of the "spirit" being given would inescapably evoke the scene in Numbers, where the "spirit" is also linked to prophetic commissioning. Let us review that passage.

In Numbers 11, we are told: "The Lord came down in the cloud and spoke to [Moses], and took of the Spirit that was on him and put it on the seventy elders. When the Spirit rested upon them, they prophesied" (Num. 11:25). What enables others to prophesy like Moses does is their reception of the Spirit that was upon him. This "Spirit" is not simply a reference to Moses's personal spirit since it comes from the Lord. The identity of this Spirit is further clarified when two others, Eldad and Medad, begin prophesying, raising complaints. Moses responds: "Would that all the Lord's people were prophets, and that the Lord would put *his Spirit* on them!" (Num. 11:29). What empowers prophecy here is not merely any "spirit" but *the* Spirit par excellence—that is, the Lord's own Spirit.

In light of the Mosaic background of the Elijah-Elisha story, it seems difficult to deny that the narrator of 2 Kings intends to convey the idea that it is this same Spirit that is transferred to Elisha. Confirmation of this reading is found in the following verses—Elijah's departure is said to be the work of

36. Mordechai Cogan and Hayim Tadmor, *II Kings*, AYB 11 (New Haven: Yale University Press, 2008), 32.

37. The most comprehensive overview of the parallels is found in Dale C. Allison Jr., *The New Moses: A Matthean Typology* (Minneapolis: Fortress, 1993), 39–50.

"the Spirit of the LORD" (2 Kings 2:16). What enables Elisha to be a prophet is the Spirit of God.[38]

The Spirit of the Lord as Anointing

That anointing is bound up with the gift of the Spirit is also attested in Isaiah 61.

> The Spirit of the Lord GOD is upon me,
> because the LORD has anointed me.
> He has sent me to bring good news to the afflicted. (Isa. 61:1)

In this passage, to be "anointed" is to have received the Spirit of God. Whom does the passage describe in its original context? Many biblical interpreters, following the Targums, have seen here a reference to the prophet Isaiah himself. This identification is well supported by the context.[39] Not only is being a prophet understood in terms of a divine anointing, but this divine anointing is also associated with the gift of the Spirit. In context, the anointing is ordered to mission—proclaiming the prophetic word. The Spirit given through anointing empowers the prophet. This may be seen in the story of Elisha, who is given the Spirit to empower his prophetic work, which involves performing miracles like his master, Elijah (cf. 2 Kings 2:9–25).

In addition, although Elijah is never explicitly called a priest in the historical books, he nevertheless carries out divinely authorized sacrifices (1 Kings 18:26–38), much as Moses presides over cultic rites in the book of Exodus (e.g., Exod. 24:4–8). Because of this, Elijah is explicitly said to be a priest in later Jewish sources. For example, *The Lives of the Prophets* says he is from Aaron's tribe and lives in a region "given to the priests" (*Lives of the Prophets* 21:1).[40] It is worth recalling that royal, priestly, and prophetic roles should not be seen as hermetically sealed categories. David and Saul, as we have seen, though kings, are given prophetic abilities. What is more, the Davidic king carries out priestly tasks (e.g., 2 Sam. 6:13) and is even designated a "priest

38. See also Volkmar Fritz, *1 & 2 Kings*, trans. Anselm Hagedorn, CC (Minneapolis: Fortress, 2003), 235.

39. See, e.g., Joseph Blenkinsopp, *Isaiah 56–66*, AB 19B (New York: Doubleday, 1988), 220–23.

40. *OTP* 2:396. See also *Rabbah Genesis* 71:9; *Rabbah Proverbs* 9; *Targum Pseudo-Jonathan* on Num. 25:11 and Deut. 30:4.

The Anointing of Adam in the Pseudo-Clementine Literature

In the fourth-century work known as the *Recognitions*, attributed to Clement of Rome but written much later than him, we read that the apostle Peter taught that Adam was a prophet. Because of this, Peter maintained that Adam was anointed in Eden. In the *Recognitions*, Peter acknowledges that this event is not narrated in Genesis but insists that readers assume it happened since every prophet must receive such an anointing.

> For although he who has recorded the law in his pages is silent as to [Adam's] anointing, yet he has evidently left us to understand these things. For as, if he had said that [Adam] was anointed, it would not be doubted that he was also a prophet, although it were not written in the law; so, since it is certain that he was a prophet, it is in like manner certain that he was also anointed, because without anointing he could not be a prophet.[a]

a. *Recognitions* 1.47 (*ANF* 8:90).

forever" (Ps. 110:4). Likewise, some prophets, such as Ezekiel and Jeremiah, are themselves priests (Jer. 1:1; Ezek. 1:3). Speaking broadly, then, we might see prophetic anointing—even if simply of a spiritual nature—as a kind of consecration that involves setting the prophet aside for doing God's own work. Like the king and priest, the prophet serves as God's own representative and can even, therefore, serve a priestly role.

The Signifying Power of Sacral Anointing

Sacral anointing—whether for kings, priests, or prophets—is therefore much more than an empty ritual in Scripture. The oil represents divine authorization and divine strengthening. It is authorization in that the king is enabled to share in and somehow exercise the kingship that properly belongs to God. It also involves divine strengthening inasmuch as it empowers the recipient to carry out this task effectively. On the one hand, oil serves as a sign designating the king as God's royal representative. On the other hand, since oil is associated with reinvigorating physical health, in certain passages it also points naturally enough to *spiritual* strengthening. The anointing is a visible sign of the invisible reality: the king receives the Spirit of God. Royal anointing is therefore carried out in certain instances with the sacral oil of the tabernacle, the place of God's presence. Biblical texts envision the newly anointed royal figure as receiving "the vital force of the deity" and "the invigorating power of God."[41] This empowers the king to act in supernatural ways—most prominently, to *prophesy*. McCarter speaks of this anointing, therefore, as a "sacramental act"—the anointing essentially effects what it symbolizes.

Priestly anointing is also more than merely symbolic. The oil again *effects* something—above all, consecration. In sacerdotal anointing, the priest shares in the holiness of the tabernacle and is enabled to enter into God's presence to offer sacrifice. This is even understood in some texts as involving a heavenly transformation.

Finally, prophetic anointing, though much less common than royal and priestly anointing, also serves an important signifying role. For one thing, prophetic anointing can symbolize prophetic succession—one figure is enabled to share in the spirit of prophecy previously given to another. Elijah is told to anoint Elisha "as prophet in your place" (1 Kings 19:16). Moreover, like royal anointing, prophetic anointing is also connected with divine strengthening or empowerment. It enables the prophet to carry out the prophetic mission, especially—though not exclusively—to speak the word of the LORD. Again, this empowerment is linked specifically to reception of the Spirit of the LORD (e.g., Num. 11:29; 2 Kings 2:16).

Sacral anointings, then, should not be dismissed as mere customs or meaningless rituals; in certain passages, they appear to *effect* what they signify—divine authorization, empowerment through the Spirit, consecration in holiness for worship, and so on. With this we see how a genuine sacramental theology emerges from Scripture. What is a "sacrament"? In chapter 2, we cited Augustine's influential definition of a sacrament: "Signs . . . are called sacraments when they are applied to divine things."[42] For Augustine a sacrament is essentially a visible sign of an invisible reality.[43] Sacral anointings

41. McCarter, *I Samuel*, 182.

42. Augustine, *Letter* 138.7; translation from Augustine, *Letters: Volume 3 (131–164)*, trans. Wilfrid Parsons, FC 20 (Washington, DC: Catholic University of America Press, 1953), 40.

43. See Augustine, *City of God* 10.5. For further discussion of Augustine's views and their influence on later sacramental theology, see William A. Van Roo, *The Christian Sacrament*, Analecta Gregoriana (Rome: Editrice Pontificia Università Gregoriana, 1992), 38–43.

are depicted as *signifying* divine realities. In the texts we have seen above, anointings are a visible sign of spiritual mysteries: the king's participation in God's divine rule, the priest's consecration, the empowerment of the prophet to speak the word of the Lord. Yet anointing is not reserved to Israel's *past*.

Certain Jewish texts evince hopes for future anointed figures—such as a royal messiah, a priestly messiah, or an eschatological fulfillment of the prophet from Isaiah 61—who will deliver God's people. In the New Testament, such hopes are viewed as fulfilled in Jesus, *the* Christ, who is portrayed as having royal, priestly, and prophetic roles. That is the subject of our next chapter. As we will show, the Church's theology of the sacrament of anointing of the sick appears deeply rooted in the recognition that Jesus himself is the Anointed One.

8

Jesus as the Anointed King, Priest, and Prophet

Christ's Fulfillment of Messianic Hopes

> God anointed Jesus of Nazareth with the Holy Spirit and with power.
>
> —Acts 10:38

> [In the Old Testament,] the anointing was reserved for the king and the priest. . . . In these two persons was prefigured one to come who should be both King and Priest, the one Christ holding both offices, and called the Christ by reason of his anointing.
>
> —Augustine[1]

In the previous chapter, we saw that sacred anointings were associated with kings, priests, and prophets. Yet Jewish sources would further develop the role of anointed figures. By Jesus's day, expectations seem to have reached a fever pitch for an anointed figure or figures. Here we turn to messianic hopes.

1. Augustine, "Second Discourse on Psalm 26," in *St. Augustine: On the Psalms*, vol. 1, *Psalms 1–29*, trans. Scholastica Hebgin and Felicitas Corrigan, ACW 29 (New York: Paulist Press, 1960), 261.

At the outset, it is important to avoid the danger, often found in older scholarship, of treating Israel's expectations in terms of a monolithic "messianic hope." As has been well documented, Jewish hopes for Israel's coming deliverance through the hand of a future "anointed one" took different forms. As John Collins explains, the dominant strand was likely that of a coming figure from the line of David.[2] Still, there is evidence that some believed a priestly messiah would emerge, perhaps alongside a royal messiah. Other sources indicate the belief that an eschatological prophet would arise in the latter days. Moreover, we should not imagine these as distinctly separate categories; sources combine passages that refer to different kinds of figures.

The New Testament writers announce that expectations for a future anointed one have been realized—Jesus is proclaimed to be not only "*a* messiah" but "*the* Messiah" par excellence. In this chapter, then, we examine the way that Jesus is presented as the long-awaited anointed one.[3] For the New Testament writers, Jewish hopes for a coming royal, priestly, and prophetic anointed one are fulfilled in Jesus.

Jesus as the Royal Messiah

The New Testament begins with the Gospel of Matthew. In its opening verse, we read: "The book of the genealogy of Jesus Christ, the son of David, the son of Abraham" (Matt. 1:1). Here Jesus is identified explicitly as "Christ"—that is, the "Messiah" or "Anointed One." What is more, his status as "Messiah" is bound up with his legal descent from the royal line of David. Other New Testament writers also spotlight Jesus's Davidic identity. Furthermore, just as kings are anointed in the Old Testament, New Testament authors explicitly link Jesus's status as "Christ" to the descent of the Spirit upon him, which in some places is explicitly depicted as an "anointing." In all of this, Jesus is seen to fulfill the messianic hopes anchored in the scriptures of Israel.

Jewish Hopes for a Coming Davidic Figure

It is not difficult to understand how hopes emerged for a royal messiah from the line of David. According to the scriptures, God promised David: "Your

2. John J. Collins, *The Scepter and the Star*, ABRL (New York: Doubleday, 1995), 209.

3. For an in-depth study, see Joshua Jipp, *The Messianic Theology of the New Testament* (Grand Rapids: Eerdmans, 2020).

house and your kingdom will be made sure *forever* before me" (2 Sam. 7:16; cf. 1 Chron. 17:11–14; Pss. 89:3–4, 35–37; 132:11–12). This hope provided a basis for the conviction that the defeat of the son of David at the hands of the Babylonians in 587 BC could not be the definitive end of the Davidic kingdom. As John Goldingay writes, "The drive of messianic expectation in Israel issues from Yhwh's promise to David."[4]

Various prophetic passages therefore speak of God raising up the Davidic line after it appears to have been cut down. Take, for instance, Isaiah 11:

> A shoot shall come out from the stump of Jesse,
> and a branch shall grow from his roots.
> The Spirit of the LORD shall rest on him,
> the Spirit of wisdom and understanding. (Isa. 11:1–2)

In using the imagery of "the stump of Jesse"—a reference to David's father (1 Sam. 16:1–13)—the prophet indicates that David's line has been "cut down." Yet out of this "stump" a figure identified as a "branch" will one day emerge. Although he is not explicitly said to be "anointed," the language of the Spirit coming to "rest on him" likely evokes the memory of royal anointings (e.g., 1 Sam. 16:13). In addition, by associating him with "wisdom" the passage evokes Solomon, known for his great wisdom (cf. 1 Kings 3:3–28; 4:29–34; 11:41; Wis. 7:7; Sir. 47:12; etc.). Using imagery similar to Isaiah 11, later prophets would identify the future ruler as a "branch" (Jer. 23:5; Zech. 6:12). The prophet Amos speaks of the restoration of the Davidic kingdom in terms of God repairing "the booth of David that is fallen" (Amos 9:11). Other prophetic texts affirm God's promise of the enduring nature of the Davidic kingdom (Isa. 9:7; Jer. 33:25; Ezek. 37:24–26).

Against the background of the exile, the royal psalms would have also taken on deeper significance. Take, for instance, Psalm 2, which speaks of the king as God's "anointed one" and definitive victory over the nations. The LORD announces:

> "I have installed my king on Zion, my holy hill."
> I will declare the decree of the LORD:
> He said to me, "You are my son,
> today I have begotten you."

4. John Goldingay, *Old Testament Theology*, vol. 1, *Israel's Gospel* (Downers Grove, IL: IVP Academic, 2003), 560.

> Ask of me, and I will make the nations your inheritance,
> and the ends of the earth your possession. (Ps. 2:6–8)

Some have suggested that this psalm was originally understood as a description of the future Messiah,[5] yet this is unlikely. The psalm was likely originally used for the installation of a new Davidic king.[6] Nonetheless, the song's promise that the Davidic king would be given lasting victory over the nations was interpreted by Jews in Jesus's day as referring to a future coming figure, a royal son, who would win a definitive and final victory over Israel's gentile oppressors. This interpretation is evident, for example, in the nonbiblical Jewish work *Psalms of Solomon* 17, which can be dated to the first century BC, as well as in the Dead Sea Scrolls.[7] Such hopes clearly form the background of the New Testament depiction of Jesus's messianic identity.

Jesus as the Messianic Son of David in Paul

The earliest Christian writer, Paul, repeatedly affirms Jesus's messianic status, referring to him over 270 times as "Christ" (*christos*).[8] Especially important is the apostle's description of Jesus in the introduction to his letter to the Romans. Here Paul speaks of "Jesus Christ" as God's "Son, who was *descended from David according to the flesh*" (Rom. 1:3; cf. 2 Tim. 2:8). That Jesus's divine sonship is closely related to his Davidic pedigree makes sense given that the royal son was frequently spoken of as God's son (2 Sam. 7:14; 1 Chron. 17:13; Pss. 2:7; 89:27). Still, for Paul, Jesus's divine sonship goes beyond anything kings of the past enjoyed. The Davidic king was God's adopted son and served as God's representative, but Jesus is far greater than any king before him.

In Philippians 2, Paul indicates that Jesus existed *prior* to becoming human:

> though he was in the form of God,
> [he] did not consider equality with God

5. See, e.g., Norman Whybray, *Reading the Psalms as a Book* (Sheffield: Sheffield Academic, 1996), 90.

6. See, e.g., S. E. Gillingham, "The Messiah in the Psalms: A Question of Reception History and the Psalter," in *King and Messiah in Israel and the Ancient Near East*, ed. John Day, LHBOTS 270 (1998; repr., London: Bloomsbury T&T Clark, 2013), 212–14.

7. *4QFlorigelium* (4Q174) fragment 1, 1:21; 2:10–13; *4QCommentary on Genesis A* (4Q252) 5:1–4. For fuller discussion, see Collins, *The Scepter and the Star*, 49–73.

8. For a full discussion, see Brant Pitre, Michael P. Barber, and John A. Kincaid, *Paul, a New Covenant Jew: Rethinking Pauline Theology* (Grand Rapids: Eerdmans, 2019), 96–101.

> as something to be exploited,
> but he emptied himself,
> by taking the form of a slave,
> being born in human likeness. (Phil. 2:6–7)

In suggesting Jesus was "in the form [*morphē*] of God," Paul is not simply saying Jesus was in the "image of God" like humanity is at creation (Gen. 1:26–27). Paul goes on to clarify what this means by speaking of Jesus enjoying "equality with God" (Phil. 2:6).[9] As we have seen, Paul identifies Jesus as the "Lord" (*kyrios*), the God of Israel (Rom. 10:8–13), and as the one Creator LORD of the *Shema* (1 Cor. 8:5–6). At the same time, in Philippians 2 Paul *also* affirms Jesus's humanity, saying Jesus took the "form [*morphē*] of a slave" in being born as a man (Phil. 2:7). From Romans 1 we see that Paul's understanding of Jesus's messiahship is bound up with his *Davidic* lineage, his humanity. Jesus is both, therefore, divine *and* human, but his status as "anointed one" is especially linked to his humanity.

In the previous chapter we saw that the anointing of the king marked him out as God's representative. Paul does not speak of a literal anointing of Jesus, yet he does seem to refer to an "installation" of Jesus as the messianic son of God. Paul speaks of Jesus as "[God's] Son . . . who was *designated* [*horisthentos*] Son of God in power according to the Spirit of holiness by the resurrection from the dead" (Rom. 1:3–4). Jesus is "designated" or "installed" in some way by the Spirit at his *resurrection*. It is important to stress the following: Paul's point cannot be that Jesus became God's Son only at his resurrection. Elsewhere, Paul indicates that Jesus was *already* God's Son when he was crucified (cf. Rom. 5:10). Nevertheless, for Paul, Jesus's royal "enthronement" is particularly linked to his resurrection. It seems, then, that what physical anointing signified in ceremonial royal anointings is here attributed to the work of the Spirit in the resurrection. In rising from the dead, Jesus's identity as ruler is made manifest. Support for this reading of Paul is found elsewhere in his epistle to the Romans.

In Romans 8, Paul announces: "It is Christ Jesus who died and, even more, who was *raised*, and who is at *the right hand of God*, who also intercedes for us" (Rom. 8:34). Once again, Paul here speaks of Jesus as "Christ" or "Messiah." In this passage, however, Jesus's resurrection is understood as involving him taking his seat at God's "right hand." The terminology here is widely

9. See Pitre, Barber, and Kincaid, *Paul, a New Covenant Jew*, 102–28.

Tertullian on Christ's Anointing as Proof of His Incarnation

At the beginning of the third century, the Christian writer Tertullian points to Jesus's status as "anointed one" as evidence that Jesus truly became human. Against the claims of those who insisted Jesus only appeared to be human, Tertullian writes:

> For Christ means *anointed*, and *to be anointed is certainly an affair of the body.* He who had not a body, could not by any possibility have been anointed; he who could not by any possibility have been anointed, could not in any wise have been called Christ.[a]

For Tertullian, Jesus's identity as "Christ" is therefore evidence of the truth of his incarnation; Jesus did not disdain our humanity but took a human nature to himself so that it could receive divine anointing. Other early Christian writers similarly affirm that Jesus's anointing relates to his humanity.[b]

a. Tertullian, *Against Marcion* 3.15 (*ANF* 3:334 with some emphasis added). For the dating of this work, see Geoffrey D. Dunn, *Tertullian*, The Early Church Fathers (London: Routledge, 2004), 8.
b. See, e.g., Hillary of Poitiers (d. AD 367). *On the Trinity* 11.18–19.

accepted as drawing from Psalm 110, where the Lord tells the Davidic king, "Sit at my right hand" (Ps. 110:1). Jesus's resurrection is therefore inseparably united to his heavenly enthronement, which is described in terms of the Davidic king in Psalm 110. We might say, then, that while Jesus already enjoys "equality with God" *prior* to his taking human form (Phil. 2:6–7), through the resurrection the Spirit empowers or glorifies him *in his humanity* so that his messianic identity is recognized by others and so that he can be enthroned as a truly *human* anointed one—having a human body and reigning over the final enemy to be defeated, death (1 Cor. 15:53–57). He is thus the Davidic "anointed one" par excellence.

Finally, it is worth pointing out that Paul connects Jesus's status as "anointed one" to the Spirit. In 2 Corinthians 1, he writes, "It is God who confirms us together with you into the *anointed one* ["Christ"] and who *anointed* ["christened"] us, who also sealed us and gave us the down payment of the *Spirit* in our hearts" (2 Cor. 1:21–22).[10] We will return to this rich passage later, in chapter 9. For now, let us simply note that Jesus's identity as "anointed one" is connected to the gift of the Spirit.

Jesus as the Messianic Son of David in the Gospels and Acts

Numerous aspects of the portraits of Jesus in the Gospels also evoke Davidic messianic expectations.[11] To name a few examples:

- *Descendant of David.* In Matthew and Luke, Jesus is explicitly said to be born of a virgin (Matt. 1:18–25; Luke 1:26–38), underscoring his identity as the divine Son of God. Nevertheless, Jesus's Davidic identity is secured through Joseph, who is recognized as his legal father.[12]
- *Born in the city of David.* Matthew and Luke portray Jesus as being born in Bethlehem, the city of David's birth (Matt. 2:1; Luke 2:4–7; cf. 1 Sam. 16:1). Matthew insists that the scribes knew the birthplace of the Messiah from the scriptures, citing a prophecy from Micah (Matt. 2:4–6; cf. Mic. 5:2).
- *Healer and exorcist.* In all three Synoptic Gospels, Jesus's healing and exorcistic activities are explicitly tied to his identity as "Son of David" (Matt. 20:30–31//Mark 10:47–48//Luke 18:38–39; cf. Matt. 9:27; 12:22–23; 15:22; 21:14–15). These traditions evoke the figure of Solomon, who was remembered as the consummate healer and exorcist (cf. Wis. 7:17–21).[13]

Much more could be said here.[14] Suffice it here to note that Jesus's Davidic identity explains much of what we find in the Gospels' portraits of him.

10. Adapted from the translation by Matthew V. Novenson, *Christ among the Messiahs: Christ Language in Paul and Messiah Language in Ancient Judaism* (New York: Oxford University Press, 2012), 147.

11. For a fuller discussion of Jesus's Davidic identity, see Michael Patrick Barber, *The Historical Jesus and the Temple: Memory, Methodology, and the Gospel of Matthew* (Cambridge: Cambridge University Press, 2023), 115–56.

12. See W. D. Davies and D. C. Allison, *A Critical and Exegetical Commentary on the Gospel according to Saint Matthew*, 3 vols., ICC (London: T&T Clark, 1988–97), 1:185.

13. See also Josephus, *Jewish Antiquities* 8.45–49; Jiří Dvořáček, *The Son of David in Matthew's Gospel in the Light of Solomon as Exorcist Tradition*, WUNT 2/415 (Tübingen: Mohr Siebeck, 2016); Wayne S. Baxter, "Healing and the 'Son of David': Matthew's Warrant," *NovT* 48, no. 1 (2006): 36–50.

14. See, e.g., Nicholas G. Piotrowski, *Matthew's New David at the End of Exile: A Socio-Rhetorical Study of Scriptural Quotations*, NovTSup 170 (Leiden: Brill, 2016); Max Botner, *Jesus Christ as the Son of David in the Gospel of Mark*, SNTSMS 174 (Cambridge: Cambridge

Since we have already noted that Jesus's identity as "Christ" is understood in pneumatological terms in Paul, we should also observe that something similar is found in the Gospels and Acts. Just as Solomon was anointed in the Gihon spring, Jesus's baptism takes place in the river Jordan (Matt. 3:13//Mark 1:9; cf. Luke 4:1; John 1:28). Although Jesus is not physically anointed with oil in this scene, the Spirit descends on Jesus at his baptism (Matt. 3:16//Mark 1:10//Luke 3:22; cf. John 1:33), just as the Spirit came upon David at his anointing. It is also worth noting that just as Solomon is said to have been anointed by the priest Zadok (1 Kings 1:39), in the Gospel of Luke, Jesus's baptizer, John, is revealed to have been from the tribe of Levi, the son of a priest (cf. Luke 1:5–23). The book of Acts is even more explicit about identifying the Spirit as Jesus's anointing. In Acts 10, Peter speaks of how "God anointed Jesus of Nazareth with the Holy Spirit and with power" (Acts 10:38).

In the previous chapter, we mentioned the Davidic king's close connection to the temple. The Gospel narratives also appear informed by these traditions.[15] This is perhaps most apparent in the way that all three Synoptic writers place the most famous temple story about Jesus—the so-called "temple cleansing" episode—immediately after his Solomonic-like entry into Jerusalem.[16]

Jesus as Messianic Heavenly High Priest

Jesus is depicted in the New Testament not only as a royal messiah but also as a priestly one. In fact, he is portrayed as a *heavenly* priest. This is especially underscored in the Letter to the Hebrews, but we find evidence for Jesus's priestly messianic status in other New Testament works as well.

University Press, 2019); Yuzuru Miura, *David in Luke-Acts*, WUNT 2/232 (Tübingen: Mohr Siebeck, 2005); Margaret Daly-Denton, *David in the Fourth Gospel: The Johannine Reception of the Psalms* (Leiden: Brill, 2000).

15. For a much fuller discussion of Jesus's relationship to the temple, see Barber, *Historical Jesus and the Temple.*

16. Notably, when questioned about his authority in the temple, Jesus asks questions about Ps. 110, which he and his hearers recognize as a messianic prophecy (Matt. 22:41–46//Mark 12:35–37//Luke 20:41–44). Some have tried to argue that Jesus uses the psalm to reject the Davidic pedigree of the Messiah, yet this is mistaken. Rather, Jesus uses the psalm to demonstrate the Messiah's *superiority* over David. Notably, given the questions about his actions in the temple, it is important to recall that the passage explicitly speaks of the king as "a priest forever according to the order of Melchizedek" (Ps. 110:4). See Barber, *Historical Jesus and the Temple*, 142.

Jesus as Priest in the Order of Melchizedek in Hebrews

Luke reveals that Elizabeth, Mary's relative, was from the line of Aaron (Luke 1:5). On this basis, some early Christians believed Mary herself was a Levite, thus making it possible for Jesus to possess both a royal genealogy (through Joseph) and priestly pedigree (through his mother). For example, belief in Jesus's mixed genealogy is attested in the *Testament of the Twelve Patriarchs*, which can be dated to the second century.[17] Referring to a single coming figure, the patriarch Simeon declares: "For the Lord will raise up from Levi someone as high priest and from Judah someone as king" (*Testament of Simeon* 7:2).[18] The New Testament, however, shows no awareness of Jesus's Levitical descent.

The author of the Epistle to the Hebrews expressly deals with the challenge that Jesus's non-Levitical lineage would pose for viewing him as a priest. The author writes, "For it is clear that our Lord has sprung from Judah, and in connection with that tribe Moses said nothing about priests" (Heb. 7:14). If Jesus is from Judah, how is he capable of being priest in the new covenant? For the author, the answer is found in Psalm 110 and its reference to the priesthood of Melchizedek. Let us briefly sum up the author's argument.

First, the author of Hebrews points out that, according to the book of Genesis, Abraham paid tithes to Melchizedek, the priest-king of Jerusalem, and was blessed by him. This indicates that Abraham recognized Melchizedek's superiority: "It is beyond dispute that the inferior is blessed by the superior" (Heb. 7:7). Since Levi comes from Abraham, this must mean that Melchizedek's priesthood surpasses the Levitical priesthood (Heb. 7:1–10).

Next, the author asks a question: "If therefore perfection had been through the Levitical priesthood, for the people received the law about this priesthood, what need would there still be for a different priest to arise according to the order of Melchizedek instead of one said to be according to the order of Aaron?" (Heb. 7:11). In other words, if perfection were found through the Levitical priesthood, one would not expect the psalmist to speak of a *different* priest, one who will be a "priest forever according to the order of Melchizedek" (Ps. 110:4). The author then explains that Jesus's resurrection

17. For further discussion, see William Adler, "On the Priesthood of Jesus," in *New Testament Apocrypha: More Noncanonical Scriptures*, ed. Tony Burke and Brent Landau (Grand Rapids: Eerdmans, 2016), 1:71. See also the early Christian writer Origen, *Adnotationes Numeros* (*Homilies on Numbers*) (PG 12:584C).

18. *OTP* 1:787.

makes him uniquely qualified for this priesthood that will last "forever," since he has obtained "indestructible life" (Heb. 7:16). Whereas the priests of the Old Testament were prevented from serving in perpetuity because of physical death (Heb. 7:23), Jesus "holds his priesthood permanently, because he continues forever" (Heb. 7:24). Because of his resurrection, then, Jesus is uniquely qualified to fulfill the requirements of Melchizedek's priesthood—he can truly be "priest forever."

The author, then, views Jesus as not merely a priest but, like Melchizedek, a priest-king. Although the author does not state this explicitly, that Jesus could be both priest and king seems possible given his *Davidic* identity since, as we have seen, Davidic kings were known to have performed priestly duties. Indeed, Psalm 110 is about a *Davidic* king. Noticeably, then, in the first chapter of the letter, the author speaks of Jesus's identity as an *anointed* royal figure:

> But to the Son he says,
>
> "Your throne, O God, is forever and ever,
> and the righteous scepter is the scepter of your kingdom.
> You have loved righteousness and hated lawlessness.
> Therefore *God, your God, has anointed you*
> *with the oil of gladness* beyond your companions."
> (Heb. 1:8–9; cf. Ps. 45:6–7)

In the original Hebrew psalm, it is clear that the passage is addressed to God. In Hebrews, however, the author uses the passage to indicate that *Jesus* is addressed as "God" by God.[19] The anointed Davidic king was God's representative, but Jesus is more than that; he truly is the divine Son. Like Melchizedek, Jesus is both king *and* priest.

Moreover, it is worth observing that Jesus's anointing seems to come *after* his enthronement in heaven (cf. Heb. 1:3–4). Jesus, then, is the subject of a *heavenly anointing* such as those described in Jewish sources examined in the previous chapter. Jesus is a heavenly high priest superior to all other priests.

Finally, the Letter to the Hebrews is relevant to our discussion for another reason. In the last chapter we looked at Jewish beliefs about the priests' access to heavenly realities. These traditions are picked up in the letter as well.

19. Craig R. Koester, *Hebrews*, AB 36 (New Haven: Yale University Press, 2001), 194.

Hippolytus on Christ's Royal and Priestly Anointing

In a commentary on Daniel, typically attributed to Hippolytus and likely written between AD 202 and 204,[a] we are told: "*For all kings and priests were called christs on account of them being anointed with holy oil*, which Moses arranged long ago."[b] We see, then, that very early on sacral anointings in the Old Testament were recognized as important prefigurations of the coming of Jesus, the Messiah.

a. See the up-to-date discussion on authorship and dating in T. C. Schmidt and Nick Nicholas, *Hippolytus of Rome: Commentary on Daniel and "Chronicon,"* Gorgias Dissertations 67, GSECP (Piscataway, NJ: Gorgias, 2017), 1–33.

b. Translation from Schmidt and Nicholas, *Hippolytus of Rome*, 161.

Jesus's identity as a priest in the order of Melchizedek in Hebrews 7 sets up the author's "main point," which is laid out in chapter 8:

> Now the main point in what has been said is this: we have such a high priest, one who is seated at the right hand of the throne of the Majesty in the heavens, a minister in the sanctuary, that is, the true tabernacle that the Lord, and not any human, has set up. . . . Now if he were on earth, he would not be a priest at all, since there are priests who offer gifts according to the law. They minister in a sanctuary that is a representation and shadow of the heavenly one. . . . But Jesus has now obtained a more excellent ministry. (Heb. 8:1–6)

Jesus has now entered into the heavenly sanctuary, of which the earthly tabernacle was merely a "representation." Jesus's priesthood is superior to the Levitical priesthood mandated under the Mosaic law since Jesus has ascended to God's right hand and serves forever in the heavenly temple, the "true tabernacle" of the Lord. In sum, Jesus is presented as the "anointed" priest par excellence, who carries out the ministry that the Levitical priesthood was meant to foreshadow.

Jesus as Messianic Heavenly Priest Elsewhere in the New Testament

As we have seen, Jesus's priesthood in Hebrews is bound up with his ascension into heaven. Something similar, however, may be detected in the

Gospel of Luke. Before Jesus ascends into heaven, the evangelist says: "And he led them out as far as to Bethany, and, *lifting up his hands, he blessed them*" (Luke 24:50). Jesus's actions are evocative of the high priest's blessing. We read in Leviticus: "Aaron *lifted up his hands* toward the people and blessed them" (Lev. 9:22). Likewise, in the book of Sirach the high priest Simon "*lifted up* his hands over the whole congregation" to "give the *blessing*" (Sir. 50:20). Jesus, then, seems to be imparting a priestly blessing as he goes up into heaven.[20] Acts goes on to interpret Jesus's ascension as the messianic fulfillment of Psalm 110 (Acts 2:33–36), the psalm that describes the messianic king as a priest "according to the order of Melchizedek." Thus, in Luke and Acts, Jesus is also presented as a messianic—"anointed"—heavenly priest-king.

Jesus's identity as high priestly Messiah is emphasized in the Apocalypse. From the very first verse, he is identified as "Jesus *Christ*" (Rev. 1:1)—that is, as the long-awaited "Anointed One" or "Messiah." Yet Jesus is not simply a royal Messiah in the book of Revelation. In the opening chapter, John relates a vision in which Jesus is presented as a priestly figure: "I saw seven golden lampstands, and in the midst of the lampstands one like a son of man, clothed with a long robe [*podērē*] and with a golden sash around his chest" (Rev. 1:12–13). A long robe was worn by the high priest (Exod. 28:4; 29:5; Wis. 18:24; Sir. 45:8), as was a girdle (Exod. 28:4; 39:29; Lev. 16:4), which corresponds to the "golden sash" worn by Jesus. While some commentators have chafed at a priestly identification of Christ's garment on the basis that the word used to describe it is *podērēs* rather than *chitōn*, the word often used to describe the priest's vestment in the Septuagint, the objection does not hold up. In reality, *podērēs* is also a word evoking a priestly vestment. David Aune writes: "The term *podērēs* occurs twelve times in the LXX and always refers to a garment worn by the high priest."[21] Moreover, that a priestly reading is intended is further suggested by the fact that Jesus stands among "lampstands." The combined imagery suggests that Jesus is being portrayed as a priest in a heavenly temple.[22]

20. See, e.g., John T. Carroll, *Luke: A Commentary*, NTL (Louisville: Westminster John Knox, 2012), 495–96.

21. David E. Aune, *Revelation 1–5*, WBC 52A (Dallas: Word, 1997), 93.

22. See, e.g., G. K. Beale, *The Book of Revelation*, NIGTC (Grand Rapids: Eerdmans, 1999), 209.

Jesus as Messianic Prophet

We noted in the previous chapter that even though the scriptures of Israel refrain from describing prophetic ceremonial anointings, prophets are nonetheless recognized as recipients of a spiritual anointing. Significantly, in the New Testament the Christ—Jesus—is not simply portrayed as a royal and priestly Messiah but is also portrayed as a prophetic figure. As with Jesus's Davidic and priestly role, this aspect of the New Testament's portrayal is anchored in Jewish expectations.

Jewish Hopes for a Messianic Prophet

In the Synoptic Gospels, we encounter the idea that Elijah will come prior to the arrival of the Messiah. For example, in Mark the disciples ask Jesus: "Why do the scribes say that Elijah must come first?" (Mark 9:11; cf. Matt. 17:10). This expectation has a scriptural basis. In the book of Malachi, we are told: "Behold, I will send you the prophet Elijah before the great and awesome day of the LORD comes" (Mal. 4:5).[23] The book of Sirach picks up this tradition, announcing that Elijah will come "to restore the tribes of Jacob" (Sir. 48:10).[24]

The book of 1 Maccabees also attests to a Jewish hope for the coming of a future prophetic figure. The book tells us that it was decided that Simon Maccabee should be ruler over the people "until a trustworthy prophet should arise" (1 Macc. 14:41). Elijah is not explicitly mentioned here. Nevertheless, here we once again find the anticipation of a coming prophet.

The hope for the coming of a future prophetic figure is rooted in a text from Deuteronomy. Moses announces: "The LORD your God will raise up for you a prophet like me from among your own people. You shall listen to him" (Deut. 18:15). In the Dead Sea Scrolls (*4QTestimonia* [4Q175]), this passage appears to have been understood as an eschatological prophecy. The belief in a future return of Elijah may be related to Deuteronomy's prophecy since, as we have seen, Elijah is portrayed in the scriptures as a kind of new Moses.

Expectations of a coming eschatological prophetic figure may also be found in another of the Dead Sea Scrolls. In a text known as *4QMessianic Apocalypse* (4Q521), we read about a figure identified as God's "messiah." The passage begins by describing how "the heavens and the earth will listen to his

23. In some editions of the English Bible, following the Hebrew Bible, this verse is Mal. 3:23.

24. For further discussion of eschatological hopes involving a prophetic figure, see Collins, *The Scepter and the Star*, 116–22.

anointed one" (*4QMessianic Apocalypse*, fragment 2, column 2, 1). It goes on to say, "And the Lord will perform marvelous acts such as have not existed, just as he said, for he will heal the badly wounded and will make the dead live, he will proclaim good news to the poor . . . and enrich the hungry" (*4QMessianic Apocalypse*, fragment 2, column 2, 11–13).[25] This passage affirms that the future figure it envisions "will proclaim good news to the poor." This line is a quotation from Isaiah 61:1.[26] It is unclear if *4QMessianic Apocalypse* is describing *physical* healings or merely the restoration of Israel in symbolic terms. The text could be read either way.[27] Given the emphasis on God performing unprecedented acts—"marvelous acts such as have not existed"—it is difficult to insist the passage is speaking only metaphorically. Elijah raised the deceased son of a widow (1 Kings 17:17–24). Is the eschatological age to involve something less? Indeed, later Jewish texts expressly connect the hope for the resurrection of the dead to Elijah.[28]

In *4QMessianic Apocalypse*, a number of traditions we have been exploring are brought together: (1) hopes for a "messiah" figure, (2) hopes involving the anointed figure of Isaiah 61, and (3) Elijah traditions (raising the dead). Does this text identify the "messiah" as both the figure from Isaiah 61 *and* as Elijah *redivivus*? That is unclear. The one who raises the dead is not specifically the "messiah," but God. In addition, there are no other Second Temple sources that identify Elijah as the messiah; this would be an exceptional case. Still, since prophetic figures are identified as "anointed ones" elsewhere in the Dead Sea Scrolls (*Damascus Document* [CD-A] 2:12; *1QWar Scroll* [1QM] 11:7), a "messianic" or "anointed" prophet would not be altogether extraordinary. Whatever we make of the precise identity of the "messiah" in *4QMessianic Apocalypse*, what is clear is this: it draws together traditions important to New Testament authors.

Jesus as Messianic Prophet in the Gospels

In the Synoptic Gospels, John the Baptist is understood to fulfill hopes for the return of Elijah (e.g., Matt. 17:9–13; Luke 1:17). Yet Jesus is also identified as

25. Translation slightly adapted from *DSSSE* 2:1045.

26. See, e.g., James VanderKam, *The Dead Sea Scrolls and the Bible* (Grand Rapids: Eerdmans, 2012), 129.

27. See Eric Eve, *The Jewish Context of Jesus' Miracles*, JSNTSup 231 (London: Sheffield Academic, 2002), 189–96.

28. *Mishnah Sotah* 9; *Jerusalem Talmud Sheqalim* 3:3; *Jerusalem Talmud Ketubbot* 12:3; *Pesiqta of Rab Kahana* 76a.

both a new Elijah figure and as the fulfillment of Isaiah 61. Perhaps nowhere are these aspects of his messianic mission more evident than in the Gospel of Luke.[29]

When Jesus reads from the scriptures in the synagogue of Nazareth, he begins with the first verse of Isaiah 61: "The Spirit of the Lord is upon me . . ." (Luke 4:18; Isa. 61:1). Having completed the reading, he sits down and boldly announces: "Today, this scripture is fulfilled in your hearing" (Luke 4:21). Jesus, therefore, explicitly identifies himself with the prophetic figure described in Isaiah 61. Given that this follows shortly after the baptism scene, in which the Spirit descends upon Jesus (Luke 3:22), Luke likely expects the reader to view Jesus's baptism as fulfilling Isaiah 61.[30]

Jesus's prophetic role is reinforced in other ways. After announcing that Isaiah 61 has been fulfilled in their hearing, Jesus reminds his audience that the prophets Elijah and Elisha went not to their own people but to gentiles (Luke 4:24–27). As part of this, he declares: "Amen, I say to you, *no prophet* is accepted in his own town" (Luke 4:24). The line, which also appears in the other Gospels (Matt. 13:57//Mark 6:4//John 4:44), is clearly a self-reference; Jesus himself is rejected in his hometown. In all three Gospels, then, Jesus—the Christ—is portrayed as a prophet.

Jesus's identity as a prophet is emphasized in still other ways, particularly in his mighty deeds. For example, in a story that parallels Elijah's act of raising the dead child of a widow to life (1 Kings 17:8–24), Jesus raises a widow's dead son (Luke 7:11–17). That the scene is meant to evoke Elijah's miracle is reinforced by the crowd's response: "A great *prophet* has risen among us!" (Luke 7:16). Given that Luke has already had Jesus implicitly compare himself with Elijah (Luke 4:24–26), the reference to Jesus being a "great prophet" in raising the dead makes an Elijah allusion irresistible. Later, Elijah himself will appear in the story of the Transfiguration (Luke 9:28–37), where he and Moses speak to Jesus of Jesus's coming "exodus"—a Jewish way of speaking of death (cf. Wis. 3:2)—"which he was about to fulfill in Jerusalem" (Luke 9:31).

Jesus also speaks of his rejection at Jerusalem in connection with his identity as a prophet, explaining, "It is impossible that a prophet should perish

29. See, e.g., Craig A. Evans, "Luke's Use of the Elijah/Elisha Narratives," *JBL* 106 (1987): 75–83; Thomas L. Brodie, "A New Temple and a New Law: The Unity and Chronicler-Based Nature of Luke 1:1–4:22a," *JSNT* 5 (1979): 21–45; Brodie, "Luke 7,36–50 as an Internalization of 2 Kings 4,1–37: A Study in Luke's Use of Rhetorical Imitation," *Biblica* 64 (1983): 457–85.

30. Of course, for Luke, Jesus's status as Messiah is not *merely* the result of the Spirit coming down upon him at his baptism. Luke tells us that Jesus's conception occurred by the Spirit (Luke 1:35).

outside of Jerusalem" (Luke 13:33). Jesus's prophetic identity is linked, therefore, to his conflict with the Jerusalem leadership. Of course, the mention of Jesus meeting his demise in Jerusalem also calls to mind the Transfiguration, where, as mentioned above, Jesus's death at Jerusalem is the subject of the conversation between Jesus, Moses, and Elijah (Luke 9:31).

Furthermore, throughout the Gospels and Acts, Jesus's prophetic identity is confirmed by the fact that he is presented as uttering prophecies of things that come to pass. Jesus foretells many events:

- His passion, death, and resurrection (Matt. 16:21//Mark 8:31//Luke 9:22; Matt. 17:22–23//Mark 9:31//Luke 9:44; Mark 10:45; 14:21)
- The coming destruction of Jerusalem (Matt. 23:37–39//Luke 13:34–35; Matt. 24:1–2//Mark 13:1–2//Luke 21:5–6; Luke 19:41–44; John 2:19–20; 4:21–23)
- Judas's betrayal (Matt. 26:21–25//Mark 14:18–21//Luke 22:21–23; cf. John 13:21–30)
- The disciples' abandonment of Jesus (Matt. 26:31//Mark 14:27)
- Peter's denial (Matt. 26:34//Mark 14:30//Luke 22:34//John 13:38)

Jesus is portrayed as a reliable prophetic figure.

Given that Jesus says and does things evocative of prophets, it is no wonder that in the Synoptic Gospels he is identified as a prophet by others (Matt. 14:5; 21:11, 46; Matt. 21:26//Mark 11:32//Luke 20:6; Luke 7:16, 39; 24:19). During his passion, Jesus's reputation as a prophet is taken up by those who mock Jesus (Matt. 26:68//Mark 14:65//Luke 22:64). Notably, in all three instances, the derision he receives is set within the larger context of his being condemned as claiming to be the Messiah.

Jesus's Prophetic Signs

Yet, as is often pointed out, being a prophet involved more than merely predicting the future. As Luke Timothy Johnson masterfully shows, prophecy was more than forecasting; it also involved other dimensions.[31] This is especially seen in the Gospel of Luke.

31. See especially Luke Timothy Johnson, *Prophetic Jesus, Prophetic Church: The Challenge of Luke-Acts to Contemporary Christians* (Grand Rapids: Eerdmans, 2011), 39–71.

First, prophecy was also understood as living a manner of life governed by the Spirit of God. As we have seen, the spirit of prophecy caused figures such as Saul to *behave differently* (1 Sam. 10:9–13). The Spirit guides Elijah (1 Kings 18:12) and "lifts up" Ezekiel (Ezek. 2:2; 3:24; cf. 11:5). Notably, Jesus is also "led" by the Spirit (Luke 4:1). Second, the prophet not only foretells events but, more broadly, *receives God's word*[32] and *speaks it to others*.[33] Jesus also preaches the "word of God" to others (Luke 5:1). Third, prophets *embody* and *enact* God's message by performing symbolic signs.[34] It is this latter point that I wish to emphasize.

Examples of prophetic signs in the Old Testament abound. Here we can mention some examples:

- Samuel tears Saul's garment to indicate that the kingdom has been torn away from him (1 Sam. 15:27–28).
- Ahijah tears his garment to signify that the kingdom will be torn into pieces (1 Kings 11:30–31).
- Elisha performs several prophetic actions: he kills oxen to symbolize his commitment to follow Elijah (1 Kings 19:21); he parts the waters of the Jordan with Elijah's cloak (2 Kings 2:12–18); he directs Joash to shoot arrows to symbolize how God will give him victory over his enemies (2 Kings 13:14–19).
- Hosea takes a wife to symbolize God's relationship with Israel (Hosea 1:2–3) and gives his children names that foretell God's coming judgment on Israel (Hosea 1:4–9). He is later told to marry a prostitute, who symbolizes Israel's infidelity to God (Hosea 3:1–5).
- Isaiah gives his son a name with prophetic value (Isa. 7:3; 8:1–4) and walks around naked for three years to foretell the humiliation Egypt and Ethiopia will experience at the hand of the Assyrians (Isa. 20:1–6).
- Micah goes naked to embody the shame coming upon Judah (Mic. 1:8).

Prophecy, then, is not simply about using words. Of course, the prophet par excellence is Moses. In the final lines of the book of Deuteronomy, Moses's

32. E.g., Isa. 38:4; Jer. 1:2, 4, 11; Ezek. 1:3; 6:1; 11:14; 13:1; Hosea 1:1; Joel 1:1; Zeph. 1:1; Hag. 1:1; Zech. 1:1.

33. E.g., Isa. 1:10; 28:14; 38:5; Jer. 2:4; 7:2; 10:1; 43:1; 49:7; Ezek. 3:4; 6:11; 13:1–2; 37:4; Hosea 4:1; Amos 3:1; 5:1; 7:16; Mic. 6:1; Zech. 4:6; 7:8.

34. An impressive overview of the use of prophetic signs is found in Scot McKnight, "Jesus and Prophetic Actions," *BBR* 10, no. 2 (2000): 201–5.

status as the greatest prophet of all time ("Since then there has not arisen a prophet in Israel like Moses," Deut. 34:10) is specifically connected to his role as a worker of "signs and wonders" (Deut. 34:11). Above all, however, it is Jeremiah and Ezekiel who are especially known for their prophetic actions.[35]

To be clear, some examples of prophetic actions resist being explained away as mere *embodiments*. An example of a sign that would seem to do more is Zechariah's account of breaking his staff: "I took my staff Grace, and I broke it, annulling the covenant that I had made with all the peoples. So it was annulled on that day, and the sheep sellers, who were watching me, knew that it was the word of the LORD" (Zech. 11:10–11). The natural reading of this passage is that the action of breaking the staff actually *effects* the annulment of the covenant. Likewise, Moses's act of elevating his staff surely had more to do with Israel's success in the battle than simply signifying it—the narrative seems to indicate that it *caused* it (cf. Exod. 17:8–13). The safest route, therefore, is to recognize that categories for understanding prophetic actions (e.g., predictive, embodiment, efficacious) are not rigid and that prophetic signs often had multiple purposes.

Many of Jesus's deeds—the cursing of the fig tree (Matt. 21:18–19//Mark 11:12–14), his temple action (Matt. 21:12–16//Mark 11:15–19//Luke 19:45–48; cf. John 2:13–16), and his actions at the Last Supper (Matt. 26:26–29; Mark 14:22–25; Luke 22:17–20; 1 Cor. 11:23–26)—have been understood as similar "prophetic acts" reminiscent of symbolic deeds performed by prophets. That such parallels were recognized by others is confirmed by Matthew, who tells us that some believed Jesus was Jeremiah *redivivus* (Matt. 16:14).[36]

In the Gospel of John, frequent expression is also given to the hope of a coming figure known as "the prophet" (*ho prophētēs*; e.g., John 1:21, 23). It is Jesus's *actions* that raise questions among the crowds about whether he is in fact this figure. When Jesus feeds the five thousand, the crowd announces that Jesus is "the prophet who is to come into the world" (John 6:14) as they seek to "make him king" (John 6:15). This suggests that the crowds believe the eschatological prophet could also be a royal figure. Later, however, things get murkier. In the following chapter, the crowd is divided

35. See Kelvin G. Friebel, *Jeremiah's and Ezekiel's Sign Acts: Rhetorical Nonverbal Communication*, JSOTSup 283 (Sheffield: Sheffield Academic, 1999).

36. Morna D. Hooker, *The Signs of a Prophet: The Prophetic Actions of Jesus* (Harrisburg, PA: Trinity Press International, 1997); Michael Knowles, *Jeremiah in Matthew's Gospel: The Rejected-Prophet Motif in Matthean Redaction*, JSNTSup 68 (Sheffield: Sheffield Academic, 1993).

as to whether Jesus "is really the prophet" or whether he is "the Messiah" (John 7:40–41).

That expectations in John lack systematization is hardly surprising. What we find here reflects the situation of the first century, where, as we have seen, Jewish expectations were variegated. We must remember that royal, priestly, and prophetic identities often overlapped. David acts as a priest and is identified as a prophet. Priests can serve in prophetic roles. Prophets can act as priests. That Jesus can be seen in the New Testament as a royal, priestly, and prophetic figure is not at all surprising. For the New Testament authors, the point is clear: Jesus is *the* Christ and the fulfillment of hopes for a coming "anointed one."

Yet while Jesus is *the* Christ, New Testament authors—preeminently, Paul—also indicate that believers are "in Christ" and participate in his work. Jesus reigns, but believers reign in him (Rom. 5:17). If Jesus offers sacrifice, believers can also offer sacrifices in him (Rom. 12:1). If Jesus performs acts that can be understood as "signs and wonders," so can believers. Not surprisingly, then, believers are also said to be "anointed." This is the subject of our next chapters, which bring us into the heart of the theology of the sacrament of anointing of the sick.

9

Believers as "Anointed Ones" in Christ

Participation in Christ's Royal, Priestly, and Prophetic Mission

> It is God who confirms us together with you into Christ and who anointed us.
>
> —2 Corinthians 1:21

> All who have been regenerated in Christ are made kings by the sign of the cross and consecrated priests by the anointing of the Holy Spirit.
>
> —Leo the Great (d. 461)[1]

That the Church celebrates a sacrament involving *anointing* the sick is not surprising. The concept of an "anointed one" is at the heart of the gospel message: Jesus is *the* Christ. Within the context of Second Temple Judaism, this had specific implications for the early believers. In the Jewish scriptures,

1. Leo the Great, *Sermon* 4.1; translation from Leo the Great, *Sermons*, trans. Jane Patricia Freeland and Agnes Josephine Conway, FC 93 (Washington, DC: Catholic University of America Press, 1996), 25.

sacral anointing was especially connected to three types of figures: kings, priests, and prophets. Not surprisingly, then, the New Testament not only portrays Jesus as a messianic figure in the abstract but affirms in different ways that he fulfills hopes that have emerged for a messianic king, priest, and prophet.

But what does the fact that Jesus is anointed have to do with the sacrament of anointing of the sick? To answer that question, we need to explore first another aspect of the New Testament's teaching—namely, that believers are also "anointed ones." To be more exact, believers are anointed by being *in* Christ. In other words, believers are said to share in Christ's messianic anointing; they are thus appropriately called "Christians." What is more, believers are also said to share in Christ's threefold mission as they participate in his royal reign, his priestly sacrificial offering, and his prophetic mission.

Anointed in the Anointed One

Above we saw that Paul links Jesus's identity as "Christ" to the "anointing" that those who are united to him receive from God (2 Cor. 1:21). What does this entail? First, it is important to explore Paul's teaching that believers are "in Christ." Second, within this context, we better understand how believers are themselves said to be "anointed." Moreover, it is not only Paul who teaches that believers are "anointed," but the idea is also found in 1 John.

Believers as "in Christ"

Throughout his letters, Paul emphasizes that believers are "in Christ." Consider some of the following passages:

> There is now no condemnation for those who are *in Christ Jesus*. (Rom. 8:1)

> If anyone is *in Christ*, there is a new creation. (2 Cor. 5:17)

> All of you are one *in Christ Jesus*. (Gal. 3:28)

From these verses we learn that those "in Christ" are (1) no longer under "condemnation," (2) "a new creation," and (3) "one" together. The phrase "in Christ" occurs about sixty-one times. Relatedly, the apostle speaks of being "in the Lord" (*en kyriō*) thirty-nine times and uses expressions such as "in" or "with" Christ numerous times as well.[2] But what does it mean to be "in Christ"?

When Paul speaks of being "in Christ," he is not simply speaking metaphorically. For Paul, believers are truly united to Jesus. This is realized through faith—Christ dwells in believers "through faith" (Eph. 3:17). At the same time, union with Christ is accomplished "sacramentally," by which I mean that it is bound up with rites the Christian tradition identifies as sacraments: baptism and eucharist. In his teaching in Romans 6, Paul writes:

> Do you not know that those of us who were *baptized into Christ Jesus* were baptized into his death? We were therefore buried with him through baptism into death in order that, as Christ was raised from the dead by the glory of the Father, so we too might walk in newness of life. (Rom. 6:3–4)

To be baptized is to share in both Christ's death and resurrection. This is not the work of the believer, but of God. As Christ was raised "by the Father," so too—through baptism—the believer is inserted into life with Christ. It is union with Christ effected in this rite that enables believers to walk in newness of life. Paul talks about baptism as what unites believers to Christ elsewhere in his letters, such as in Galatians 3: "Those of you who were baptized into Christ have clothed yourselves with Christ" (Gal. 3:27).[3]

Believers are effectively united to Christ through the eucharist as well.[4] In 1 Corinthians 10, Paul explains that the eucharistic cup is "a communion [*koinōnia*] in the blood of Christ" and the eucharistic bread is "a communion [*koinōnia*] in the body of Christ" (1 Cor. 10:16). For the apostle, it is the eucharistic bread itself that *effects* union with Christ and his body. The Lord's Supper does more than serve as a reminder of Jesus's sacrificial death. Notice Paul's language: "Because [*hoti*] there is one bread, we who are many are one body, for [*gar*] we all eat of the one bread" (1 Cor. 10:17). Paul is not saying, "Because we are one body, we share in the one bread." Instead, it is

2. See James D. G. Dunn, *The Theology of Paul the Apostle* (Grand Rapids: Eerdmans, 1998), 396–97; Brant Pitre, Michael P. Barber, and John A. Kincaid, *Paul, a New Covenant Jew: Rethinking Pauline Theology* (Grand Rapids: Eerdmans, 2019), 21–23.

3. See Isaac Augustine Morales, "Baptism and Union with Christ," in *"In Christ" in Paul: Explorations in Paul's Theology of Union and Participation*, ed. Michael J. Thate, Kevin J. Vanhoozer, and Constantine R. Campbell, WUNT 2/384 (Tübingen: Mohr Siebeck, 2014), 157–77.

4. See Pitre, Barber, and Kincaid, *Paul, a New Covenant Jew*, 211–50.

Augustine on Christ as the Name of a Sacrament

As part of a discussion of anointing in the Old Testament, Augustine notes that just as figures prior to Christ were anointed, so too does this occur in the age of the new covenant. He writes: "Christ is the name of a sacrament. Just as one may be called a prophet or one may be called a priest, so Christ is commended as one who has been anointed, in whom there was the redemption of the whole people of Israel."[a] Here Augustine describes sacred anointing—"Christ"—as a "sacrament." Here we see the way "sacrament" was used in different ways by Augustine. In this passage, Augustine uses the term to describe the sign of spiritual anointing on consecrated individuals. There is no sense here in which anointing, then, must be *either* a ritual *or* a spiritual reality. Augustine thinks anointing can be both, using the term "sacrament" for both.

a. Augustine, *Homilies on 1 John* 3.6. Translation from Augustine, *Homilies on the First Epistle of John*, trans. Boniface Ramsey, WSA I/14 (Hyde Park, NY: New City Press, 2008), 56.

the eucharistic elements that effect communion: "*Because there is one bread*, we who are many are one body." In his later work, E. P. Sanders therefore concludes: "Christians are *one person* with Christ and *participate* in him through *baptism* and the *Lord's Supper*. These two Christian rites were taking on a 'mystical' or 'sacramental' meaning."[5] For Paul, then, the sacramental rites of the Church do not merely *symbolize* union with Christ but *effect* it. We saw something analogous to this when we discussed certain prophetic actions of the prophets; in some cases, these acts seem to *effect* what they symbolize (see pp. 141–43).

This union with Christ, moreover, involves sharing in Christ's Spirit. Indeed, Paul will go on to explain that Christians are also, like Christ, "anointed" in him. These two ideas seem interrelated.

5. E. P. Sanders, *Paul: The Apostle's Life, Letters, and Thought* (Minneapolis: Fortress, 2015), 329 (emphasis original).

Anointed and Sealed in Christ by the Spirit

In the opening chapter of 2 Corinthians, Paul writes:

> For the Son of God, Jesus Christ, the one proclaimed among you by us, Silvanus and Timothy and I, was not "Yes" and "No." Rather, in him it is always "Yes." For however many are God's promises, they have their "Yes" in him. Therefore it is also through him that we say the "Amen" to the glory of God. But now it is *God who confirms us together with you into Christ* and who *anointed* ["christened"] us, who also *sealed* us and gave us the down payment of the *Spirit* in our hearts. (2 Cor. 1:19–22)

We examined a line from this passage in the previous chapter to show that Paul connects Jesus's identity as "Christ" to the Spirit. Here we also see that believers are "confirmed" or "established" (*bebaioō*) "together . . . into Christ." Participation in Christ is the basis for his teaching. Much more needs to be said about this passage, however.

First, Paul insists that believers are united with Christ *by God* and *with others*: "Now it is God who confirms us together with you into Christ" (2 Cor. 1:21). That the promises of God are fulfilled in Jesus is not the end of the story. Believers are to be incorporated into Christ. The word translated "confirms," *bebaioō*, has the connotation of "strengthening." In 1 Corinthians, Paul uses the same word to speak of how believers will be "sustained" to reach the "end"—that is, the day of Christ's return (cf. 1 Cor. 1:7–8). Notice, however, that this is in the passive sense—believers do not confirm *themselves*. Rather, it is *God* who confirms believers in Christ. Moreover, participation with Christ is not individualistic or understood simply in terms of a private reality. Rather, one is "confirmed" or "strengthened" in Christ *by God* and *with others*. All of this is especially emphasized in the sacraments of baptism and confirmation, in which the believer receives the rite from someone else.

Second, being confirmed in Christ is bound up with being "anointed"—or "christened"—in him. The play on words points to a theological truth: those in the Anointed One—"Christ"—are anointed themselves. Believers are "christs" in *the* Christ. This idea is closely connected to being "sealed" (*sphragizō*) and receiving "the down payment of the Spirit in our hearts" (2 Cor. 1:22). Both of these ideas need to be considered carefully.

What does the language of being "sealed" indicate? Sealing can signify different things, including ownership (Rom. 15:28) and safely securing

Augustine on the Prophets as "Full of Christ"

Given that the New Testament presents Christ as the "Anointed One" par excellence, it should be no surprise that, reading the Old Testament in light of the New, Augustine maintains that Christ himself was present in the prophets. The anointing of the prophets is therefore not simply identified with the Spirit but—to a certain extent—can be connected to Christ himself: "In the prophets he was proclaiming himself, for he is the Word of God, and everything they said was full of the Word of God. The prophets were full of Christ, and Christ it was whom they announced."[a]

a. Augustine, *Exposition of Psalm 142*. Translation from Augustine, *Expositions of the Psalms 121–150*, trans. Maria Boulding, WSA III/20 (Hyde Park, NY: New City Press, 2000), 400.

something (Matt. 27:66; Rev. 20:3). Especially important parallels to the language of 2 Corinthians 1, however, are found in the Letter to the Ephesians.[6] Among other things, the letter identifies the "seal" believers receive with the Holy Spirit:

> In [Christ] you also . . . were *sealed* with the promised *Holy Spirit*. (Eph. 1:13)
>
> And do not grieve *the Holy Spirit* of God, with which you were *sealed* for the day of redemption. (Eph. 4:30)

Whereas 2 Corinthians 1 connects the gift of the Spirit with the seal received by believers, in Ephesians the Spirit is explicitly identified as that seal. Moreover, as in 2 Corinthians, the first passage from Ephesians connects this sealing with being "in Christ." Those in communion with Christ, then, are not simply "anointed" in Christ but also "sealed" in the Spirit.

6. Whether Paul himself wrote Ephesians is debated among scholars. For a detailed overview of the arguments, see Ernest Best, *Ephesians*, ICC (London: T&T Clark, 1998), 6–35. If the Letter to the Ephesians is not written by Paul, the letter at the very least shows us what the earliest interpretation of Paul's theology looked like. Here we simply identify the author as "Paul" without prejudice to debates about authorship.

Anointed by the Holy One

Another important New Testament source for our discussion of the anointing of believers is found in 1 John. The author warns his readers that an "antichrist" is coming, announcing that "many antichrists have arisen" (1 John 2:18). These have left the community and, in so doing, make it manifest that "they did not belong to us" (1 John 2:19). The reason his readers have not fallen away is due to their "anointing": "But you have been anointed by the Holy One, and you all have knowledge" (1 John 2:20).

The word "anointed" here translates the Greek term *chrisma*. Is the idea that believers have received physical "oil" or that they have been anointed in a spiritual sense? The Greek is open to both meanings. The consensus among scholars is that the language refers to the Spirit. First, the author says that believers receive this anointing "from him" (1 John 2:27)—namely, from God, which coheres with the distinctive way the author speaks of the Spirit as a gift to believers: "the Spirit that he has given us" (1 John 3:24). Unlike the spirits associated with the false prophets, the Spirit that believers receive is "from God" (1 John 4:1).[7] Second, the anointing is described as a *teacher*: "His anointing teaches you about all things [*didaskei hymas peri pantōn*]" (1 John 2:27). Scholars widely agree that 1 John is to be read as coming from the same community responsible for the Fourth Gospel. With that in mind, note that in the Gospel of John, Jesus announces that "the Paraclete, the Holy Spirit . . . *will teach you all things* [*hymas didaxei panta*]" (John 14:26). While the language is not precisely the same, it is impossible to overlook the conceptual overlap; both the Spirit and anointing "teach" believers in Johannine theology.[8] Finally, as we have seen elsewhere, following Isaiah, other New Testament writers seem to identify the Spirit as "anointing." This is most explicit in Acts 10:38: "God anointed [*echrisen*] Jesus of Nazareth with the Holy Spirit." First John indicates that by receiving the Spirit as "anointing"—in Greek, *chrisma*—believers share in the status of Jesus, the *Christos*.

7. See Urban C. von Wahlde, *The Gospel and Letters of John*, 3 vols., ECC (Grand Rapids: Eerdmans, 2010), 3:93.

8. See Raymond E. Brown, *The Epistles of John*, AB 30 (Garden City, NY: Doubleday, 1982), 343. Significantly, in the Dead Sea Scrolls the Spirit is also associated with the "true counsel of God" (1QS 3:6; *DSSSE* 1:75). The Johannine identification of the Spirit as teacher would thus seem to be rooted in Jewish soil.

Origen on the Anointing of Head and Body

In his work *Against Celsus* (AD 248), Origen discusses the way believers share in Christ's status as "Anointed One":

> [Christ] took the first-fruits of the anointing, even, so to speak, the whole anointing of "the oil of gladness" [Ps. 45:7]; whereas his fellows, each one as he had the capacity, shared in his anointing. That is why, since Christ is the head of the Church [Col. 1:18], so that Christ and the Church are one body, the oil on the head descended upon the beard of Aaron, the signs of a full-grown man, and why this oil descended till it reached the skirts of his garment [Ps. 133:2].[a]

For Origen, the image of oil flowing from Aaron's head to the rest of his body is taken as a spiritual reference to the anointing of Christ flowing from him as head to the members of his body, the Church.

a. Origen, *Against Celsus* 6.79. Translation from Origen, *Contra Celsum*, trans. Henry Chadwick (Cambridge: Cambridge University Press, 1953), 392.

Participation in Christ's Royal Reign

We saw above that the New Testament views Jesus not only as the "Anointed One" but also as having the roles typically associated with sacral anointings—king, priest, and prophet. The New Testament indicates, however, not only that those who are in Christ are "anointed ones" but that they also share in Christ's royal reign, in his priestly identity, and in his prophetic role. We begin by looking at passages that speak of believers sharing in Christ's royal reign.

Sharing in Jesus's Messianic Rule

As we have seen, in 2 Corinthians 1, Paul speaks of believers as sharing in Christ's status as "anointed ones" (2 Cor. 1:21–22). As Joshua Jipp explains, "It seems likely that Paul is punning on the meaning of God's consecration of the Messiah as king and the church's consecration *into* the same *royal* identity."[9]

9. Joshua Jipp, *The Messianic Theology of the New Testament* (Grand Rapids: Eerdmans, 2020), 140.

Not surprisingly, then, in 2 Corinthians believers also are portrayed as sharing in an aspect of Christ's *royal* activity—namely, judgment.

Jipp shows that, for Paul, the concept of judgment is closely bound up with Christ's role as king. This connection is evident in 2 Corinthians: "For we all must appear before the judgment seat of Christ that each one may receive a recompense, whether good or bad, for what he has done in the body" (2 Cor. 5:10). Here the judge is Christ, whom Paul elsewhere identifies as the royal Messiah.[10]

A similar idea is found in Romans 8.[11] The apostle writes:

> Who will bring charges against God's chosen ones? It is God who justifies. Who is to condemn? It is Christ Jesus, who died and, even more, who was raised from the dead. It is also he who is at the right hand of God and who even intercedes for us. (Rom. 8:33–34)

Paul asks a rhetorical question: Who could bring charges against God's chosen ones when it is God himself who decides their legal status? God renders the ultimate verdict because he "justifies" the elect, vindicating them from legal charges against them.[12] Paul therefore asks another rhetorical question: "Who is to condemn?" Believers need not fear condemnation from any judge since God has already justified the righteous, effectively holding them in the right. The apostle draws from Psalm 110, reminding us that Jesus has been enthroned "at the right hand of God." In other words, as the enthroned royal judge, Jesus has the capacity to condemn but does not do so. Those in Christ can be confident that their Lord not only is not going to condemn them but is even actively interceding before God on their behalf. All of this is bound up with his identity as *Christ* Jesus—Jesus is the enthroned royal judge.

What is especially important for our study is that Paul also indicates believers share in Christ's work of judgment. For example, this expectation undergirds Paul's teaching in 1 Corinthians. Paul castigates the Corinthians for bringing civil charges against one another in secular courts. In this, Paul sees a

10. See Jipp, *Messianic Theology*, 175.

11. For what follows, see Jipp, *Messianic Theology*, 177–79; Jipp, *Christ Is King: Paul's Royal Ideology* (Minneapolis: Fortress, 2015), 270.

12. For the juridical backdrop of Paul's language of justification and its implications for his thought, see James B. Prothro, *A Pauline Theology of Justification: Forgiveness, Friendship, and Life in Christ*, Lectio Sacra (Eugene, OR: Cascade Books, 2023); Prothro, *Both Judge and Justifier: Biblical Legal Language and the Act of Justifying in Paul*, WUNT 2/461 (Tübingen: Mohr Siebeck, 2018).

failed recognition of the way believers are united in Christ's reign. He writes: "Do you not know that *the saints will judge* the world? . . . Do you not know that *we will judge the angels*?" (1 Cor. 6:2, 3). According to the apostle, the saints will somehow share in Christ's judgment even over the angels. That he goes on to speak of "inheriting the *kingdom* of God" places all of this under the banner of Christ's royal rule. Believers are therefore not only "anointed" *in* the Anointed One par excellence, they also share in the Messiah's reign.

In Romans 5, believers' participation in Christ's royal reign overcomes the powers of sin and death. Due to Adam's disobedience, "death reigned" (Rom. 5:17), such that "sin reigned in death" (Rom. 5:21). Yet the tyranny of sin and death has been toppled by the obedience of Christ. Paul writes: "If, by the trespass of one man death reigned through that one man, much more will those who receive the abundance of grace and the free gift of righteousness *reign* in life through the one man, Jesus Christ" (Rom. 5:17). Whereas death previously had "dominion" or "reigned," believers now reign—though this is possible only "through the one man, Jesus Christ." Believers reign, though they do so only through participation in Christ.

A similar idea may be found in 2 Timothy. There we read: "Because of this I endure all things for the sake of the chosen in order that they also may obtain salvation, which is in Christ Jesus with eternal glory. The saying is trustworthy: If we have died with him, we will also live with him; if we endure, we will also *reign with him* [*symbasileusomen*]" (2 Tim. 2:10–12). In this passage, salvation is explicitly found "in Christ Jesus"—that is, "in the Messiah." Not surprisingly, then, royal imagery follows—those who endure will "reign with him." Again, believers exercise royal power but only with Christ.[13]

Enthronement with Christ and Freedom from Sin

An idea related to reigning with Christ found in some New Testament books is the imagery of believers being enthroned with him. For example, in Colossians we are told:

> If, therefore, you have been raised together with Christ, seek the things above, where Christ is seated at the right hand of God. Set your mind on things above, not on things on earth, for you have died and your life is hidden with Christ

13. 2 Tim. 2:12 uses imagery strikingly similar to 1 Cor. 4:8. See Luke Timothy Johnson, *The First and Second Letters to Timothy*, AB 35A (New York: Doubleday, 2001), 376.

> in God. When Christ who is your life is revealed, then you too will be revealed with him in glory. (Col. 3:1–4)

The logic here is straightforward. Jesus is said to be enthroned in heaven via the language of Psalm 110:4: Jesus is "seated at the right hand of God" (Col. 3:1). Believers should set their minds on heavenly things because they have been "raised together with Christ" and their "life is hidden with Christ in God." In other words, believers already have a share in Christ's heavenly reign. The passage does not explicitly say that those in Christ are enthroned with him, but the idea seems to be nonetheless implied: Christ is enthroned, and believers' heavenly existence is "hidden with Christ."

But there is more. The affirmation that believers share in Christ's heavenly reign serves as the basis for the call to renounce sin: "*Put to death*, then, whatever in you is earthly: sexual immorality, impurity, passion, evil desire, and greed, which is idolatry" (Col. 3:5). As in Romans, sharing in Christ's reign has an inverse effect—namely, overcoming sin. To reign with Christ is ultimately expressed in overcoming the power of sin.

The Letter to the Ephesians contains nearly identical material. We read that God has "made us alive together with Christ—by grace you are saved—and raised us up together with him and *seated us together with him in the heavenly places in Christ Jesus*" (Eph. 2:5–6). Believers are *enthroned* with Christ by virtue of their union with him, and so, as Ernest Best explains in his landmark commentary on Ephesians, they "participate in Christ's reign."[14] In context, this co-reigning with Christ is contrasted with the life believers had prior to faith in him, a life in which "you were dead through the trespasses and sins in which you once walked" (Eph. 2:1–2). Again, as in Romans and Colossians, to share in Christ's reign is to be saved from sin.

Furthermore, while Colossians seems to imply that believers are enthroned with Christ by saying that Christ sits at God's right hand and believers' lives are "hidden with Christ in God" (Col. 3:3), Ephesians is more explicit. Here we read that God has "seated us together with [Christ]" (Eph. 2:6). The explicit imagery of co-enthronement with Christ in Ephesians could be read as a fuller expression of what is found in Colossians.[15]

14. Best, *Ephesians*, 222.

15. It is well known that the two epistles share numerous similarities (e.g., compare Col. 4:7–8 with Eph. 6:21–22; Col. 2:19 with Eph. 4:15–16), though their precise relationship may ultimately be unknowable. For a discussion, see Best, *Ephesians*, 20–25.

Finally, the book of Revelation is even more explicit about believers' enthronement with Christ. There Jesus promises, "I will grant to the one who conquers the right to sit with me *on my throne*, just as I myself have conquered and have sat down with my Father on his throne" (Rev. 3:21).[16] Here victory in Christ is nothing less than sitting with him on the divine throne, sharing in his divine reign.

Participation in Christ's Priesthood

In addition to passages that suggest believers have a share in Christ's royal prerogatives, there are also texts that indicate that they have a priestly role. This is rooted in Jewish expectations. In the book of Isaiah, the following statement is made to the people of God restored from exile: "You will be called priests of the LORD; you will be named ministers of our God" (Isa. 61:6). Since the New Testament books frequently draw from Jewish restoration hopes, it is no surprise that we find believers described in priestly terms—the eschatological people of God are a priestly people. Moreover, certain texts appear to connect the priestly role of believers to the idea of their union with the Messiah, the Anointed One—Christ.[17]

Paul's Exhortation to Offer One's Body as a Sacrifice

To be sure, Paul never speaks of believers as "priests" in a general sense. Nevertheless, in Romans 15, the apostle explicitly identifies his own ministry as "priestly." He speaks of "the grace that has been given to me by God to be a minister of Christ Jesus to the gentiles, serving as a priest [*hierourgounta*] of the gospel of God, in order that the offering of the gentiles may be acceptable, sanctified by the Holy Spirit" (Rom. 15:15–16). We will have more to say about this passage later, but for now let us simply focus on Paul's role in it.

In the verses that follow, Paul emphasizes that his priestly work is possible only through his union with Christ: "Therefore, I have a reason for boasting *in Christ Jesus* regarding my work for God. For I will not dare to speak about anything except *what Christ has accomplished through me*" (Rom. 15:17–18).

16. Martin Hengel, "Sit at My Right Hand!," in *Studies in Early Christology*, trans. Rollin Kearns (London: T&T Clark, 1995), 148–58.

17. Here I limit myself to passages not only where believers are portrayed in priestly terms but also where traces of participationist themes might be found.

What has been accomplished in Paul is nothing less than Christ's own work. If Paul is "serving as a priest," it would follow that Christ is in some way a priestly figure. In fact, earlier in the letter, Paul uses temple imagery to describe Jesus's own act of obedience in dying on the cross. In Romans 3, Paul explains that Jesus was put forward by God "as a sacrifice of atonement [*hilastērion*]" (Rom. 3:25). The language here draws from Israel's sacrificial worship (Exod. 25:17; Ezek. 43:14, 17, 20 LXX). The point seems to be that the suffering of Christ functions in an atoning way, in some way analogous to the rites of the temple.[18] Romans 15, then, makes two points about Paul: (1) he performs a priestly service; and (2) this is possible only because of his union with Christ, whose death is to be understood as a sacrificial act.

Paul also suggests a priestly role for himself in 1 Corinthians. The apostle explains that he has a right to receive food as part of his apostolic service. He goes on to justify this in a remarkable way—he compares himself to the Jewish priests: "Do you not know that those who work the temple services eat the things from the temple, and those who minister at the altar share in the sacrifices on the altar? In the same way too the Lord commanded that those who proclaim the gospel should get their living from the gospel" (1 Cor. 9:13–14). The Torah supplies helpful background for Paul's language: priests received their provisions from the sacrifices offered in the sanctuary (Num. 18:8–20). In other words, just as priests receive their sustenance from the sacrifices offered in the sanctuary, those who proclaim the gospel should receive their living from their work. Implicit in all of this is the idea, fleshed out further in Romans 15, that those who proclaim the gospel are in some way performing a priestly work.

Let us now return to the description of the gentiles in Romans 15. Paul speaks of "the offering of the gentiles" (*hē prosphora tōn ethnōn*; Rom. 15:16). Here the gentiles are said to be a sacrificial offering to God. The language likely builds on material that occurs earlier in the Letter to the Romans. In Romans 12, the apostle exhorts his readers, "Present [*parastēsai*] your bodies as a living sacrifice, holy and acceptable to God, which is your reasonable worship" (Rom. 12:1). In Greek, the word translated "present" is a form of the verb *paristēmi*, a term that has sacrificial resonances.[19] This appeal is set

18. See Michael Patrick Barber, *The Historical Jesus and the Temple: Memory, Methodology, and the Gospel of Matthew* (Cambridge: Cambridge University Press, 2023), 192–95. Significantly, the same term used by Paul is used for the death of the Jewish martyrs in 4 Macc. 17:22.

19. See, e.g., Josephus, *Jewish War* 2.89; *Jewish Antiquities* 4.113.

within a context in which Paul uses participationist language in reference to the Church. He goes on to explain that "we who are many are one body [*sōma*] in Christ" (Rom. 12:5). Paul, then, has a priestly role inasmuch as he serves as a minister to the gentiles, a task he performs in union with Christ. Specifically, Paul exhorts the gentiles into the spiritual worship that consists of offering their "bodies" to the Lord through the one *body* (singular). In other words, they are to offer their individual bodies as members of the one body of "Christ," whose own death is construed as a sacrifice (Rom. 3:25).

The priestly imagery in Romans might also be seen as paralleled in the Letter to the Colossians. There we read: "But now [Christ] has reconciled you by his death in his fleshly body, to *present* [*parastēsai*] you *holy* and unblemished and irreproachable before him" (Col. 1:22). The word translated "present," *parastēsai*, is the same verb used in Romans 12 for presenting a sacrificial offering. That the verse speaks of being "holy" (*hagious*) and "blameless" (*amōmous*), terms connected with sacrificial offerings (e.g., Lev. 1:3; 2:3, 10), reinforces the sacrificial imagery.[20] Some have resisted such a reading, noting that juridical symbolism is present[21] or observing that the primary thrust of the passage is entering into God's presence. Yet one should not pit a sacrificial backdrop against others. For one thing, some biblical traditions suggest the temple is the locus of judgment (e.g., Deut. 17:8–13; Ezek. 44:24).[22] In addition, offering sacrifice was understood to be a way of approaching God's presence (e.g., Exod. 29:42–46).[23] Furthermore, to recognize sacrificial echoes in Colossians 1 is not to deny the passage's multivalent meaning. It seems temple and juridical imagery are combined here.

Colossians 1 does differ from Romans 15 in a striking way, however. In Colossians, *Christ* "presents" the gentiles to the Father. In Romans 15, it is *Paul* who, in Christ, facilitates the offering of the gentiles. Yet before we press that difference too much, we should note that later the author says: "It is [Christ] whom we proclaim by admonishing every person and teaching every person with all wisdom, in order that we may *present* [*parastēsōmen*] every person *perfect* [*teleion*] in Christ" (Col. 1:28). The Greek term I have

20. See, e.g., James D. G. Dunn, *The Epistles to the Colossians and to Philemon*, NIGTC (Grand Rapids: Eerdmans, 1996), 109–10.

21. Jerry L. Sumney, *Colossians*, NTL (Louisville: Westminster John Knox, 2008), 85–86.

22. See, e.g., Moshe Weinfeld, *The Place of the Law in the Religion of Ancient Israel*, VTSup (Leiden: Brill, 2004), 96.

23. See, e.g., Jonathan Klawans, *Purity, Sacrifice, and the Temple: Symbolism and Supersessionism in the Study of Ancient Judaism* (Oxford: Oxford University Press, 2006), 68–72.

rendered here "perfect," *teleios*, is used in Exodus to describe the sacrificial Passover lamb (Exod. 12:5 LXX). The related word *teleiōsis* ("perfection") is used throughout the scriptures in reference to sacrifices (Exod. 29:22–34; Lev. 8:22–33 LXX). Combined with the verb meaning "to present" (*paristēmi*), the language suggests that once again sacrificial symbolism is intended.[24] Though Christ was the one who "presented" the gentiles a few verses earlier, here it is Paul and his co-workers who present others as "perfect" sacrifices. While Paul is not explicitly described as a "priest" here, the conceptual connections with Romans 12 and 15 are difficult to avoid.[25]

The Priesthood of Believers in 1 Peter

Paul describes himself in priestly terms and suggests his readers offer sacrifices, but he never explicitly identifies believers in general as priests. In 1 Peter, however, the priesthood of believers is made explicit. In 1 Peter 2, we read:

> . . . coming to him, a living stone, rejected by humans but chosen and precious in the sight of God. And you yourselves, as living stones, are being built into a spiritual house, to be a holy priesthood, to offer spiritual sacrifices acceptable to God through Jesus Christ. (1 Pet. 2:4–5)

It is necessary to consider different aspects of this passage.

First, to whom are believers "coming"? The answer is undoubtedly Jesus. The epistle opens by speaking of "the God and Father of our Lord Jesus Christ" (1 Pet. 1:3). Jesus is thus already spoken of as "Lord." Moreover, the end of the passage explains that believers are to offer sacrifices through "Jesus Christ." Believers are therefore to draw near to Christ to offer sacrifices in him.

Second, the imagery here is assuredly that of believers as a temple. Christ himself is described as "a living stone" (*lithon zōnta*) who is "rejected" (*apodedokimasmenon*; 1 Pet. 2:4). The language here is drawn from the Greek version of Psalm 118: "The stone [*lithon*] that the builders *rejected* [*apedokimasan*] has become the very head of the corner" (Ps. 118:22 [117:22 LXX]). That Psalm 118:22 is the source for 1 Peter's language is impossible to dispute; the author goes on to quote the verse directly (1 Pet. 2:7). The language of a "spiritual house" follows from the connection to Psalm 118, a psalm which is

24. See Paul Foster, *Colossians*, BNTC (London: Bloomsbury T&T Clark, 2016), 230.
25. Foster, *Colossians*, 230.

itself set within the temple: "We bless you from the *house of the Lord*" (Ps. 118:26). The Mishnah and other later Jewish works connect the psalm to the temple.[26] The psalm even appears in Ezra 3, where it is used in the context of the rebuilding of the temple (Ezra 3:11; Ps. 118:29).

Third, consonant with the temple symbolism in play, believers are identified as a "holy priesthood" who "offer spiritual sacrifices [*anenenkai pneumatikas*]" (1 Pet. 2:5). This teaching later is anchored in the description of Israel's calling in Exodus—"You shall be for me a kingdom of priests and a holy nation" (Exod. 19:6; cf. 1 Pet. 2:9). With this we come to the critical point this overall section is seeking to highlight—namely, the idea that believers have a priestly identity.

Is the priesthood of believers related to the notion of being "in Christ"? A good case can be made for this reading. Elsewhere, the author uses the expression found throughout the Pauline literature.[27] For example, the author explicitly speaks of believers' "good conduct *in Christ* [*en christō*]" (1 Pet. 3:16). The phrase appears again in the conclusion of the letter, where we read that God has "called you to his eternal glory *in Christ* [*en christō*]" (1 Pet. 5:10). In their commentary on the letter, Travis Williams and David Horrell see here usage that is "coherent with the distinctively Pauline flavour of the phrase," identifying this as one of many examples where 1 Peter shows the influence of Pauline thought.[28] With this in mind, let us return, then, to the imagery of 1 Peter 2:5, which indicates that believers "offer spiritual sacrifices acceptable to God *through Jesus Christ*." It is only in association with Christ—again, the "Anointed One"—that believers are able to offer acceptable offerings to God. The community, then, is identified in priestly terms, yet they offer their sacrifices to God by union with Christ. Other aspects of the passage confirm this reading.

At the beginning of this section, we read that believers are "stones" built into a temple with Christ, "a living stone." Believers are thus able to function as priests inasmuch as they form one temple with Christ. Moreover, Christ is said to be "chosen" (*eklekton*; 1 Pet. 2:4). Notably, this section of the letter climaxes with the description of believers using the same term: believers are "chosen

26. *Mishnah Pesahim* 5:5–7; 10:6–7; *Mishnah Sukkah* 3:9; 4:5; *Tosefta Pesahim* 4:10–11; *Babylonian Talmud Pesahim* 95b.

27. For a balanced overview of the letter's relationship to Pauline literature, see Travis B. Williams and David G. Horrell, *1 Peter*, 2 vols., ICC (London: Bloomsbury T&T Clark, 2023), 1:63–74.

28. See Williams and Horrell, *1 Peter*, 2:597.

[*eklekton*], a royal priesthood" (1 Pet. 2:9). Christ's "chosenness" is thus shared with believers, which is in turn explicitly connected with their priesthood.

Believers' participation in Christ is suggested by 1 Peter 4: "Because Christ therefore suffered in the flesh equip yourself with the same intention for *the one who has suffered in the flesh has ended sin* [*ho pathōn sarki pepautai hamartias*]" (1 Pet. 4:1). Most English translations render the Greek in such a way that the passage presents Christ as merely an exemplar. Yet, as Grant Macaskill shows, the passage goes on to use the language of participation explicitly: "But rejoice insofar as you *share* [*koinōneite*] in the sufferings [*pathēmasin*] of Christ" (1 Pet. 4:13). Macaskill rightly observes: "All of this suggests that Peter is not calling for mimesis of an exemplary suffering, but for consciousness of participation in a foundational event that gives significance and moral shape to the believer's own experience of suffering."[29] A participationist outlook, therefore, shapes the teaching of 1 Peter, including its presentation of the priesthood of believers.

The Kingdom of Priests in the Apocalypse

The Apocalypse likewise draws on traditions relating to Israel's vocation to be a priestly nation. Above, we saw that the book describes Jesus as a heavenly high priest. We also noted that those Christ saves are made a "kingdom" and "priests." We are told: "To him who loves us and freed us from our sins by his blood, and *made us a kingdom, priests to his God and Father*, to him be glory and dominion forever and ever. Amen" (Rev. 1:5–6). It is widely accepted that this passage is shaped by Exodus 19:6.[30] Yet the priestly nature of the saints seems to be further reinforced in other ways in the book of Revelation.

In Revelation 4, John has a vision of God's throne in which he sees a mysterious group of figures: "Round the throne were twenty-four thrones, and seated on the thrones were twenty-four elders, clothed in white garments, and on their heads were golden crowns" (Rev. 4:4). There are many possible ways to interpret the twenty-four elders.[31] A number of interpreters have identified them as angelic beings.[32] This, however, seems unlikely.

29. Grant Macaskill, *Union with Christ in the New Testament* (Oxford: Oxford University Press, 2013), 279.

30. See, e.g., G. K. Beale, *The Book of Revelation*, NIGTC (Grand Rapids: Eerdmans, 1999), 193–95.

31. See the overview in David E. Aune, *Revelation 1–5*, WBC 52A (Dallas: Word, 1997), 288–92.

32. Craig R. Koester, *Revelation*, AYB 38A (New Haven: Yale University Press, 2014), 362–63.

It seems more likely that the twenty-four elders represent the martyrs. Given that martyrs are elsewhere depicted as wearing the same attire—they receive crowns (Rev. 2:10) and wear white robes (Rev. 19:8)—it is difficult to imagine that the reader is not intended to see the twenty-four elders as martyrs. It appears, then, that Revelation 4 depicts those who "conquer" with Christ (Rev. 3:21; cf. 5:5) by "not loving their lives" in the face of death (Rev. 12:11) as those who reign with him. This is an ancient view. It finds support in Caesarius of Arles's homilies on the Apocalypse, which date to sometime between 508 and 537.[33]

What further suggests that the twenty-four elders in Revelation 4 are the saints, however, is the priestly imagery that connects them to the description of believers as "priests" in Revelation 1:5–6. That there are *twenty-four* elders is significant. There have been many suggestions as to the meaning of this number, but as David Aune observes, "the most cogent explanation" is that the number is derived from 1 Chronicles 23–24, where we read that the Jerusalem priesthood was arranged into *twenty-four* divisions (1 Chron. 23:6; 24:7–18).[34] According to Chronicles, these priestly figures play musical instruments—most notably, "harps" (1 Chron. 25:6–31). In addition, as sons of Aaron, they offer incense in the temple, as is clear from Luke's description (Luke 1:8–9; cf. 1:5). The imagery in Revelation 4, therefore, coheres remarkably well with the Chronicler's account of the priests: the twenty-four elders are seen "holding a harp" and also hold vessels "full of incense" (Rev. 5:8). That the elders offer incense seems to decisively shift the balance in favor of viewing these figures as priestly representatives. In a cultic setting, offering incense would have been a task normally reserved for priests (Exod. 30:7–10; Lev. 10:1–2; Num. 16:38–40). While angels are described as having a priestly role in the Apocalypse, even offering incense (Rev. 8:3), the parallels with the martyrs point away from an angelic interpretation.

Moreover, many have argued that Revelation 6 applies sacrificial imagery to the martyrs: "When he opened the fifth seal, I saw underneath the altar the souls of those who had been slain for the word of God and for the witness

33. Caesarius of Arles, *Exposition on the Apocalypse* 3. On the dating of these homilies, see William C. Weinrich, trans. and ed., *Latin Commentaries on Revelation: Victorinus of Petovium, Apringius of Beja, Caesarius of Arles, and Bede the Venerable*, ACT (Downers Grove, IL: IVP Academic, 2011), xxxvii.

34. See Aune, *Revelation 1–5*, 288–89; Beale, *Book of Revelation*, 324.

that they had given" (Rev. 6:9). As G. K. Beale writes, "The mention of the 'altar' here in association with those slain evokes the sacrificial nature of their suffering."[35] Indeed, the combination of slaughtered victims with the appearance of an "altar" makes viewing the martyrs as sacrificial offerings unavoidable.

That the martyrs would be depicted as both priests and sacrificial offerings coheres well with the broader imagery of the book. As we have seen above, the Apocalypse portrays Jesus as a priest (Rev. 1:12–13). In addition, the book portrays him as a sacrificial lamb: "I saw between the throne and the four living creatures and between the elders a Lamb standing as if it had been slain" (Rev. 5:6). Moreover, Christ is not merely any kind of lamb but the *Passover* lamb. The paschal nature of his identity is suggested by the song sung to him by the four living creatures and the twenty-four elders: "You were slaughtered and by your blood you purchased for God saints from every tribe and language and people and nation; you have made them a kingdom and priests" (Rev. 5:9–10). The coordination of "blood" with a "lamb" in connection with a people that are "purchased" seems unmistakably paschal.

The foregoing discussion helps to explain what it means that Christ—portrayed as both priest and king—is declared in the opening lines of the Apocalypse to have "*made us a kingdom, priests to his God and Father*" (Rev. 1:6). I would suggest that believers are, in a sense, to become like Christ—sacrificial victims who come to reign with him. Moreover, we have already noted participationist language in the Apocalypse's depiction of the royal dimension of the reward given to those who conquer with Christ—they are enthroned *with* him: "I will give a place *with me* on my throne" (Rev. 3:21). We might also note that participationist language is used in connection with the suffering of the saints: "I, John, your brother and *co-sharer* [*synkoinōnos*] in the affliction and the kingdom and the patient endurance in Jesus . . ." (Rev. 1:9). The author emphasizes that he is a "co-sharer "or "participant" with his readers in the "affliction" that is also "in Jesus" (*en Iēsou*). It seems the author is indicating that believers share in the suffering of Jesus. Furthermore, that suffering is portrayed in liturgical terms. Not surprisingly, then, as Christ is priest and king, believers are priests and kings because, like him—and *in* him—they make a priestly sacrifice of themselves.

35. Beale, *Book of Revelation*, 391.

Participation in Christ's Prophetic Mission

Finally, we come to the idea that believers share in Christ's prophetic mission. First, we will look at the Pauline letters. We will also consider other New Testament works that speak of believers as prophets. As will see, there are places in the New Testament where the prophetic capacity of believers is anchored in their communion with Jesus, the Messiah.

The Gift of Prophecy in Paul

Paul explains that "there are distributions of gifts but the same Spirit" (1 Cor. 12:4).[36] Going on, Paul lists different gifts, saying:

> To one is given through the Spirit a word of wisdom, and to another a word of knowledge by the same Spirit, *to another faith by the same Spirit*, to another gifts of healing by the one Spirit, to another the working of powerful deeds, *to another prophecy*, to another discernment of spirits, to another varieties of tongues, to another the interpretation of tongues. (1 Cor. 12:8–10)

What is most important here for our purposes is the affirmation that believers are given a gift of "prophecy."

At first glance, Paul seems to suggest that not all believers can prophesy but that prophecy is one of the various gifts given through the Spirit to different people. This reading would seem to be confirmed by the rest of the chapter. Paul explains that members of the body do not complain that they do not have different functions within it, saying, for example: "If the foot should say, 'Because I am not a hand, I am not of the body,' that would not make it any less a part of the body" (1 Cor. 12:15). The apostle's overall point is that just as a body has different members with different parts to play in it, so too it is with Christ and his body. Paul then asks a series of rhetorical questions: "Are all apostles? Are all prophets? Are all teachers? Do all work powerful deeds? Do all possess gifts of healing? Do all speak in tongues? Do all interpret?" (1 Cor. 12:29–30). The implication is *some* are apostles, but others are not. Likewise, *some* are prophets and others are not.

36. Most translations understand the noun we have translated "distribution" (*diairesis*, from the verb *diaireo*) to refer to "different" gifts or "varieties" of gifts, contrasting with the idea of "one Spirit." Yet see the nuanced treatment in Soeng Yu Li, *Paul's Teaching on the Pneumatika in 1 Corinthians 12–14: Prophecy as the Paradigm of* ta Charismata ta Meizona *for the Future-Oriented Ekklēsia*, WUNT 2/455 (Tübingen: Mohr Siebeck, 2017), 233–34.

What problematizes the reading suggested above, however, is that one of the gifts mentioned in 1 Corinthians 12 is "faith" (1 Cor. 12:9). It is unthinkable that Paul holds that some believers have faith and others do not. For Paul, faith is a constitutive aspect of being united to Christ; believers must *believe* (e.g., Rom. 3:30; 5:1; 10:17; 12:3; 1 Cor. 2:5; 13:13; 2 Cor. 1:24).

It is probably best, then, to make some distinctions: the Spirit's gifts are provided *in different ways* for the upbuilding of the body, and, therefore, there are different roles in the Church; one such role is being a "prophet." This does not mean, however, that only some are capable of prophesying, for Paul later says, "Strive for the spiritual gifts, especially that you may prophesy" (1 Cor. 14:1). Paul seems to think that prophecy is something *all believers* should hope to do. Paul's teaching in Romans offers further confirmation for this approach. In Romans 12, the apostle writes:

> We, who are many, are one body in Christ, and individually members of one another. But we have gifts that differ according to the grace given to us: *prophecy, according to the proportion of his faith*; service, in serving; the teacher, in teaching; the exhorter, in exhorting; the giver, in sincerity; the leader, in diligence; the one who shows mercy, in cheerfulness. (Rom. 12:5–8)

Notice here that Paul indicates that a believer prophesies in relation to the "proportion of his faith" (Rom. 12:6). Paul cannot mean that only some are capable of this. For certainly, the list he provides cannot be understood as indicating that only some are called to be givers in sincerity or that only some are to show mercy in cheerfulness. For example, in 2 Corinthians Paul tells his readers: "Each one of you must give as you have decided in your heart, not from regret or from compulsion, for God loves a cheerful giver" (2 Cor. 9:7).

It should also be observed that, for Paul, the believers' ability to prophesy is closely linked *to union with Christ and the gift of the Spirit*. As we have seen, in 1 Corinthians 12 the gift of prophecy is one of the "gifts" of the Spirit, and later, in 2 Corinthians, Paul identifies the Spirit as the "anointing" believers have in Christ (2 Cor. 1:21). Moreover, Paul's discussion of the spiritual gifts in 1 Corinthians 12 leads into his teaching about the church as the body of "Christ" (1 Cor. 12:12–13). Likewise, revisiting the passage again from Romans 12, we see that, just prior to speaking of the gifts (which include prophecy), the apostle underscores the way believers are "one body in Christ" (Rom. 12:5–8). So, Paul affirms (1) that believers exercise the gift of prophecy and (2) that this activity is related to participation in Christ.

Believers as Prophets in Acts

Above we saw that the Gospel of Luke especially emphasizes Jesus's identity as a prophet. Not surprisingly, its sequel, the book of Acts, also stresses the way believers share in Jesus's prophetic task. This dynamic is underscored near the beginning of the book and is presented as one of the clear indicators that the eschatological age has dawned. After the Spirit is poured out on Jesus's disciples, enabling them to speak in foreign languages, the people of Jerusalem are perplexed at what they are hearing. Some suggest that the apostles are drunk (Acts 2:13). Peter responds: "This is what was spoken through the prophet Joel: 'And it will happen in the last days, God says, I will pour out my Spirit on all flesh, and your sons and your daughters will *prophesy*'" (Acts 2:16–17; see Joel 2:28). The disciples' ability to prophesy is evidence that the age of redemption has dawned.

Once again, what Jesus does in his personal body in his ministry in the Gospel of Luke is continued in his ecclesial body in Acts. Just as Jesus foretold future events in Luke (e.g., Luke 5:10; 9:44; 17:22–37; 21:5–24), believers are gifted with the ability to predict the future in Acts. Agabus announces a coming famine, which he "foretold by the Spirit" (Acts 11:28). Likewise, Agabus announces Paul's suffering, using the phrase "Thus says the Holy Spirit" (Acts 21:11). We also read that the deacon Philip's daughters "prophesied" (Acts 21:9). Luke Timothy Johnson rightly observes: "From the beginning of the Acts narrative to the end . . . Jesus' prophetic successors are directed and empowered by the same Holy Spirit that was at work in the prophet Jesus."[37] To be sure, the disciples' prophetic activity is not portrayed as separable from Jesus. Rather, in context, the Spirit given is the "Spirit of the Lord" (Acts 5:9) and "the Spirit of Jesus" (Acts 16:7), who remains active among them through the Holy Spirit.

Moreover, as we mentioned above, prophecy is more than merely foretelling the future. First, it involves living a life that is directed by the Spirit. The disciples' activity, then, is consistently presented as being informed by the Spirit. Just as Jesus is "led" by the Spirit in Luke (Luke 4:1), the movements

37. Luke Timothy Johnson, *Prophetic Jesus, Prophetic Church: The Challenge of Luke-Acts to Contemporary Christians* (Grand Rapids: Eerdmans, 2011), 64.

of the disciples are guided by the Spirit in Acts. Philip is literally "carried away" by the Spirit and taken to Azotus (Acts 8:39–40). Peter reports that he went to Caesarea to meet Cornelius because "the Spirit told me to go" (Acts 11:12). Paul later explains that he is "bound by the Spirit" to go to Jerusalem (Acts 20:22).

Second, just as Jesus spoke the word of God as the prophets did, so too do the disciples in Acts. Peter and the apostles are depicted as speaking and preaching "the word of God" (Acts 4:31; 6:2). Paul proclaims "the word of God" in Antioch of Pisidia and Thessalonica (Acts 13:46; 17:13). Similarly, he remains in Corinth for a year and a half, "teaching the word of God" (Acts 18:11).

Finally, just as Jesus performed prophetic signs like the prophets of the past, the disciples in Acts are said to work "signs and wonders" (Acts 5:12; cf. 6:8; 8:6, 13; 14:3; 15:12). The disciples' act of shaking off from their feet the dust of the towns that reject them also seems to serve as a prophetic act of judgment against them (Acts 13:51; cf. Luke 10:11). We might also see the healings they effect—such as the healings effected by handkerchiefs touched by Paul (Acts 19:12)—as prophetic signs that point to the apostles' divinely authorized mission.

Believers as Prophets in the Apocalypse

We bring this section to a close by noting that believers have a prophetic charism in the book of Revelation. First and foremost, since the book itself is described as containing "prophecy" (Rev. 1:3; 22:7), it is clear that its author, John, is presented as a prophet. At one point, John is explicitly told, "It is necessary for you to *prophesy* again about peoples and nations and tongues and many kings" (Rev. 10:11). At the end of the book, an angel also refers to "your brothers the prophets" (Rev. 22:9), indicating that John has fraternity with them. It should be noted that John's ability to prophesy seems bound up with the Spirit's activity (Rev. 1:10; 4:2; 17:3; 21:10).

Yet, according to the Apocalypse, it is not simply John who prophesies. In Revelation 19, John begins to worship at the feet of an angel, who stops him. The heavenly messenger explains, "Do not do that! I am a fellow slave with you and your brothers who hold to the testimony of Jesus. Worship God! For *the testimony of Jesus is the spirit of prophecy*" (Rev. 19:10). Notice here that bearing testimony to Jesus is also identified with "the spirit of prophecy." Craig Koester explains that the latter expression indicates that "God's Spirit communicates the prophecy."[38] Inasmuch as believers witness to Jesus, then, they are prophets. The Spirit of God works through them to enable them to testify to Jesus. Here it is important to underscore that, according to the Apocalypse, Jesus himself is the witness par excellence; he is "the faithful and true *witness*" (Rev. 3:14). As we have already seen above, the Apocalypse bears evidence of the conviction that believers somehow participate in Christ (Rev. 1:9; 3:21). It would seem, then, that believers also share a role in testifying or witnessing to Christ, which is understood as having a prophetic dimension.

In Revelation 11, we read about the future age, which will involve "rewarding your servants, the prophets and saints and all who fear your name" (Rev. 11:18). The passage could be read as indicating that all of God's servants—that is, all the faithful in Christ—are in some way "prophets." That bearing testimony to Jesus is identified with the spirit of prophecy in Revelation 19 is strongly suggestive of this reading.[39]

In the New Testament, then, believers share in Christ's royal, priestly, and prophetic roles. In patristic sources, this relates in concrete ways to the Christian life. For example, commenting on Paul's teaching that Christ has "anointed" believers and given them the Spirit (2 Cor. 1:21–22), John Chrysostom observes that the Spirit was given in the Old Testament, "making at once prophets and priests and kings, for in old times these three sorts were anointed." He then applies this to believers:

> For we are both to enjoy a kingdom and are made priests by offering our bodies for a sacrifice—for, he says, "present your members a living sacrifice unto God" (Rom. 12:1)—and additionally we are constituted prophets too, for what "eye has not seen, nor ear heard" (1 Cor. 2:9) has been revealed to us. And in another way too we become kings, if we have the mind to get dominion over our unruly thoughts.[40]

First, Christians are priests inasmuch as they make themselves a spiritual sacrifice. Second, they are prophets since to them has been revealed divine truths. Finally, they are kings by overcoming sinful tendencies.

38. Koester, *Revelation*, 732.

39. See Beale, *Book of Revelation*, 616–17.

40. John Chrysostom, *Homilies on Second Corinthians* 3 (at 2 Cor. 3:21–22); adapted from *NPNF*[1] 12:290.

This sharing in Christ's threefold mission, I would suggest, is crucial for advancing our understanding of the sacrament of anointing of the sick. This sacrament is not merely about "strengthening" in the sense of overcoming difficulties, nor should it be understood merely as preparation for death. Rather, the sacrament of anointing involves nothing less than conformity to the crucified and risen Lord, who is king, priest, and prophet.

10

Anointing of the Sick and Participation in Christ's Threefold Mission

A Biblical Reframing of the Sacrament's Effects

> The Anointing of the Sick should not be held to be almost "a minor sacrament" when compared to the others.
>
> —Pope Benedict XVI[1]

> *The Anointing of the Sick completes our conformity to the death and Resurrection of Christ*, just as Baptism began it. *It completes the holy anointings that mark the whole Christian life.*
>
> —*Catechism of the Catholic Church* 1523 (emphasis added)

We have seen that the New Testament indicates that not only is Jesus "Christ," but believers are also "anointed" in him. This involves sharing in Christ's royal, priestly, and prophetic identity. Moreover, the New Testament writers are clear

1. Benedict XVI, Message of the Holy Father on the Occasion of the Twentieth World Day of the Sick (February 11, 2012), §3, https://www.vatican.va/content/benedict-xvi/en/messages/sick/documents/hf_ben-xvi_mes_20111120_world-day-of-the-sick-2012.html.

that those who are "in Christ" enter into life in him not only by faith (Rom. 3:23–26; Gal. 3:26; Eph. 2:8–10) but also through baptism (Rom. 6:3–4; Gal. 3:25–28; Col. 2:11–12) and eucharist (1 Cor. 10:16–17). Union with Christ, then, has what we might call a "sacramental" dimension; that is, participation in Christ is bound up with practices that Christian tradition would later call "sacraments." Of course, for our purposes it is important to recognize that Christians in both the West and the East came to identify the anointing of the sick described by James 5 as one of these sacraments.

Catholic teaching maintains that all of the sacraments involve not only "union" with Christ but the grace to be—as Paul teaches—"conformed to the image of [God's] Son" (Rom. 8:29). Here let us consider an important paragraph about the sacraments from the *Catechism of the Catholic Church*:

> "Sacramental grace" is the grace of the Holy Spirit, given by Christ and proper to each sacrament. The Spirit heals and transforms those who receive him by *conforming* them to the Son of God. The fruit of the sacramental life is that the Spirit of adoption makes the faithful *partakers in the divine nature* [2 Pet. 1:4] by uniting them in a living union with the only Son, the Savior.[2]

Believers are "healed" and "transformed" in the sacraments through the Spirit's work of "conforming" believers to Christ. The sacraments, then, unite believers to the "Savior," who is active in the sacraments. This conviction reflects the teaching of Scripture. We read in 1 Peter that "baptism . . . now *saves* you" (1 Pet. 3:21). Of course, 1 Peter would not deny that Christ is the "Savior." The author goes on to affirm that baptism effects salvation "through the resurrection of Jesus Christ" (1 Pet. 3:21). Baptism can be said to "save" because the risen Christ is working in the sacraments through the Spirit, uniting himself to believers.[3]

The section from the *Catechism* quoted above also insists that believers are made, in the words of 2 Peter 1:4, "partakers in the divine nature." Salvation is conformity to Christ—and this involves not only sharing in his perfected humanity but sharing also in his divinity. Christian tradition therefore views

2. *CCC* 1129 (emphasis added on "conforming").

3. A detailed explanation of the way the sacraments save through "instrumental causality" cannot be provided here. Suffice it to say, the sacraments "save" because it is Christ who works through them. See Reginald M. Lynch, *The Cleansing of the Heart: The Sacraments as Instrumental Causes in the Thomistic Tradition*, Thomistic Ressourcement Series 9 (Washington, DC: Catholic University of America Press, 2017).

salvation not only as deliverance from hell but as "divinization" or *theosis*. For example, Irenaeus (d. AD 202) writes that Jesus "became what we are, that he might bring us to be even what he is."[4] Ben Blackwell helpfully characterizes this ancient Christian conviction as *christosis*, which emphasizes that believers are "divinized," but only through participation *in Christ*.[5]

Finally, notice that the quotation from the *Catechism* above maintains that there is a grace "proper to each sacrament." The question we must explore here, then, is this: In what specific way does the sacrament of anointing of the sick conform believers to Christ? I would suggest that we take our cue from the Second Vatican Council's teaching on this sacrament, which, as we saw in chapter 2, represents a genuine development of doctrine.

When it comes to explaining anointing of the sick, the council does something no previous magisterial source has ever done—it explains the sacrament's effects in terms of believers' participation in Christ's suffering and death. The council cites the teaching of 1 Peter: "Rejoice insofar as *you share in the sufferings of Christ*, so that at the revelation of his glory you may also rejoice" (1 Pet. 4:13).[6] It also cites 2 Timothy: "*If we died with him*, we also *live with him*" (2 Tim. 2:11).[7] Through the sacrament of anointing, the sick can be said to offer themselves in Christ, "uniting themselves to the passion and death of Christ."[8] Church teaching, therefore, maintains that the sacrament of anointing enables believers to see their suffering as "a participation in the saving work of Jesus."[9]

4. Irenaeus, *Against Heresies* 5.preface.1. Translation from Ben C. Blackwell, *Christosis: Engaging Paul's Soteriology with His Patristic Interpreters* (Grand Rapids: Eerdmans, 2016), 48n60.

5. See Blackwell, *Christosis*, 266: "As a relatively new term christosis . . . allows us to focus on the christo-form nature of Pauline soteriology."

6. Second Vatican Council, *Lumen gentium* (The Light of the Nations), Dogmatic Constitution on the Church (November 21, 1964), §11; translation from Austin Flannery, *Vatican Council II: The Basic Sixteen Documents, Constitutions, Decrees, Declarations*, rev. ed. (Collegeville, MN: Liturgical Press, 2014), 16.

7. Second Vatican Council, *Lumen gentium* §11.

8. Second Vatican Council, *Lumen gentium* §11. This is not to say that private theologians had not already begun to think this way. See Bernard Leeming, *Principles of Sacramental Theology* (London: Longmans, Green, 1956), 371; Émile Mersch, *The Theology of the Mystical Body*, trans. Cyril Vollert (London: Herder, 1952), 570–71. I here spare the reader the less exciting "theologianology" behind the development of the magisterium's teaching and focus instead on what is more important—namely, the way the Church's official teaching has developed out of exegesis of Scripture.

9. CCC 1521. For a recent treatment, see Roger W. Nutt, *To Die Is Gain: A Theological (re-)Introduction to the Sacrament of Anointing of the Sick for Clergy, Laity, Caregivers, and Everyone Else* (Steubenville, OH: Emmaus Academic, 2022), 119–26.

Additionally, more recent Church teaching has especially emphasized the way the sacrament of anointing of the sick must be viewed in continuity with the anointings received in the sacraments of baptism and confirmation. The *Catechism* explains,

> *The Anointing of the Sick completes our conformity to the death and Resurrection of Christ*, just as Baptism began it. *It completes the holy anointings that mark the whole Christian life*: that of Baptism which sealed the new life in us, and that of Confirmation which strengthened us for the combat of this life.[10]

The sacraments are not to be understood atomistically. Anointing of the sick not only effects "conformity" to the crucified Lord, but it does so in a way that somehow "completes" what begins at baptism. Something similar is taught by the Council of Trent, which insists that the sacrament of unction is "considered by the Fathers *the consummation* [*consummativum*] . . . *of the whole Christian life*."[11] Anointing of the sick brings to "consummation" the life in Christ that begins in baptism. But how does anointing of the sick go beyond and complete what happens in baptism? This is the question this chapter seeks to address. What will be suggested here is that the best way to understand the sacrament of anointing's effects is to view it through the lens of participation in Christ's priestly, royal, and prophetic mission, something which the believer is first initiated into through baptism.

Anointed to Share in Christ's Priestly Sacrifice

We have noted that in Scripture, anointing is associated with priestly consecration. Since Christ is presented as the messianic—"anointed"—priest, it is natural to ask whether the sacrament of anointing has a connection to this aspect of Jesus's mission. Indeed, over the course of the last century or so, recent theological work on anointing of the sick has begun emphasizing the way the sacrament involves participation in Christ's priestly work.[12] This

10. *CCC* 1523 (emphasis added).

11. Council of Trent, Session 14, Doctrine on the Sacrament of Extreme Unction, (foreword). Translation from Heinrich Denzinger, *Compendium of Creeds, Definitions, and Declarations on Matters of Faith and Morals*, ed. Peter Hünermann, 43rd ed. (San Francisco: Ignatius, 2012), 408 (§1694).

12. See, e.g., J. Augustine DiNoia and Joseph Fox, "Priestly Dimensions of the Sacrament of Anointing of the Sick," *The Priest* 62 (2006): 10–13.

has been confirmed by aspects of official Catholic magisterial teaching. One recent curial source even goes so far as to insist that "anointing represents a deeper, priestly self-offering which joins the person intimately with the final offering of Jesus on the Cross."[13]

Participation in Christ's Sacrificial Suffering

We have already seen that Scripture indicates that believers have a participation in Christ's priesthood. The Second Vatican Council, which draws together many ideas and biblical texts we examined in the previous chapter, emphasizes this idea:

> Christ the Lord, high priest taken from the midst of humanity (see Heb. 5:1–5), made the new people "a kingdom of priests to God, his Father" (Rev. 1:6; see 5:9–10). The baptized, by regeneration and *the anointing of the Holy Spirit*, are *consecrated* to be a spiritual house and a holy priesthood, that through all their Christian activities they may offer spiritual sacrifices (cf. 1 Pet. 2:4–10). . . . Therefore all the disciples of Christ . . . should present themselves as a sacrifice, living, holy and pleasing to God (see Rom. 12:1).[14]

The council affirms that Christ is the "high priest," referencing Hebrews 5. Through his high priesthood, Christ makes the whole people of God "a kingdom of *priests*," an idea drawn from 1 Peter and the book of Revelation.

Note, though, that the council emphasizes that participation in Christ's priesthood is bound up with baptism. The passage above refers not simply to "the faithful" but to the "baptized." The anointing received at baptism is said to "consecrate" believers. That this anointing is *priestly* in character is further emphasized in that this consecration is interpreted in light of 1 Peter 2: the faithful are made a temple ("a spiritual house") and a "holy priesthood" (1 Pet. 2:5, 7). The passage goes on, then, to explain that the baptized are therefore called to, in the words of Paul, present themselves as a "living sacrifice" to God (Rom. 12:1).

13. Apostolic Penitentiary, Address of Major Penitentiary, Cardinal J. Francis Stafford, to the Annual General Conference of the Society for Catholic Liturgy, Mary Immaculate Center, Northampton, PA (September 21, 2006), https://www.vatican.va/roman_curia/tribunals/apost_penit/documents/rc_trib_appen_doc_20060921_stafford-reconciliation_en.html.

14. Second Vatican Council, *Lumen gentium* §10. Slightly adapted from Flannery, *Vatican Council II*, 14.

But how does this teaching about baptism relate to the sacrament of anointing of the sick? As we have seen, according to the Second Vatican Council, anointing of the sick enables believers to share in Christ's passion. To make this point, the council references Romans 8: "[We are] heirs of God and fellow heirs with Christ, if indeed we suffer together with him so that we may also be glorified together with him" (Rom. 8:17). Paul emphasizes that though believers share in Christ's inheritance, a contingency is involved with this: "if indeed we *suffer together with him*" (Rom. 8:17). How can Paul say such a thing when he affirms elsewhere that salvation is a "gift" by grace and not based on human works (Rom. 11:6; Eph. 2:8)? Here, because it is so often misrepresented, a brief explanation of Catholic soteriology is needed.

Notwithstanding claims to the contrary made by anti-Catholic polemicists, it should be emphasized that Catholic teaching maintains that the initial gift of grace received by the believer is entirely unmerited and in no way based on human works.[15] The gratuitous nature of salvation is especially emphasized through the Catholic practice of infant baptism.[16]

At the same time, Catholic teaching underscores the effect of grace. Once it is received, grace brings union with Christ so that Christ truly lives in the believer. As Paul writes, "It is no longer I who live, but Christ who lives in me" (Gal. 2:20). The believer's works are therefore no longer simply his or her own. The Christian's good works are also truly *Christ's*. For Catholic theology, the implications of this are immense. Good works cannot bring about the initial gift of salvation. Still, the value of works done by the person united to Christ must be understood to be of a radically different nature than those done apart from Christ. To say the works done by one united to Christ are not salvific would be to insist that Christ's *own* works are not salvific—a claim that contradicts Paul's teaching.[17] Good works cannot earn the initial gift of grace. Nevertheless, good works done in Christ must be recognized as performed *with him*. Paul therefore teaches: "*Work out your own salvation* with fear and trembling, *for God is working within you*" (Phil. 2:12–13). For

15. See, e.g., Council of Trent, *Decree on Justification*, Chapter 8: "We are said to be justified gratuitously because nothing that precedes justification, neither faith nor works, merits the grace of justification; for 'if it is by grace, it is no longer on the basis of works; otherwise (as the same apostle says), grace would no longer be grace' (Rom 11:6)." Translation from Denzinger, *Compendium of Creeds*, 378.

16. See CCC 1250.

17. See Michael P. Barber, "A Catholic Perspective," in *Four Views on the Role of Works at the Final Judgment*, ed. Alan Stanley (Grand Rapids: Zondervan, 2013), 161–84, especially 180–81.

those in Christ, divine and human agency are not competitive. It is not as if the believer's works somehow threaten to displace the priority or necessity of grace. Rather, by grace, human agency is "transformed."[18]

But why does Paul emphasize the role of *suffering* in Romans 8? And how does suffering relate to sharing in Christ's priestly role? First, that suffering has redemptive value and can be offered up for others is taught in the scriptures. Above all, it is emphasized in Isaiah's description of the Suffering Servant:

> He has borne our infirmities
>   and carried our diseases,
> yet we regarded him as stricken,
>   struck down by God and afflicted.
> But he was wounded for our transgressions,
>   crushed for our iniquities.
> Upon him was the punishment that made us whole,
>   and by his stripes we are healed. (Isa. 53:4–5)

The Servant's suffering effects the healing of *others* and can be offered for their transgressions. The passage goes on to speak of the Servant as a "guilt offering" (Isa. 53:10), one of the types of sacrifice described by the book of Leviticus (Lev. 5:14–6:7).[19] Suffering is thus both redemptive (or atoning) *and* sacrificial. In the New Testament, Isaiah's prophecy is recognized as fulfilled in Christ. For example, Isaiah 53 is widely acknowledged as informing Paul's statement in Romans 4:25 that Christ was "put to death for our trespasses."[20]

It is necessary to add that, for Paul, Christ's suffering is redemptive not simply because Christ endured suffering but because he did so *out of love*: "I live by faith in the Son of God, *who loved me and gave himself for me*" (Gal.

18. See Brant Pitre, Michael P. Barber, and John A. Kincaid, *Paul, a New Covenant Jew: Rethinking Pauline Theology* (Grand Rapids: Eerdmans, 2019), 166–69.

19. Many insist that the passage does not evoke sacrificial imagery. See, e.g., Bernd Janowski, "He Bore Our Sins: Isaiah 53 and the Drama of Taking Another's Place," in *The Suffering Servant: Isaiah 53 in Jewish and Christian Sources*, ed. Bernd Janowski and Peter Stuhlmacher, trans. Daniel P. Bailey (Grand Rapids: Eerdmans, 2004), 48–74. While I do not concur with all of his conclusions, I must agree with Klaus Baltzer that "it is impossible to overlook the fact that *'asham* as 'guilt offering' is a technical term for a special form of sacrifice" (*Deutero-Isaiah*, trans. Margaret Kohl, Hermeneia [Minneapolis: Fortress, 2001], 421). Moreover, the use of the passage in Matt. 26:28 makes best sense as a cultic reading of the passage (see above, pp. 90–92). For more, see Hans Moscicke, *The New Day of Atonement: A Matthean Typology*, WUNT 2/517 (Tübingen: Mohr Siebeck, 2020), 193–96.

20. See, e.g., Robert Jewett, *Romans*, Hermeneia (Minneapolis: Fortress, 2007), 342–43, who speaks of the "consensus" on the influence of Isa. 53 in early Christianity.

2:20). Christ's self-giving is ultimately an expression of divine love (Rom. 5:8). Ephesians helps fill out the Pauline message: "Be imitators of God, as beloved children, and *walk in love just as Christ loved us* and gave himself for our sake, an offering and a *sweet-smelling sacrifice* to God" (Eph. 5:1–2). Christ's suffering and death entails the perfect act of love, which is presented to the Father as a "sacrifice." Christ transforms suffering into sacrifice by offering it up as an expression of love.

Catholic tradition recognizes that believers are called into this mystery of suffering, not because God desires to see human beings suffer, but because the faithful are to be conformed to Christ in love. This is the heart of a soteriology rooted in *theosis*. Believers are to love precisely because God is love. This is spelled out in 1 John:

> Whoever does not love does not know God, *for God is love*. The love of God was revealed among us in this way: God sent his only begotten Son into the world in order that we might live through him. In this is love, not that we have loved God but that he loved us and sent his Son to be the atoning sacrifice for our sins. Beloved, since God loved us in this way, we also ought to love one another. . . . If we love one another, God remains in us, and his love is perfected in us. (1 John 4:8–11, 12)

The point here is that true love is not human love, but God's love. Christ reveals this true divine love on the cross. In offering himself, he is the "atoning sacrifice" (*hilasmos*; 1 John 4:10). The language of "atonement" evokes the imagery of paying a "ransom" or debt.[21] But the debt that must be repaid is, in the final analysis, a debt of love. Christ pays that debt, not so that believers do not have to, but to show what they must learn. In loving others, believers make evident that God "remains" or "dwells" (*menei*) within them. The purpose of God's love thereby reaches its goal—it is "perfected" (*teteleiōmenē*)—as it transforms believers into God-like lovers (1 John 4:12). Christ's suffering is redemptive because it expresses divine love for us, revealing the lengths to which he will go to save us. Sherri Brown and Francis Moloney beautifully sum up the message here: "God's love is witnessed by the gift of the atoning sacrifice of his Son and is perfected in the ongoing mutual indwelling love of the community."[22]

21. See Pitre, Barber, and Kincaid, *Paul, a New Covenant Jew*, 146–52.

22. Sherri Brown and Francis J. Moloney, *Interpreting the Gospel and Letters of John: An Introduction* (Grand Rapids: Eerdmans, 2017), 326.

We are now in a better place to understand Paul's teaching in Romans 8. Believers are "heirs of God" (Rom. 8:17) inasmuch as they are to be "conformed to the image of his Son" (Rom. 8:29) by suffering. This is why the apostle says that believers are heirs "if indeed we suffer with him" (Rom. 8:17).

But how is suffering related to priestly imagery? Those in Christ are called to become self-sacrificial lovers in imitation of Christ (Eph. 5:1–2) because salvation is *more* than mere deliverance *from* sin. Rather, salvation is nothing less than learning to love like Christ the Lord. Paul speaks of Christ's death in terms of *kenosis*—"self-emptying" (see Phil. 2:7). Learning this kind of love is what constitutes salvation. As Jesus explains: "For whoever would save his life will lose it, but *whoever loses his life for my sake will find it*" (Matt. 16:25). Salvation is becoming like Christ, including learning to suffer out of love as he did. We can therefore speak of *theosis* through *kenosis*.[23]

All of this illuminates the Church's theology of anointing of the sick. In explaining the sacrament, the Second Vatican Council cites a passage from 1 Peter: "But rejoice insofar as you share in the sufferings of Christ, so that at the revelation of his glory you may also rejoice" (1 Pet. 4:13). In the same epistle, we are told: "You may have to suffer various trials, so that *the genuineness of your faith*, more precious than gold which though perishable *is tested by fire*" (1 Pet. 1:6–7). Faithfulness is tested by affliction; suffering has a kind of purging effect. We therefore go on to read in 1 Peter 4: "Whoever has suffered in the flesh has finished with sin" (4:1). Paul also points to the perfective nature of suffering when he writes, "Suffering produces endurance" (Rom. 5:3). The sacrament is thus intended to enable the believer to participate in Christ's sufferings through their affliction.

Sacrificial Suffering for the Sake of Christ's Body

Participation in Christ's sufferings should not be viewed as merely an individualistic reality. For Paul, suffering in Christ has an ecclesial dimension. Emphasizing that the Church is the body of Christ and believers are individual "members" of it, Paul insists: "If one member suffers, all suffer together; if one member is honored, all rejoice together" (1 Cor. 12:26). Likewise, "*If we are afflicted, it is for your comfort and salvation. . . .* As *you share in our*

23. I am especially indebted here to Khaled Anatolios, *Deification through the Cross: An Eastern Christian Theology of Salvation* (Grand Rapids: Eerdmans, 2020); Michael J. Gorman, *Inhabiting the Cruciform God: Kenosis, Justification, and Theosis in Paul's Narrative Soteriology* (Grand Rapids: Eerdmans, 2009).

sufferings, you will also share in our comfort" (2 Cor. 1:6–7). Because the body of Christ is united, what happens to one member affects the others. This conviction that suffering in Christ involves an ecclesial aspect underlies the Catholic understanding of anointing of the sick. *Pastoral Care of the Sick* explains, "The sacrament of anointing effectively expresses the share that each one has in the sufferings of others."[24] This needs to be further unpacked.

The ecclesial aspect of suffering in Christ is especially highlighted in Colossians. Here we read: "Now I rejoice in my sufferings for you, and *I fill up in my flesh what is lacking of the afflictions of Christ for his body, which is the church*" (Col. 1:24). How can Paul speak of something "lacking" in Christ's afflictions? Are we being told that Jesus's suffering on the cross was somehow inadequate? In his commentary on Colossians, Thomas Aquinas forcefully rejects such a reading. He says that the verse must not be read as suggesting Christ's passion "was not sufficient for our redemption, and that the sufferings of the saints were added to complete it."[25] Instead, Aquinas goes on to explain that what is "lacking" is found not in Christ's personal sufferings but only in the ecclesial body's participation in Christ's redemptive work.

Aquinas writes, "What was lacking was that just as Christ had suffered in his own body, so he should also suffer in Paul, his member, and in similar ways in others."[26] The key idea, then, is that each member contributes to the growth of the whole body in their own suffering. Suffering in Christ is not meaningless or pointless. By virtue of union with the body of Christ, believers suffer with Christ *for others*, especially the other members of the body. Paul therefore says that his sufferings are "for your sake" (Col. 1:24).[27]

This brings us back to anointing of the sick. In its explanation of this sacrament, the Second Vatican Council explicitly cites Colossians 1:24.[28] Christians

24. *Pastoral Care of the Sick: Rites of Anointing and Viaticum* (Totowa, NJ: Catholic Book Publishing, 1983), 82 (§98).

25. Thomas Aquinas, *Commentary on Colossians* §61, in Thomas Aquinas, *Commentary on the Letters of Saint Paul to the Philippians, Colossians, Thessalonians, Timothy, Titus, and Philemon*, ed. John Mortensen and Enrique Alarcón, Latin/English Edition of the Works of St. Thomas Aquinas 40 (Lander, WY: The Aquinas Institute for the Study of Sacred Doctrine, 2012), 96.

26. Aquinas, *Commentary on Colossians* §61, in Aquinas, *Commentary on the Letters of Saint Paul*, 96.

27. For further discussion by a non-Catholic scholar, see M. David Litwa, *We Are Being Transformed: Deification in Paul's Soteriology* (Berlin: De Gruyter, 2012), 215–16.

28. Second Vatican Council, *Lumen gentium* §11, in Flannery, *Vatican Council II*, 16.

already have a share in Christ's death and resurrection through baptism. In the sacrament of anointing of the sick, however, they are empowered to offer their suffering in union with Christ's. As we have seen, Paul exhorts the Romans to "present your *bodies* as a living *sacrifice* . . . which is your reasonable worship" (Rom. 12:1). Believers offer their *bodies* (plural) as a "living sacrifice" (singular) because, in Christ, they are *in communion with one another* as one offering.[29] Since Christ's sacrificial suffering is redemptive and believers participate in that one offering, their suffering is also redemptive—though only through union with Christ. Anointing of the sick is seen as a way of entering into the mystery of participation in Christ's death, which begins at baptism. In the eucharist, the faithful also unite their suffering to that of Christ's.[30] In his or her sickness, the believer is more fully conformed to Christ crucified by being anointed.

As we have seen, suffering is closely connected to sin in the scriptures. The Suffering Servant suffers—including bearing "infirmities" and carrying "our diseases" (Isa. 53:4)—in a way that is redemptive for others. We are told, "Upon him was the punishment that made us whole . . . by his stripes we are healed" (Isa. 53:5). Christian faith recognizes that this is fulfilled in the person of Christ. In his important study on soteriology in Eastern Christian traditions, Khaled Anatolios writes about how the Gospel of Matthew portrays Jesus as the Suffering Servant, explaining: "Jesus heals by taking upon himself our infirmities and diseases ([Matt.] 8:17). . . . Jesus heals people from the consequences of sin by taking these consequences upon himself."[31] For Anatolios, this aspect of Jesus's redemptive mission is expressed in the baptism of Jesus. He shows that the evangelists not only link John the Baptist's baptism with repentance and forgiveness of sins (Matt. 3:6, 11; Mark 1:4; Luke 3:3; cf. Acts 13:24), they also connect Jesus's baptism with his death (Mark 10:38; Luke 12:50; cf. Mark 1:10–11 with Mark 15:38–39). This makes it possible, then, to view Jesus's baptism in terms of his acceptance of death on behalf of humanity's sin. Jesus, though sinless himself (2 Cor. 5:21; Heb. 4:15), thus serves as the perfect representative of contrition for sin. There is no glorification apart from contrition (repentance) and suffering—including suffering *for others* out

29. See, e.g., Colin D. Miller, *The Practice of the Body of Christ: Human Agency in Pauline Theology after MacIntyre* (Eugene, OR: Pickwick, 2014), 174.

30. Second Vatican Council, *Lumen gentium* §34.

31. Anatolios, *Deification through the Cross*, 157.

of love. Anatolios thus speaks beautifully of salvation in Christ in terms of "doxological contrition."[32]

Yet, as we have seen, Christians are invited to participate in Christ's work. Catholic theology understands, then, that by being anointed the sick person is empowered to participate in Christ's redemptive sacrificial suffering. Christ dies for our sins, but believers share in that work with him. Pope John Paul II, therefore, writes that anointing of the sick "is a sign of definitive conversion to the Lord and of total acceptance of suffering and death as penance for sins."[33] This helps to further illuminate the Church's teaching that anointing of the sick is not only the completion of sacramental anointings but also the "consummation . . . of penance."[34]

In this sense, Vatican II can speak of how the sick person who receives anointing of the sick is enabled to "contribute to the good of the people of God by freely uniting themselves to the passion and death of Christ (see Rom. 8:17; Col. 1:24; 2 Tim. 2:11–12; 1 Pet. 4:13)."[35] They do so by offering their suffering in union with Christ so that "it becomes a participation in the saving work of Jesus."[36] The sick, precisely in their suffering, are truly empowered to contribute to the Church's mission. Benedict XVI writes, "The Anointing of the Sick, for its part, unites the sick with Christ's self-offering for the salvation of all, so that they too, within the mystery of the communion of saints, can participate in the redemption of the world."[37]

Not surprisingly, then, the Church's teaching about anointing of the sick recalls the *priestly* nature of the believer's participation in Christ, first established at baptism. For example, Church teaching maintains that, through anointing of the sick, the sick person is "*consecrated* to bear fruit by configuration to the Savior's redemptive Passion."[38] The language here of "consecration" evokes the Church's teaching on baptism, which we quoted above. This

32. See especially Anatolios, *Deification through the Cross*, 140–66.

33. John Paul II, *Reconciliatio et penitentia* (Reconciliation and Penance), Apostolic Exhortation on Reconciliation and Penance in the Mission of the Church Today (December 2, 1984), §27.

34. Council of Trent, Session 14, Doctrine on the Sacrament of Extreme Unction, Foreword, in Denzinger, *Compendium of Creeds*, 408 (§1694).

35. Second Vatican Council, *Lumen gentium* §11, in Flannery, *Vatican Council II*, 16.

36. *CCC* 1521.

37. Benedict XVI, *Sacramentum Caritatis* (The Sacrament of Charity), Post-synodal Apostolic Exhortation on the Eucharist as the Source and Summit of the Church's Life and Mission (February 22, 2007), §22. Quoted from Pope Benedict XVI, *The Sacrament of Charity* (Ijamsville, MD: The Word Among Us Press, 2007), 35.

38. *CCC* 1521 (emphasis added).

teaching uses the terminology of "consecration" directly in connection with the common "priesthood" of the baptized: the baptized are "*consecrated* to be a spiritual house and a holy priesthood" that they may offer "spiritual sacrifices."[39]

That priestly imagery would be used to describe all of this also coheres well with Colossians 1. Just before describing how his sufferings "complete . . . what is lacking in the sufferings of Christ," Paul speaks of how Christ has "reconciled you by his death in his fleshly body, to *present* [*parastēsai*] you *holy* [*hagious*] and *unblemished* [*amōmous*] and irreproachable before him" (Col. 1:22). The language here involves sacrificial imagery. For example, it uses the same verb found in Romans 12, where Paul tells believers to "present" (*parastēsai*) themselves as a "living sacrifice . . . acceptable to God" (Rom. 12:1). Likewise, the language of "holiness" evokes Israel's worship. Finally, believers are said to be "unblemished," the same term used for acceptable sacrifices in the scriptures—sacrificial animals must be "unblemished" (*amōmos*; Exod. 29:1; Lev. 1:3; 4:3; 5:15 LXX). While these terms can be used apart from Israel's liturgical worship, their use together makes an allusion to Israel's sacrificial liturgy difficult to avoid.[40] All of this reinforces the idea that sharing in Christ's affliction involves a *sacrificial* dimension.

To the best of my knowledge, the significance of the sacrificial imagery that surrounds Colossians 1:24 has been ignored in theological treatments of anointing of the sick. Nevertheless, it is worth noting that, in a more general way, theologians have been moving toward a greater appreciation of the way the sacrament of anointing relates to the exercise of the common priesthood received at baptism. For example, in his landmark book on ecclesiology, which heavily influenced magisterial teaching in the twentieth century,[41] the French theologian Émile Mersch not only emphasizes the way anointing of the sick relates to James 5, he writes of how it "unites [the sick] to the dying Christ" and incorporates them into the "sacrifice" of Christ's body.[42] In his 1993 study of the sacrament, Andrew Cuschieri writes, "In the Anointing of the Sick, the sick person is consecrated into *the priesthood of Christ* who was at

39. Second Vatican Council, *Lumen gentium* §10, in Flannery, *Vatican Council II*, 14.
40. See Paul Foster, *Colossians*, BNTC (London: Bloomsbury T&T Clark, 2016), 206–7.
41. See Amanda C. Osheim, "The Christian Faithful," in *The Cambridge Companion to Vatican II*, ed. Richard R. Gaillardetz (Cambridge: Cambridge University Press, 2020), 214–15.
42. Mersch, *Theology of the Mystical Body*, 571.

once victim and priest."[43] Likewise, in a 2006 article, Augustine DiNoia and Joseph Fox write that the sacrament involves "an *act of worship* in which the recipient of the sacrament is joined to the *priestly* self-offering of Christ."[44]

The Res et Sacramentum *of Anointing and Priestly Imagery*

Focusing on the sacrament's relationship to the believer's share in Christ's priesthood, which is first realized in baptism, can also help clarify another aspect of the sacrament that has been seen as underdeveloped in theological reflection—namely, the dimension of the sacrament known as its *res et sacramentum*. Here some background explanation in sacramental theology is necessary.[45]

Since at least the time of Augustine, there has been a recognition that sacraments involve multiple dimensions. First, there is the visible dimension of the sacrament, which symbolically points beyond itself. This is known as the *sacramentum tantum*, "the (visible) sign only." To give an example, in baptism, the visible sign is the water, which symbolizes spiritual washing. Sacraments, however, involve not only visible realities but also spiritual effects. This conviction is expressed by Augustine, who writes, "A sacrament is one thing, quite another is the effect [*virtus*] of the sacrament."[46] In baptism, the spiritual reality is forgiveness of sins and new life in union with Christ and his body.

A pastoral crisis, however, caused Augustine to realize that yet another aspect of sacraments must be recognized. A group known as the Donatists went into schism, and Augustine reflected on what bringing them back would entail. He understood that the Donatists who returned to the Church should not be rebaptized. After all, Scripture maintains that there is "one baptism" (Eph. 4:5). Moreover, the Council of Constantinople (381) taught that heretics such

43. Andrew Cuschieri, *Anointing of the Sick: A Theological and Canonical Study* (Lanham, MD: University Press of America, 1993), 76 (emphasis added).

44. DiNoia and Fox, "Priestly Dimensions," 13 (emphasis added).

45. For a fuller account of what follows, see Lawrence Feingold, *Touched by Christ: The Sacramental Economy* (Steubenville, OH: Emmaus Academic, 2021), 225–305. Feingold's treatment, which shapes the one presented here, is especially commendable due to his careful engagement with the scriptural bases of sacramental theology. See also P. F. Palmer, "The Theology of the *Res et Sacramentum* with Particular Emphasis on Its Application to Penance," in *Readings in Sacramental Theology*, ed. C. Stephen Sullivan (Englewood Cliffs, NJ: Prentice Hall, 1964), 104–23.

46. Augustine, *Tractates on John* 26.11 (John 6:41–59); slightly adapted from Augustine, *Homilies on the Gospel of John 1–40*, trans. Edmund Hill, WSA III/12 (Hyde Park, NY: New City Press, 2009), 458.

as the Arians were not to be rebaptized if they joined the Church.[47] Despite their sin of schism, then, Augustine came to hold that the Donatists did not entirely lose what baptism imparts. He therefore developed the idea, which was already present in earlier patristic sources, that baptism imprints a spiritual "seal" or "character" on the soul.[48] The imagery is taken in part from biblical passages that speak of the believer being "sealed" by the Spirit (2 Cor. 1:22; Eph. 1:13; 4:30). Even if one commits mortal sin (1 John 5:15–16)—that is, a grave sin that causes the believer to be "severed" from Christ and so be in a state in which they have "fallen away from grace" (Gal. 5:4)—Augustine remained convinced that the seal of baptism remains. To explain this, he likens the spiritual seal imparted in baptism to a tattoo received by soldiers in an army that marks their affiliation to their king. Even should a soldier desert in warfare, he would not lose the mark.

Moreover, if a deserting soldier were granted forgiveness by the king and rejoined his army, the soldier would not receive a second tattoo. Augustine writes: "From the fact that the sacrament is not readministered to a deserter when he returns, it is clear that he could not have lost it when he withdrew."[49] Augustine therefore held that a new sealing in baptism is not necessary. Through the baptismal seal, grace can be reactivated in the soul of one who falls away. Theologians have come to refer to this dynamic as *reviviscence* or "revivification"—the believer returns to life. This occurs through the reality and hidden sign—the *res et sacramentum*—of the baptismal seal, which is an abiding reality that is never lost.

Later theologians would therefore add a third dimension to the sacraments. In addition to the *sacramentum tantum* (the visible sign only) and the *res tantum* (the hidden reality only), a further concept emerged: the *res et sacramentum*. This third aspect of the sacraments refers to the "(hidden) reality and sign" in each sacrament. According to official magisterial teaching, all seven sacraments involve all three elements: (1) a *sacramentum tantum*, (2) a *res et sacramentum*, and (3) a *res tantum*.[50] For many of the sacraments these are all clearly defined.

47. See Council of Constantinople, Canon 7.

48. Irenaeus, *Against Heresies* 3.17; Clement of Alexandria, *Extracts from the Prophets* 86.

49. From a sermon by Augustine on baptism published in *Miscellanea Agostiniana* (1930), in Augustine, *Commentary on the Lord's Sermon on the Mount with Seventeen Related Sermons*, trans. Denis J. Kavanaugh, FC 11 (Washington, DC: Catholic University of America Press, 1951), 334.

50. See Innocent III, *Cum Marthae circa*, Letter to Archbishop John of Lyon (November 29, 1202); cf. Denzinger, *Compendium of Creeds*, 783.

In baptism, the *res et sacramentum* refers to the baptismal seal imprinted on the soul.[51] In the eucharist, it refers to the body and blood of Christ, which are present under the visible signs of bread and wine (*sacramentum tantum*) and through which believers receive the grace of union to Christ and his sacrifice (*res tantum*). In anointing of the sick, the *sacramentum tantum*—the visible sign—is easily identified with the oil, which symbolizes healing and strengthening through the Spirit. The *res tantum* is also not hard to define: it is the grace of the Spirit symbolized by the oil. But what is the *res et sacramentum* of anointing of the sick? Theologians have disagreed. Exasperated by the discussion, one theologian wrote in 1900 that "one can only guess" what it would be.[52] Much more work has been done on this question, however, since then.

Some have spoken of the *res et sacramentum* of anointing of the sick as an interior strengthening.[53] This, however, seems to confuse the *res tantum* with the *res et sacramentum*. Moreover, it fails to identify an abiding reality that remains even if the sinner is improperly disposed to the sacrament.[54] A more attractive explanation is that anointing of the sick's *res et sacramentum* involves the concept of consecration to the crucified Lord mentioned above. This idea is anchored in the work of previous theologians such as Mersch. The idea would be that the sick person is consecrated to the crucified and risen Christ in their particular illness. Indeed, as we have seen, the *Catechism* explicitly teaches that, in anointing of the sick, the sick person "in a certain way is consecrated to bear fruit by configuration to the Savior's redemptive Passion."[55] Although the *Catechism* does not explicitly identify this effect of the sacrament as its *res et sacramentum*, other theologians have made the connection.[56] For example, Roger Nutt explains: "The anointing with oil in the Sacrament of the Sick is viewed as bestowing a special consecration of the sick person to Christ's Passion (*res et sacramentum*)."[57]

51. See, e.g., Hugh of St. Victor, *On the Sacraments of the Christian Faith* 2.8.7; Peter Lombard, *Sentences* 4.8.7 §§1–2.

52. Alex MacDonald, "Sacramental Causality," *AER* 22, no. 6 (1900): 578.

53. See Felix M. Cappello, *Tractatus Canonico-Moralis de Sacramentis*, vol. 3, 3rd ed. (Taurini: Marietti, 1949), 145.

54. Feingold, *Touched by Christ*, 284.

55. CCC 1521.

56. Feingold (*Touched by Christ*, 284n24) cites not only the *Catechism of the Catholic Church* but also DiNoia and Fox, "Priestly Dimensions"; Palmer, "Theology of the *Res et Sacramentum*," 113.

57. Roger Nutt, *General Principles of Sacramental Theology* (Washington, DC: Catholic University of America Press, 2017), 171.

Lawrence Feingold argues that viewing the *res et sacramentum* of anointing of the sick in terms of a consecration that configures the believer to the crucified Lord is fitting due to the sacrament's use of oil: "An anointing with olive oil is frequently used to consecrate persons and objects in the liturgy."[58] I would go further and point out that, given what we have seen, we can identify here a specific connection to Old Testament *priestly* consecration. This is especially fitting since the New Testament presents Christ's own suffering as a *priestly* sacrificial offering. Moreover, since believers are presented as sharing in that offering in "Christ"—the "Anointed One"—it is significant that when *deadly* suffering threatens them, they are anointed with oil. In anticipation of ending his or her life as Christ did, the believer offers his or her suffering in union with Christ, participating in his redemptive work. Their lives are to end as Christ's did.

This understanding also helps to explain why anointing of the sick, unlike baptism and confirmation, can be repeated. The *res et sacramentum* involves a consecration of the person in danger of death for the duration of the affliction. In this state, the person is especially configured to Christ.[59] It is healing because it involves conformity to Christ. But this *necessarily* entails participation in the mystery of the cross. Physical healing may result, which points beyond itself to both forgiveness of sins—spiritual healing—and the hope of new life in the resurrection of the dead. Yet physical healing is only temporary. Either way, the believer is called into the paschal mystery of Christ, which involves suffering for sins out of love for God and others through anointing—a rite that symbolizes the help and empowerment of the Spirit. And so, anointing of the sick consecrates suffering and turns it into an act of worship in Christ.

Anointed to Share in Christ's Reign over Sin and Death

Yet as we have seen, anointing is also linked to the royal dimension of Christ's mission. Here I believe the Church's teaching can be further developed. The effects attributed to anointing of the sick seem to map nicely onto the concept of participation in Christ's royal rule, a reality that believers are initiated into by baptism.

58. Feingold, *Touched by Christ*, 284.

59. See also Jean-Hervé Nicolas, *Catholic Dogmatic Theology: A Synthesis*, trans. Matthew K. Minerd (Washington, DC: Catholic University of America Press, 2024), 3:628.

Anointed to Share in Christ's Dominion over Sin and Death

We saw in the last chapter that the New Testament presents believers as sharing not only in Christ's priesthood but also in his royal and prophetic mission. Since initiation into participation in Christ is associated with baptism, it is no wonder that this sacrament is understood in Christian tradition as enabling believers to share in these aspects of his mission. Reflecting on baptism, Gregory of Nazianzus (d. AD 390) writes, "We call it . . . *anointing* for it is *priestly* and *royal* as are those who are anointed."[60] The Second Vatican Council therefore teaches that "by Baptism" the faithful are "incorporated into Christ" and "made sharers in their own way in the priestly, prophetic, and kingly office of Christ."[61] Likewise, the *Catechism* affirms, "By Baptism they share in the priesthood of Christ, in his prophetic and royal mission."[62]

In the previous chapter, we saw that the believer's participation in Christ's royal dominion is depicted in the New Testament in various ways. In particular, the faithful's share in Christ's reign is connected to overcoming sin. This is especially emphasized in Romans 5, where Paul explains that while sin and death reigned through Adam's disobedience, those who have received the grace of Christ "reign in life through the one man, Jesus Christ" (Rom. 5:17). Likewise, in Colossians and Ephesians to reign with Christ is to be "saved" and to overcome sin (Eph. 2:1–6; Col. 3:1–5).

That the baptized participate in Christ's kingship has been emphasized in various ways since the Second Vatican Council. For example, John Paul II explicitly links this aspect of the Christian's vocation to overcoming sin:

> Because the lay faithful belong to Christ, Lord and King of the Universe, they share in his kingly mission and are called by him to spread that Kingdom in history. They exercise their kingship as Christians, above all in the spiritual combat in which they seek to overcome in themselves the kingdom of sin (cf. Rom. 6:12).[63]

60. Gregory of Nazianzus, *Oratio* 40.3–4 (PG 36:361C), quoted in CCC 1216 (emphasis original).

61. Second Vatican Council, *Lumen gentium* §31, in Flannery, *Vatican Council II*, 48.

62. CCC 1268.

63. John Paul II, *Christifideles laici* (The Lay Faithful of Christ's People), Post-synodal Apostolic Exhortation on the Lay Faithful in the Church and in the World (December 30, 1988), §14, https://www.vatican.va/content/john-paul-ii/en/apost_exhortations/documents/hf_jp-ii_exh_30121988_christifideles-laici.html.

For John Paul II, following Paul, participation in Christ's royal dominion is understood in terms of "spiritual combat" in which the believer seeks victory over the "kingdom of sin." Anointing of the sick is easily seen as related to this. As we have seen, James explicitly connects anointing the sick with forgiveness of sins.

Specifically, James explains, "Confess your sins to one another" (James 5:16). Because of this, ancient Christians in both the East and the West understood that forgiveness of postbaptismal sins is realized through the sacrament of penance, which involves oral confession of sins.[64] Yet since James indicates that forgiveness of sins is also associated with the prayer that accompanies the anointing of the sick person, the sacrament of anointing is understood to bring about forgiveness of sins in cases where the sacrament of penance is not able to be administered.[65] It is presumed that someone unable to receive the sacrament of penance would do so if he or she were capable of doing so. In cases where the sick person is unconscious, the sacrament of anointing is therefore given to those who "requested it at least implicitly when they were in control of their faculties."[66] It cannot be administered to a nonpracticing Catholic who has persisted in public acts that are contrary to the Church's teaching and has exhibited no desire to return to the faith.[67] The sacrament, then, is closely bound up with repentance and the hope for remission of sins. It is therefore recognized as "completion" of both baptism and penance,[68] sacraments that bring about forgiveness of sins.[69] This is fitting given that the sacrament of

64. On forgiveness of sins through sacramental penance (and confession) in the early Church, see examples in the following: *Didache* 14:1; Origen, *Homilies on Leviticus* 2.4.5; Tertullian, *On Penance* 4.2; Cyprian, *The Lapsed* 28; Basil of Caesarea, *Letter 199* (Canonical Penances), Canon 34; John Chrysostom, *On the Priesthood* 3.5; Council of Florence, Session 8, Bull of Union with the Armenians (November 22, 1439). For a biblical approach to this sacrament, see James B. Prothro, *The Bible and Reconciliation: Confession, Repentance, and Restoration*, CBTS (Grand Rapids: Baker Academic, 2023).

65. *CCC* 1532.

66. *CIC* 1006. See also *Pastoral Care of the Sick: Rites of Anointing and Viaticum* (Totowa, NJ: Catholic Book Publishing, 1983), 22 (§14).

67. See the sources cited and discussion in John C. Kasza, *Understanding Sacramental Healing: Anointing and Viaticum* (Chicago: Hillenbrand Books, 2007), 95–96.

68. On baptism, see *CCC* 1523. On penance, see Council of Trent, Session 14, Doctrine on the Sacrament of Extreme Unction, Foreword, in Denzinger, *Compendium of Creeds*, 408 (§1694).

69. This has long been received as Christian doctrine. On forgiveness of sins in baptism, aside from the teaching of Scripture (such as Acts 2:38), see also *Shepherd of Hermas* 4.3.1; Origen, *Exhortation to Martyrdom* 5.30; First Council of Constantinople (AD 381), *Exposition of the 150 Fathers*; Augustine, *City of God* 13.7; Council of Florence, Session 8, Bull of Union with the Armenians (November 22, 1439).

the sick involves being *anointed*, a reality bound up with royal associations in Scripture. If being anointed involves sharing in Christ's royal reign, anointing is therefore easily seen as effecting participation in Christ's reign over sin.

Anointing and Christ's Rule over Sin's Effects

In addition to bringing about forgiveness of sins, anointing of the sick is also understood as addressing the "remains of sin"—or perhaps better put, the "aftereffects" of sin.[70] The fundamental idea here is that even after one is forgiven of sins, their psychological and physiological consequences do not immediately vanish. To be truly "saved" from sin, one would need to be delivered not only from sin itself but also from its wounds. The aftereffects of sin have therefore been understood to include the following: the inclination to sin (which has a physiological component when the sin involves things such as addictive substances), memories of sin and the illicit pleasures they brought, evil habits, and mental obscurities (that is, inability to think with clarity about what constitutes sin).[71]

As we have seen, sin is inextricably bound up with physical death in the scriptures. It is therefore also appropriate that anointing of the sick is associated with physical restoration. James 5, we have seen, specifically has in mind those who are gravely ill. Yet James describes how the sick person who is anointed and prayed over by the elders will be "saved" (James 5:15). This language is used elsewhere in the New Testament to describe the return to a healthy state (e.g., Luke 8:48). Therefore, not only has the fact that the sacrament of anointing can involve physical healing been explicitly affirmed by Church Doctors such as Aquinas[72] and by ecclesiastical councils,[73] this understanding also continues to be upheld in more recent Church teaching. For example, the *Catechism* maintains that the sacrament can result in physical healing, "if it is conducive to the salvation of [the sick

70. I here use the language employed by Colman E. O'Neill, *Meeting Christ in the Sacraments*, rev. ed. (Staten Island, NY: Alba House, 1991), 279, 288.

71. See especially the summary of different theological opinions found in Stanislaus J. Brzana, *Remains of Sin and Extreme Unction according to Theologians after Trent* (Rome: Catholic Book Agency, 1953), 80–98.

72. Thomas Aquinas, *Summa Contra Gentiles* 4.73.

73. Fourth Lateran Council of 1215, Canon 22: "Sickness of the body may sometimes be the result of sin—as the Lord said to the sick man he had cured, 'Go and sin no more, lest something worse befall you' [John 5:14]." Translation from Norman Tanner, ed., *The Decrees of the Ecumenical Councils*, 2 vols. (Washington, DC: Georgetown University Press, 1990), 1:245 (with minor changes; Tanner incorrectly attributes the verse to John 8).

person's] soul."[74] When such healing occurs, the sacrament makes evident the believer's share in Christ's reign over sin, which includes victory over sickness and death, the aftereffects of sin.

Yet even in cases where physical health is not fully restored, Catholic tradition holds that the sacrament of anointing of the sick also results in lesser forms of nonspiritual healing, including psychological and emotional revitalization.[75] In other words, the sacrament often imparts a sense of peace, strengthening, and courage. These enable the sick person to endure their afflictions faithfully.[76] This dimension of anointing of the sick can be viewed as part of the sacrament's *sacramentum tantum*—that is, the visible dimension of the sacrament that points beyond itself to its invisible effects. It also makes evident the believer's union with Christ, who reigns over sin and overcomes its consequences.

Notably, that the sacrament's capacity to bring about healing is related to Christ's royal rule is emphasized by the rite of anointing of the sick itself. The prayer over the oil asks God, "Make this oil a remedy for all who are anointed with it; heal them in body, in soul, and in spirit, and deliver them from every affliction. We ask this through our Lord Jesus Christ, your son, who lives *and reigns* with you and the Holy Spirit, one God, for ever and ever."[77] Of course, the mention of healing "in soul" could be seen as referring to spiritual healing—that is, forgiveness of sins. However, the prayer clearly wants to emphasize healing in "body" and "deliverance from every affliction," while speaking of Christ's royal *reign*.

Anointed to Share in Christ's Prophetic Mission

What has received less attention is the way anointing of the sick also relates to the believer's share in the prophetic aspect of Christ's mission. This seems to be a major lacuna in the theology of this sacrament. Nevertheless, its

74. CCC 1532. See also Council of Trent, Session 14, Chapter 2.

75. It is important to recall that, in Catholic tradition, emotions—identified more properly as "passions"—pertain to the body and are not, strictly speaking, "spiritual." See Steven J. Jensen, *The Human Person: A Beginner's Thomistic Psychology* (Washington, DC: Catholic University of America Press, 2018), 67.

76. See CCC 1520. In addition, see the Council of Florence, Session 8, Bull of Union with the Armenians (November 22, 1439), which teaches that the effect of the sacrament of unction "is to *cure the mind* and, in so far as it helps the soul, also the body." Translation from Tanner, *Decrees of the Ecumenical Councils*, 1:549.

77. Liturgy of Anointing, Prayer over the Oil, Option A. Taken from *Pastoral Care of the Sick*, 115.

prophetic dimension could be deduced from the sacrament's association with baptism and other clear dimensions of the Church's teaching about it and the role of the sick in the Church.

Anointed to Share in Christ's Prophetic Role

According to the Church's teaching, the baptized participate not only in Christ's royal and priestly offices but also in his prophetic identity. We have already provided patristic support for this view in John Chrysostom, who wrote: "We are constituted prophets too, for what 'eye has not seen, nor ear heard' (1 Cor. 2:9) has been revealed to us."[78] Other sources could also be mentioned. For example, Augustine brings together the anointing of the prophets in the Old Testament and the gift of the Spirit bestowed on believers in baptism:

> Those who believed in him and who were cleansed by the sanctifying power of his baptism have been anointed, not in a limited number as formerly under the Old Law, but all, in addition to prophets, priests, and kings. By the symbolism of this anointing we are admonished as to the sort of people we should be, so that holiness of life may be evident in those upon whom this anointing has been conferred. From the mystery of this anointing, both the word and the name of Christ and of all Christians, that is, of those believing in Christ, have come down to us.[79]

According to Augustine, Christians are anointed by the Spirit in baptism in a way analogous to the anointing received by "prophets, priests, and kings." They can thus be rightly called "Christians." In addition, the Syriac writer Ephrem (d. AD 373) speaks of the oil of anointing in connection with the anointings of Old Testament figures such as Elijah, Christ as the anointed one, and the gift of the Spirit in baptism.[80] We see, then, that the link between baptism, anointing, and prophecy is well established in the Greek, Latin, and Syriac traditions, representing a truly "catholic" perspective.

78. John Chrysostom, *Homilies on Second Corinthians* 3 (at 2 Cor. 3:21–22); adapted from *NPNF*[1] 12:290.

79. Augustine, *The Christian Life* 1; translation from Augustine, *Treatises on Various Subjects*, trans. Mary Sarah Muldowney, FC 16 (Washington, DC: Catholic University of America Press, 1952), 11 (slightly adapted). Elsewhere, Augustine also explains that just as God spoke through the prophets, he now speaks through Christians through "the gift of God," citing Jesus's words to disciples, "It is not you who speak" (Matt. 10:20). Augustine, *Sermon* 2.5.

80. Ephrem, *Hymns on Virginity and on the Symbols of the Lord* 4 and 5. See Kathleen E. McVey, *Ephrem the Syrian: Hymns* (New York: Paulist Press, 1989), 275–86.

Following this, the Second Vatican Council therefore teaches that "by Baptism" the faithful are "incorporated into Christ" and "made sharers in their own way in the priestly, prophetic, and kingly office of Christ."[81] In addition, we are told: "The holy people of God shares also in Christ's prophetic office: it spreads abroad a living witness to him, especially by a life of faith and love." Going on, this is linked to the "anointing" mentioned in 1 John: "The whole body of the faithful who have received an anointing which comes from the holy one (see 1 John 2:20, 27) cannot be mistaken in belief."[82] In this, the faithful's prophetic task is recognized not simply as a participation in Christ—they share in "Christ's prophetic office"—but also corporately as his body.[83]

Yet the faithful also participate in Christ's prophetic mission in the concrete circumstances of their lives. The Second Vatican Council explains that Christ fulfills his prophetic mission "not only through the hierarchy . . . but also through the laity." This is explicitly linked to their role in "witnessing" to Christ: "[Christ] establishes them as witnesses."[84]

Recent popes have further emphasized the prophetic responsibility of the baptized. John Paul II writes: "Through their participation in the *prophetic mission* of Christ . . . the lay faithful are given the ability and responsibility to accept the gospel in faith and to proclaim it in word and deed."[85] Likewise, Pope Francis says, "Each one of us, brothers and sisters, is a prophet. In fact, with Baptism, all of us received *the gift and mission of prophecy*. . . . The prophet is the one who shows Jesus to others, who bears witness to him, who helps live today and build the future according to his designs. Therefore, we are all prophets."[86] Here Pope Francis underscores that it is through baptism

81. Second Vatican Council, *Lumen gentium* §31, in Flannery, *Vatican Council II*, 48 (emphasis added).

82. Second Vatican Council, *Lumen gentium* §12, slightly adapted from Flannery, *Vatican Council II*, 16–17.

83. It should be recognized that the magisterium itself participates in this such that the "sense of the faithful" is not simply the "sense of the laity." See International Theological Commission, Sensus Fidei *in the Life of the Church* (2014), §§76–77. See also Ormond Rush, *The Eyes of Faith: The Sense of the Faithful and the Church's Reception of Revelation* (Washington, DC: Catholic University of America Press, 2009), 246–47.

84. Second Vatican Council, *Lumen gentium* §35, slightly adapted from Flannery, *Vatican Council II*, 52.

85. John Paul II, *Christifideles laici* (The Lay Faithful of Christ's People), Post-synodal Apostolic Exhortation on the Lay Faithful in the Church and in the World (December 30, 1988), §14, https://www.vatican.va/content/john-paul-ii/en/apost_exhortations/documents/hf_jp-ii_exh_30121988_christifideles-laici.html.

86. Francis, Angelus Address, Saint Peter's Square (July 2, 2023), https://www.vatican.va/content/francesco/en/angelus/2023/documents/20230702-angelus.html.

that the faithful are helped by the Holy Spirit, whom we have seen is elsewhere identified in terms of spiritual anointing. Likewise, the prophetic role of believers is expressly connected with bearing "witness" to Jesus.

If the believer exercises a prophetic role because baptism makes them a witness to Christ, it is not difficult to understand how anointing of the sick can be seen as "completing" this aspect of the Christian's mission. The Church teaches that "the role of the sick in the Church is to be a reminder to others of the essential or higher things. By their *witness* the sick show that our mortal life must be redeemed through the mystery of Christ's death and resurrection."[87] Anointing of the sick can be seen as specifically connected to this "witness" of the sick. Through this sacrament, "faith itself is manifested."[88]

Recent papal teaching on the sacrament of anointing stresses that the recipient is called to be a "witness" to Christ. For example, addressing those about to receive the sacrament, John Paul II says, "You strengthen the Church by *the witness of your faith*."[89] Prior to another celebration of the sacrament, the same pope told those who were about to receive anointing, "You have an important role in the Church. . . . *You can proclaim the Gospel* in a very powerful way. Your joy and patience are themselves *silent witnesses* to God's liberating power at work in your lives."[90]

Moreover, when anointing of the sick is administered to a person "in advanced age," the post-anointing prayer explicitly asks that the sick person who is anointed be strengthened by the Spirit, "so that they may give us all an example of patience and joyfully *witness* to the power of your love."[91] All of this emphasizes that the sacrament is specifically intended to—among many other things—empower the sick to be faithful witnesses in their suffering. Furthermore, we might mention that if the person were to experience physical healing, this would be yet another way in which the person would serve as a prophetic witness to the reality of God's power at work in the world. In her study of anointing of the sick, then, Lizette Larson-Miller speaks about the

87. *Pastoral Care of the Sick*, 19 (§3).

88. *Pastoral Care of the Sick*, 21 (§7).

89. John Paul II, "Address of John Paul II at the Ceremony of the Anointing of the Sick," Southwark Cathedral, UK (May 28, 1982), §5, https://www.vatican.va/content/john-paul-ii/en/speeches/1982/may/documents/hf_jp-ii_spe_19820528_cattedrale-southwark.html.

90. John Paul II, "Address of John Paul II to the Sick, the Elderly and the Handicapped," Wellington, NZ (November 23, 1986), §6, https://www.vatican.va/content/john-paul-ii/en/speeches/1986/november/documents/hf_jp-ii_spe_19861123_malati-wellington-nuova-zelanda.html.

91. *Pastoral Care of the Sick*, 118, 131 (Prayer after Anointing, Option D).

"prophetic role of the sick person in our midst" who reminds the community of their own mortality.[92]

Anointing of the Sick and Participation in the "Anointed One"

In anointing of the sick, the recipient is therefore truly conformed to the "Anointed One," Christ, sharing in his messianic royal, priestly, and prophetic offices. In his study of the sacrament of anointing of the sick, John Kasza points in this direction. In the sacrament, he writes,

> the patient has the opportunity to witness to the faith community as priest, prophet, and king. As priest, the patient may offer his or her sufferings as atonement for sin. One's sufferings are joined to Christ and thus become salvific. As prophet, the patient is called to give testimony to what God has been doing in his or her life. The patient may share what he or she has learned from the illness and encourage others to bear their sufferings with humility and grace. Finally, as a king or leader of God's people, the seriously ill person . . . is capable of leading others toward Christ by an example of faith and love.[93]

While Kasza's description of the priestly dimension of anointing of the sick's conformity to Christ is on target, I would suggest that his account of the prophetic and royal dimensions of the sacrament's implications need further refinement.

First, in Kasza's account, the prophetic element involves the sick person's verbal explanation of God's working in his or her life. This, I think, is overstated since the recipient may not be able to vocalize much about his or her experience. As we saw John Paul II explain above, they can be "silent witnesses" in their suffering and yet be no less effective.

Second, Kasza's explanation of the sick person's exercise of Christ's royal mission as "leading" God's people fails to give much room for an account of the role of Holy Orders and the ministerial priesthood in the Church. Moreover, Kasza leaves no way to account for the sacrament of anointing's effects that have long been established in Church teaching—namely, healing, forgiveness of sins, and the sacrament's power to address sin's effects (that is, the "remains" or "aftereffects" of sin).

92. See Lizette Larson-Miller, *The Sacrament of Anointing of the Sick*, Lex Orandi Series (Collegeville, MN: Liturgical Press, 2005), 68.

93. Kasza, *Understanding Sacramental Healing*, 174.

The proposal put forward here is that all of the sacrament's effects can be integrated into an account that focuses on the sacrament's power to complete what begins in baptism—healing through conformity to Christ, the crucified and risen Lord. Anointing conforms the believer to Christ the High Priest, configuring the believer to the crucified Lord, consecrating the sick person to Christ's priestly offering, enabling him or her to offer his or her suffering in union with Christ's. In so doing, the sick person offers his or her affliction up with the whole ecclesial body, learning to love as God is love. Anointing also conforms the believer to Christ the King, enabling the sick person to gain forgiveness of sins. In this the sick person reigns with Christ, overcoming sin and its effects. This may or may not include physical healing. If it does, however, this would only involve a delay of what is inevitable—namely, sharing in Christ's paschal mystery through dying and rising with him. Finally, anointing conforms the sick person to Christ the Prophet, enabling him or her to bear faithful witness to hope in the risen Lord even in great affliction. If physical healing takes place, this would also involve a prophetic witness to Christ.

The outlook I am advocating here is actually a return to the roots of the Church's celebration of the sacrament. As we saw early in our study (see pp. 15–16), the earliest recorded blessing over the oil for the sick explicitly uses as its basis the observation that God used oil in the Old Testament for anointings of kings, priests, and prophets: "*As you anointed kings, priests, and prophets*, so may it give strength to all who consume it and health to all who are anointed with it."[94]

94. *Apostolic Tradition* 5:2; translation from Hippolytus of Rome, *On the Apostolic Tradition*, trans. Alistair Stewart-Sykes, 2nd ed., PPS 54 (Yonkers, NY: St. Vladimir's Seminary Press, 2015), 90 (emphasis added).

Conclusion

Healing as Conformity to Christ

> The Lord accepted the ointment upon his head for this reason: that he might breathe incorruptibility upon the church.
>
> —Ignatius of Antioch[1]

> By the sacred anointing of the sick and the prayer of her priests the whole Church commends the sick to the suffering and glorified Lord, asking that he may lighten their suffering and save them.
>
> —Vatican II[2]

We have seen that the New Testament indicates that not only is Jesus "Christ," believers are also to be "anointed ones" through union with him. Anointing of the sick, then, can be understood not simply in terms of healing but as effecting conformity to the crucified and risen Christ through union with him in the Spirit. To be clear, this perspective on the sacrament does not conflict with the idea that anointing of the sick is a sacrament of "healing." Rather, it explains what Christian healing ultimately entails. With this understanding

1. Ignatius, *To the Ephesians* 6:1, in Michael W. Holmes, *The Apostolic Fathers: Greek Texts and English Translations*, 3rd ed. (Grand Rapids: Baker Academic, 2007), 197.

2. Second Vatican Council, *Lumen gentium* (The Light of the Nations), Dogmatic Constitution on the Church (November 21, 1964), §11; slightly adapted from Austin Flannery, *Vatican Council II: The Basic Sixteen Documents, Constitutions, Decrees, Declarations*, rev. ed. (Collegeville, MN: Liturgical Press, 2014), 15–16.

in mind, I believe we can also reframe debated questions about the sacrament and provide satisfying answers to them.

At the beginning of this study, we explained that an exegetical approach to the theology of anointing of the sick can help shed light on questions that have been asked about the sacrament. Here we return to these questions. First, who are the proper recipients and ministers of anointing of the sick? Second, what is the significance of the use of oil? Third, in what way does the sacrament bring about healing? As part of this, how are we to think about the physical and spiritual effects of the sacrament? We sum up our study by returning to these questions.

The Proper Recipients and Ministers of the Sacrament

First, let us consider the question of the proper recipient and minister of anointing of the sick. Here once again the biblical data helps bring clarity to the issues involved. We will first look at the question of the recipient and then turn to the question of the identity of the sacrament's minister.

The Sick as the Recipient of Anointing

We have seen that James identifies the recipient of anointing as one who is gravely ill. As commentators frequently point out, the "elders" must be summoned to the sick person because the subject of anointing is likely unable to go to them.[3] Church teaching therefore maintains that the sacrament of anointing is to be given to those "whose health is seriously impaired by sickness or old age."[4] Here, however, pastoral concerns arise that must be addressed.

For much of Church history there has been a tendency to reserve the sacrament for those on the brink of death. This has often meant that the sacrament is administered only after the recipient has lost consciousness. In some cases, this was due to the mistaken belief that recipients of the sacrament would have to live out their lives in a state of extreme penance if they recovered their health. For example, in the Middle Ages, some people held that after

3. See, e.g., Ralph P. Martin, *James*, WBC 48 (Dallas: Word, 1988), 206; Peter H. Davids, *James*, NIGTC (Grand Rapids: Eerdmans, 1982), 192.

4. *Pastoral Care of the Sick: Rites of Anointing and Viaticum* (Totowa, NJ: Catholic Book Publishing, 1983), 21 (§8).

receiving the sacrament a person was required to live out his or her days in a permanent penitential state. Among other things, it was believed that one who was anointed and returned to health was required to renounce conjugal relations with their spouses, abstain from all meat, and give up wearing shoes. These ideas were apparently so widespread that ecclesiastical authorities felt the need to explicitly condemn them.[5]

Many in our own day avoid the sacrament of anointing out of superstitious beliefs. Pope Francis points out that some think that the priest will "bring bad luck" or "scare the sick person." He expresses concern that "the idea is floating about that the undertakers arrive after the priest."[6] Such attitudes reflect a failure to understand the Church's teaching that Christ comes in the sacrament to bless and bring comfort to the sick. Putting off the sacrament until a person is unconscious is therefore a missed opportunity. Since the sacrament is, in part, understood to enable the sick person to offer up his or her sufferings with Christ and to empower the recipient to witness faithfully to him in their illness, it is best for it to be administered to a person who is aware of what they are experiencing.

Because of these concerns, the Second Vatican Council preferred to speak of the sacrament as "anointing of the sick" rather than "extreme unction." The sacrament should not be given in an indiscriminate way—it is not for those experiencing minor ailments or for simple outpatient surgery, and it should not simply be given to everyone attending a healing Mass. Still, the effort should be made to administer it to the sick well before the sick are rendered incapable of experiencing it and the graces it imparts. The sacrament ought to be given to a person who remains conscious so that the recipient can fully participate subjectively, cooperate with the graces of the sacrament, and increase in charity. If death is a real threat because of illness or serious fragility due to old age, the sacrament should not be withheld. The Church's ministers should always err on the side of caution. If there are questions about whether it should be administered, it should be given.

5. See Andrew Cuschieri, *Anointing of the Sick: A Theological and Canonical Study* (Lanham, MD: University Press of America, 1993), 54–55; Joseph Kern, *De sacramento extremae unctionis: Tractatus dogmaticus* (Ratisbonae: Pustet, 1907), 282–85.

6. Francis, *Meeting Jesus in the Sacraments* (Huntington, IN: Our Sunday Visitor, 2015), 88. See also Christoph Schönborn, *Living the Catechism of the Catholic Church: A Brief Commentary on the Catechism for Every Week of the Year*, vol. 2, *The Sacraments* (San Francisco: Ignatius, 2000), 116–17.

The Question of Anointing Young Children

An area that needs to be explored in greater depth is a discrepancy between the way the sacrament is administered in the West and the practice of Eastern Catholic communities. The majority of Catholics, especially in the West, belong to what is known as the Latin Rite. According to the *Code of Canon Law*, which regulates the practice of these Catholics, the sacrament of anointing is to be administered only to those who have attained the age of reason.[7] There are, however, many Catholics who—though in communion with the bishop of Rome—belong to Eastern Rite communities (Byzantine, Alexandrian, Syriac, Armenian, Maronite, and Chaldean rites). These rites are governed by the *Code of Canon Law for Eastern Churches*, which is approved by the pope. Strikingly, unlike the one that governs the Latin Rite, the *Code of Canon Law for Eastern Churches* contains no age restriction for the sacrament of anointing of the sick.

Evidence suggests that prerational children received anointing of the sick until about 1200.[8] For example, Theodulf of Orléans indicates that it should be given not only to adults but also to children (*pueris*).[9] That this statement follows one about anointing those lacking rational faculties makes it more likely than not that he is referring to prerational children.

The reason the sacrament of anointing has been restricted in the West to those who have attained the age of reason is its connection to forgiveness of sins.[10] Thomas Aquinas explains that prerational children do not receive the sacrament because it addresses the effects of actual sin, "which are not in children."[11] Since those who have not attained the use of reason cannot incur guilt due to personal sin, their sicknesses cannot possibly be attributed to it. Of course, as we have seen, one should not assume that a sickness is due to personal sin. Sickness is also connected in a broader way to the general fallen condition of humanity (see especially chap. 4 above). Yet, on Thomas's account, anointing of the sick would serve no purpose here since baptism remits both the guilt and temporal punishment due to original sin.

7. *CIC* 1004.

8. See, e.g., Nicholas Omre, *Medieval Children* (New Haven: Yale University Press, 2001), 215.

9. Theodulf of Orléans, *Capitulare* 2 (PL 105:221).

10. See the Directory for the Ministry and Life of Permanent Deacons, published jointly by the Congregation for the Clergy and the Congregation for Catholic Education (February 22, 1998), §34.

11. Thomas Aquinas, *Summa Theologiae*, Supplement, q. 32, art. 4, ad 2.

How, then, might we account for the administration of the sacrament to the very young? The analogous case of baptizing infants offers one possible route. While infants are incapable of asking for the sacrament itself, "Mother Church," Augustine says, "uses for them the heart and mouth of a mother, that they may be imbued with the sacred mysteries."[12] Aquinas cites this passage from Augustine to explain how infants receive the grace of baptism. Thomas writes, "As the child while in the mother's womb receives nourishment not independently, but through the nourishment of its mother, so also children before the use of reason, being as it were in the womb of their mother the Church, receive salvation not by their own act, but by the act of the Church."[13]

Accordingly, we might say that just as the infant at baptism is united to Christ through the faith of the Church, so too a child's suffering is united in a particular way to Christ's sacrifice by the faith of the Church. Indeed, the *Catechism of the Catholic Church* emphasizes the ecclesial dimension of anointing of the sick:

> By the sacred anointing of the sick and the prayer of the priests *the whole Church commends those who are ill to the suffering and glorified Lord*, that he may raise them up and save them. And indeed she exhorts them to contribute to the good of the People of God by freely uniting themselves to the Passion and death of Christ.[14]

The child may not be rational, but the child still genuinely *suffers*. In such a case, "the whole Church commends" the child to the Lord through anointing of the sick. Moreover, this passage from the *Catechism* reminds us that the sacrament has effects other than healing and forgiveness of sins. The recipient of anointing is enabled to contribute to the good of the Church through being conformed to Christ in a particular way through his or her sufferings. Could we therefore consider the possibility that the sacrament enables the infant, who is commended to Christ through the faith of the Church, to be conformed to the crucified one in a way that participates in the ecclesial mystery of salvation?

12. Augustine, *A Treatise on the Merits and Forgiveness of Sins, and On the Baptism of Infants* 1.38 (*NPNF*[1] 5:30).

13. Thomas Aquinas, *Summa Theologiae* III, q. 68, art. 9, ad 1. Translation from Thomas Aquinas, *Summa Theologiae, Tertia Pars, 60–90*, trans. Laurence Shapcote, Latin/English Edition of the Works of St. Thomas Aquinas 20 (Lander, WY: The Aquinas Institute for the Study of Sacred Doctrine, 2012), 118.

14. CCC 1499.

If the child can be so united to Christ, this can also offer the child a share in the consolation of Christ, though in a way that "surpasses all understanding" (Phil. 4:7). As we have mentioned, anointing of the sick does more than bring about healing and forgiveness from sins. As part of dealing with the effects of sin, it also brings comfort.[15] Pope Francis explains how the sacrament brings solace from Jesus himself:

> The greatest comfort comes from the fact that it is the Lord Jesus himself who makes himself present in the Sacrament, who takes us by the hand, who caresses us as he did with the sick, and who reminds us that we already belong to him and that nothing—not even evil and death—can ever separate us from him.[16]

As Jesus brought comfort to the sick in his earthly ministry, he does this now in the Church in the sacrament of anointing.

Yet we should recall that while the sacrament is most fittingly applied to a conscious recipient, the sacrament is nonetheless administered to the unconscious. Just as the faith of the Church commends the unconscious recipient to the Lord, something analogous could be said about infants who receive the sacrament in Eastern churches.

This author readily and joyfully submits to the Church's authority to determine such matters, yet it seems the current restriction in the West could conceivably be revisited. A robust account of anointing that views the sacrament in terms of conformity to Christ as priest, prophet, and king might further explain why children are permitted to receive the sacrament in the East. As the Church supplies the act of faith for a child at baptism, something similar could be said to help explain why children in Eastern churches are permitted to receive the sacrament. An approach to anointing of the sick that views the healing it brings about merely in terms of actual sins and their effects understandably fails to account for how the sacrament can benefit young children. Yet once the sacrament is recognized as bringing comfort and consolation to the sick—a feature of the sacrament that we have connected to Christ's royal dominion over the aftereffects of sin—its reception by young children makes greater sense.

15. See *Pastoral Care of the Sick*, 20 (§4).

16. Francis, General Audience, Saint Peter's Square (February 26, 2014), https://www.vatican.va/content/francesco/en/audiences/2014/documents/papa-francesco_20140226_udienza-generale.html.

Jesus himself said, "Let the children come to me, and do not hinder them, for the kingdom of heaven belongs to such as these" (Matt. 19:14). He healed the children who were brought to him (e.g., Mark 9:14–29), and he raised Jairus's daughter (Mark 5:21–24, 35–43). While we should not be presumptuous about God's grace or advocate an age-blind inclusiveness to all of the sacraments, when it comes to the sacrament of anointing, which is closely bound up with the mystery of Jesus's healing power, the lack of restriction in the administration of the sacrament to prerational children in the Eastern churches seems to derive special support from the portrait of Jesus in the Gospels.

The Proper Minister of Anointing

As we have seen, there is evidence of lay people anointing others in Church history. Perhaps most significant is the teaching of Pope Innocent, who expressly states, "In case of emergency, this anointing is permitted not only for priests but even for all Christians."[17] The question that must be asked is whether Innocent conceives of the emergency case of lay anointing as having the same meaning as an anointing performed by a priest. As we have seen, not all anointings of the sick are necessarily understood as instances of the sacrament of anointing.

The most thorough argument in favor of the view that the sacrament of anointing could be administered by lay ministers was advanced in a 1987 study published by John J. Ziegler.[18] Ziegler recognizes that the Council of Trent explicitly denies that lay people can administer the sacrament. According to the council, James's words "show that the proper ministers of this sacrament are 'presbyters' of the church, and by this title in the text are to be understood, not the elders or leading figures among the people, but either bishops or priests duly ordained by them *by the laying on of hands of the presbyterate*."[19] The view that the "elders" may be interpreted as nonsacerdotal ministers is explicitly anathematized by the council.[20] Ziegler, however,

17. Innocent I, *Letter to Decentius* 8; translation from Martin Connell, *Church and Worship in Fifth-Century Rome: The Letter of Innocent I to Decentius of Gubbio*, GLS 50 (Piscataway, NJ: Gorgias, 2010), 47.

18. John J. Ziegler, *Let Them Anoint the Sick* (Collegeville, MN: Liturgical Press, 1987).

19. Council of Trent, Session 14, Chapter 3; translation from Norman Tanner, ed., *The Decrees of the Ecumenical Councils*, 2 vols. (Washington, DC: Georgetown University Press, 1990), 2:711.

20. See Canon 4.

argues that the council's goal was not to set forward a definitive teaching on the identity of the ministers of the sacrament. Rather, Ziegler insists that the council should be read as condemning the disobedience of the Protestant Reformers, who rejected the Church's authority to regulate the administration of the sacraments.

In addition, a major reason priests have been viewed as the primary ministers of anointing of the sick has been the sacrament's connection to forgiveness of sins. Yet baptism and eucharist are also associated with forgiveness of sins[21] and can, in certain situations, be distributed by laity.[22] Some have therefore argued that perhaps a similar exception might be allowed for anointing of the sick.

Yet hopes that lay ministers would one day be permitted to administer the sacrament of anointing of the sick were dealt a major blow by a 2005 "doctrinal note" published by the Congregation for the Doctrine of the Faith. The document explains that the priestly identity of the minister of anointing "enjoys such a degree of theological certainty that it must be described as a doctrine '*definitive tenenda*.'" In other words, the priestly identity of the minister of anointing of the sick is declared to be taught "definitively" by the Church. The document observes that the overwhelming tradition of the Church has been to interpret the "elders" mentioned by James 5 as referring to ordained clergy—namely, those who have received "laying on of hands." Moreover, we are told that Pope Innocent's letter "provides no proof of the possibility of introducing ministers who are not priests to administer the Sacrament of the Anointing of the Sick."[23]

A perspective that privileges the biblical data would especially seem to point away from the claim that *any* believer is capable of administering the anointing James envisions. After all, James specifies that the sick person is to be anointed by the "elders." There are *possible* ways of arguing that the elders are not official church leaders, but is it really probable that James uses the term "elders" to include any and all believers? No serious biblical scholar

21. On this effect of the sacrament of the eucharist, see CCC 1393–94.

22. On the capacity of non-priests to perform baptism in emergency circumstances, see *CIC* 861 §2; CCC 1256. On extraordinary ministers of the eucharist, who cannot confect the eucharist but only distribute it, see *CIC* 910 §2.

23. Congregation for the Doctrine of the Faith, "Note on the Minister of the Sacrament of the Anointing of the Sick," with Commentary (February 11, 2005), https://www.vatican.va/roman_curia/congregations/cfaith/documents/rc_con_cfaith_doc_20050211_unzione-infermi_en.html.

that I know of thinks so. While we should avoid a simplistic approach that somehow reads the precise hierarchical structure of today's Church into the New Testament period, James manifestly does not envision a scenario in which *any* Christian is capable of performing the anointing he describes.

Moreover, in their treatment of the sacrament, Augustine DiNoia and Joseph Fox observe that the need for a priestly minister to administer the sacrament is also evident due to another fact. Since the recipient is called to offer himself or herself to the priestly offering of Christ, this points to the need of a sacerdotal minister: "It requires the priest acting *in persona Christi Capitis* ["in the person of Christ the head"] to lead the worshipping community in their participation in this moment of personal self-offering on the part of one of its members."[24] The authors do not provide biblical support for this assertion, but it does exist.

Paul speaks of the need for believers to "present" (*paristēmi*) themselves as a sacrificial offering to God (Rom. 12:1). Notably, the same language occurs within the context of believers' participation in Christ's suffering in Colossians 1:24. Indeed, we can find three different uses of this term in the Pauline corpus. First, in Colossians 1:21–23, Paul speaks of how *Christ* "presents" his body to the Father. Here we might recognize an affirmation of Christ's priestly sacrificial work. Second, in Romans 12 Paul explains that believers "present" their bodies as a living sacrifice—the sacrifice of Christ's body. In this, we can find a reference to the priesthood of the baptized, who are each called to make a sacrificial offering of themselves. Third, in Colossians 1:28 Paul explains that *he* "presents" believers. Significantly, in Romans, Paul explains how he has a priestly role in facilitating Christians' sacrificial offering: the apostle speaks of how he is involved in "the priestly service of the gospel of God, so that the offering of the gentiles may be acceptable, sanctified by the Holy Spirit" (Rom. 15:16).

Following the Pauline teaching, then, we might say that while believers are to present themselves as sacrificial offerings to the Lord, they should make this offering not as mere individuals but *ecclesially*. With that in mind, there is therefore a need for another ecclesial minister who is involved in the process so as to underscore the way this occurs in an ecclesial mode. Since anointing of the sick involves such an offering—which is understood as benefitting the whole Church—it is appropriate that the minister is a duly recognized

24. Augustine DiNoia and Joseph Fox, "Priestly Dimensions of the Sacrament of Anointing of the Sick," *The Priest* 62 (2006): 13.

ecclesial minister. The use of oil blessed by the bishop would seem to further this dimension of the sacrament.

Statements from the Congregation of the Doctrine of the Faith do not enjoy the same authority as other forms of magisterial teaching. That being said, it is difficult see the 2005 statement from the Congregation of the Doctrine of the Faith being reversed. Given that James 5 specifies the ministers of the sacrament as "elders," it would seem difficult to argue that the sacrament can be administered by any member of the Church.

The Significance of Oil in Anointing of the Sick

The fundamental idea behind the sacraments is that they somehow visibly *signify* what occurs spiritually, and the spiritual reality is caused by this signification. As Augustine writes, "For, if the sacraments did not have some likeness to those events of which they are sacraments, they would not be sacraments at all. But because of this likeness they generally receive the name of the realities themselves."[25] In other words, the spiritual event of our being "washed" of sin in Christ (1 Cor. 6:11) is made visible in the washing of water and effected in baptism. What, then, can we say about the use of oil in anointing of the sick? Here let us return to what we have seen above.

Oil and Healing

Anointing of the sick is understood to be a sacrament of "healing." It is fitting that it is associated with oil, an agent used as a healing remedy in the ancient world. This use of oil is especially on display in Jesus's parable of the good Samaritan. The protagonist finds a man beaten and left for dead by the side of a road and dresses his wounds with oil: "He poured oil and wine on his wounds and bandaged them" (Luke 10:34). That James speaks of the use of oil in connection with ministering to the sick, then, is no surprise.

Yet it would be a mistake to read James's directives as envisioning *merely* a kind of natural healing technique. To ask whether James conceived of the use of oil in terms of a "natural" healing agent *or* whether he conceived of it as bound up with divine power is anachronistic. Ancient Jews attributed

25. Augustine, *Letter* 98.7; translation from Augustine, *Letters 1–99*, trans. Roland Teske, WSA II/1 (Hyde Park, NY: New City Press, 2001), 431.

the healing power of physicians to the work of God.[26] The very notion that there could be a healing apart from God's assistance is simply the result of modern presuppositions, which does not reflect the perspective of the biblical writers. James insists that the healing of the sick will occur "in the name of the Lord," an expression that likely involves an allusion to "the Lord Jesus Christ" (James 1:1). After all, in context, James seems to evoke traditions about Jesus's coming (compare James 5:7–9 with Mark 13:26–29).

Moreover, within the very context in which James speaks of anointing the sick, he also speaks of the forgiveness of sins. To maintain that James neatly separates physical healing from spiritual healing also overlooks the fact that James closely connects sin with physical affliction—namely, death: "Desire, when it has conceived, gives birth to sin, and sin, when it is fully grown, gives birth to *death*" (James 1:15). Our study has shown that the relationship between sin and sickness/death is deeply ingrained in biblical traditions. Similarly, we have explored the ways physical healing and forgiveness of sins are also inextricably bound up with one another in the scriptures of Israel and the New Testament. Given all of this, James most likely views anointing of the sick as having profound spiritual significance. In context, when he says that the sick person will be "saved" (James 5:15), it seems unlikely that he has in mind *only* physical restoration. Indeed, later sources like the *Life of Adam and Eve* explicitly connect the imagery of oil to the hope of the eschatological healing that will arrive with the coming of Christ, the Messiah (*Life of Adam and Eve* 42; *Christ's Descent into Hell* 3 [19].1, in the *Gospel of Nicodemus*).

Thomas Aquinas's teaching on the reason oil is used in the sacrament is also worth mentioning here. Aquinas observes that washing is a property natural to water, yet restoring physical health is not necessarily a natural property of oil. For this reason, the sacrament can bring about physical healing, but it does not do so necessarily. It occurs only when God deems it necessary.[27]

Oil and the Power of the Spirit

That James says the sick are to be anointed in "the name of the Lord" (James 5:14) has further important implications. The power of healing is ultimately located not in the oil but in its connection to "the Lord." We explained how James's language evokes the biblical description of the God

26. Sir. 38:6–9, 12–15; Philo, *Allegorical Interpretation* 3.178.
27. See Thomas Aquinas, *Summa Theologiae*, Supplement, q. 30, art 2.

of Israel as "the Lord," YHWH, the "Lord of life" (2 Macc. 14:46). Oil is frequently mentioned as one of the expressions of the Lord's providential and abundant care for his people (e.g., Pss. 92:10–15; 104:14–15). Oil is therefore appropriately used in caring for the sick. Because the Lord is the creator (Isa. 45:18), sustainer, and savior of life (e.g., Job 12:9–10; Pss. 3:5; 22:20–21; 36:6), believers have confidence that the prayer to God over the anointed sick person will "save" him (James 5:14–15).

In addition, biblical traditions associate empowerment by the Lord with the Spirit who is portrayed as coming upon figures that are recipients of sacred anointings. Kings are depicted being empowered by the Spirit, who enables them to receive the gift of prophecy and even personal transformation: "Then the Spirit of the LORD will come upon you in power, and you will prophesy along with [prophets], and will turn into a different person . . . for God is with you" (1 Sam. 10:6, 7). In some traditions, oil is even connected to heavenly transformation (*2 Enoch* 22:10). In the book of Isaiah, to be anointed is, in the final analysis, to be anointed by the Spirit (Isa. 61:1). The New Testament identifies the Spirit as the anointing received by Christ (e.g., Acts 10:38; 2 Cor. 1:21–22).

As we have seen, scholarly discussions of royal anointings give way to the use of "sacramental" language: "The practice [of anointing] involved a symbolic transfer of sanctity from the deity to an object or person and thus was *essentially a sacramental act*. . . . The divine virtue, believed to be especially present in living things, was directly transferred to the sanctified individual."[28] Ritual anointing is no empty ritual. Matthew Novenson writes that ancient sources such as Psalm 45 indicate that, in anointing, "oil, properly applied, confers divinely sanctioned power."[29] In the sacrament of anointing of the sick, then, the Church understands that the oil signifies not merely healing but empowerment—that is, being strengthened or empowered by the Spirit.

Here one can recognize divine pedagogy—the use of material elements such as oil in anointing guards against a spiritualist outlook that, as in Gnosticism, rejects the role of the material cosmos in God's saving plan. For Christians, the use of oil underscores the incarnational dimension of Christian faith. As Christ took to himself a human nature and used it as the instrument of

28. P. Kyle McCarter Jr., *I Samuel*, AYB 8 (New Haven: Yale University Press, 2008), 178 (emphasis added).

29. Matthew V. Novenson, *The Grammar of Messianism: An Ancient Jewish Political Idiom and Its Users* (Oxford: Oxford University Press, 2017), 47.

his divinity,[30] in an analogous way Christ continues to affirm the goodness of creation by using material elements to continue his saving work. The use of water, bread, wine, and oil expresses the hope that all creation will somehow share in Christ's redemptive work (Rom. 8:19–23).[31] Orthodox scholar Edith Humphrey writes, "Liturgical acts are not *substitutes* for personal faith, but means by which that faith is passed on and confirmed."[32] That ritual acts are no substitute for personal faith is also affirmed in Catholic tradition.

To be sure, there is no evidence that James conceives of the oil as *itself* having special power apart from the prayer. Indeed, according to Catholic teaching, while the sacrament of anointing of the sick is normally to be carried out using the oil of the sick blessed by the bishop, in the case of necessity other oil can be used.[33] Although Catholic doctrine maintains that in the eucharist, the bread and wine are substantially changed into the body and blood of Jesus, such an understanding does not apply to the material elements used in other sacraments. Baptism is performed with water; while it is "holy water" because it is blessed, its substance is not changed. Likewise, the oil used in anointing of the sick is not somehow a substantially altered element. As Augustine explains, the sacrament is constituted not only by the element(s) it uses (the sacramental "matter") but also by the prayer (the sacramental "form"): "Remove the word, and what is the water but water? The word comes to the element, and it becomes a sacrament, which itself is like a visible word."[34]

The fact that the prayer is necessary does not in any way negate the importance of the oil. Like the water of baptism, oil is important because of what is *signifies*. As with sacral anointings in the Old Testament, anointing of the sick is no empty ritual—it accomplishes what it signifies. Nevertheless, we must avoid a mechanical understanding of the sacrament.[35] Anointing is

30. See Thomas Joseph White, *The Incarnate Lord: A Thomistic Study in Christology*, Thomistic Ressourcement Series 5 (Washington, DC: Catholic University of America Press, 2017), 83.

31. See Brant Pitre, Michael P. Barber, and John A. Kincaid, *Paul, a New Covenant Jew: Rethinking Pauline Theology* (Grand Rapids: Eerdmans, 2019), 211–50.

32. Edith Humphrey, *Mediation and the Immediate God: Scriptures, the Church, and Knowing God* (Yonkers, NY: St. Vladimir's Seminary Press, 2023), 57.

33. See the discussion and sources in Cuschieri, *Anointing of the Sick*, 94.

34. Augustine, *Tractates on John* 80.3, in Augustine, *Homilies on the Gospel of John 41–124*, trans. Edmund Hill, WSA III/13 (Hyde Park, NY: New City Press, 2020), 287.

35. See, e.g., the treatment on Thomas Aquinas's teaching in Romanus Cessario, *The Seven Sacraments of the Catholic Church* (Grand Rapids: Baker Academic, 2023), 94–95.

bound up with the faith of the Church, which believes that what is signified through the use of oil is effected by the Father, Son, and Spirit, who are at work in the sacrament through the Church, Christ's Mystical Body.

But what exactly is signified in anointing of the sick? Here we turn to the third major area that requires discussion—namely, the relationship of physical healing to spiritual healing. Indeed, here it is necessary to clarify *what* spiritual healing entails.

The Healing Effected in Anointing of the Sick

If theologians prior to the Second Vatican Council emphasized the spiritual dimension of the sacrament of anointing of the sick to the neglect of its physical aspect, the proverbial pendulum had certainly swung the other way after the council. In a study of the sacrament published in 1993, Andrew Cuschieri writes: "Great emphasis is being placed on the physical healing at the risk of diminishing the very sacramentality of the Anointing of the Sick."[36] Holding together the physical and spiritual effects of the sacrament have proven challenging. The best way to maintain both the physical and spiritual effects of anointing is to recognize the *christological* dimension of the sacrament, something that can be rooted in James 5 itself.

James 5 and Conformity to the Risen Lord

James 5 explains that the anointed sick person will be "raised up" (James 5:15). The immediate context suggests that this primarily refers to the hope of physical restoration. Nevertheless, it would be irresponsible to insist that James has no other meaning but this one in mind. For James, as a Jewish writer informed by the scriptures, healing is holistic—physical well-being and spiritual well-being are inextricably bound up with one another. As we have seen, James explicitly declares that sin and death are intertwined (James 1:15). Indeed, James 5 moves from the promise of the sick person being "saved" and "raised up" to discuss that person's spiritual condition: "If he has committed sins, he will be forgiven" (James 5:15). From this, we have seen that, in accord with Israel's biblical traditions, James likely maintains that at least some forms of sickness and death are due to sin and that physical healing can be bound up with repentance from such sins.

36. Cuschieri, *Anointing of the Sick*, 71.

This is not to say that James associates *all* sickness and death with personal sin. Nor does it mean that James believes anointing can permanently stave off physical death. Nevertheless, it does challenge modern conceptions that reduce illness and death to biological realities; James has a *theological* perspective on sickness that cannot be ignored.

Moreover, James explains that the Lord will "raise up" the sick person who is anointed and prayed over by the elders (James 5:14–15). The Greek verb used for "raise up," *egeirō*, is evocative of Gospel stories in which Jesus heals people. For example, Mark tells us that taking the hand of Peter's sick mother-in-law, Jesus "raised her up [*ēgeiren*]" (Mark 1:31).[37] The verb is also used to describe those Jesus "raises" from the dead. For example, Jesus raises a dead girl by saying to her, "Arise" (*egeire*; Mark 5:41).[38] Indeed, forms of the verb are also *repeatedly* used in reference to Jesus himself—Jesus is "raised" from the dead (e.g., Mark 14:28: "after I am *raised* [*egerthēnai*]").[39]

In speaking of how the sick person who is anointed and prayed over will be "raised up," James has deliberately chosen a polyvalent term that carries the connotation of both physical healing and resurrection. James's language can be read as indicating that the sick who are anointed are conformed in a certain way to the risen Lord.

There is no reason to insist that James's use of the language of being "raised up" involves no echo of resurrection hopes. Informed by Jewish expectations,[40] there is broad evidence that early Christians expected a future day of resurrection from the dead, a belief that finds wide attestation in the New Testament.[41] It is difficult to believe James would have forgotten the word *egeirō* would have triggered such hopes. James, then, likely describes the fate of the recipient of anointing as that which his readers would have also associated with Jesus: the sick person is like Christ because, like him, he or she will be "raised up"—either in the sense of physical healing or, ultimately, in the resurrection of the dead. Whatever the outcome, then, the sick person is configured to

37. See also, e.g., Mark 2:9, 11–12; 5:41; 9:27; Acts 3:7.

38. See also Matt. 11:5//Luke 7:22; cf. Matt. 9:25; Luke 7:14; John 12:1, 9, 17.

39. See also Matt. 16:21; 17:9, 23; 26:32; 27:63–64; 28:6–7; Mark 16:6; Luke 9:22; 24:6–7, 34; John 2:19, 22; 21:14; Acts 3:15; 4:10; 5:30; 10:40; 13:30, 37; Rom. 4:24–25; 6:4, 9; 7:4; 8:11, 34; 10:9; 1 Cor. 6:14; 15:4, 12–13, 15–17, 20; 2 Cor. 4:14; 5:15; Gal. 1:1; Eph. 1:20; Col. 2:12; 1 Thess. 1:10; 2 Tim. 2:8; 1 Pet. 1:21.

40. Isa. 26:19; Dan. 12:1–3; 2 Macc. 7:14, 23, 29; *4QMessianic Apocalypse* (4Q521) 1; Pseudo-Philo, *Biblical Antiquities* 3:10; *1 Enoch* 51:1–5; 91:10; 92:3; 103:4; 104:1–2; *Mishnah Sanhedrin* 10:1.

41. Matt. 22:29–31//Luke 20:35–36; Luke 14:14; John 5:28–29; 11:24; Acts 24:15; Rom. 8:11; 1 Cor. 6:14; 15:12–24, 52–57; 2 Cor. 4:14; Phil. 3:10–11, 21.

Christ—the "Anointed One"—through anointing. As with the Messiah, the anointed sick person's sufferings will give way to a state of being "raised up." In his or her suffering, then, the sick is conformed to Christ in hope.

Similarly, when James speaks of how the sick person who is anointed and prayed over will be "saved," he most likely first has in mind the restoration of physical health. Still, we cannot rule out that other meanings of the word are also intended. Patrick Hartin writes, "While the concept of salvation relates first of all to healing or the restoring to fullness of health in this present life, there is also the further implication of eschatological salvation, as occurs elsewhere."[42]

Hartin highlights three key passages in James where the language of salvation points to something beyond physical restoration. First, James 1 speaks of the need to put aside moral impurity and to "welcome the implanted word that is able to save your souls [*psychas*]" (James 1:21). There is nothing here that suggests physical restoration. As Dale Allison writes, "The focus is not upon being saved from evil in this life but upon finding salvation in the next."[43] Second, James 2 teaches that faith apart from works cannot "save" (James 2:14). The meaning here can hardly be viewed as referring to preserving biological life. Again, to quote Allison, "The issue here is manifestly eschatological salvation."[44] Finally, eschatological realities are suggested in James 4, where the author speaks of God as the judge who is able "to save and to destroy" (4:12).[45]

Therefore, to read the instructions pertaining to anointing the sick in James 5 as promising physical restoration alone presses the text too far. As Allison explains, "Given that bodily and spiritual health were scarcely distinct categories for early Christians, an exclusive emphasis upon the physical may assume a false dichotomy."[46] Allison is characteristically cautious here, but that James is concerned with both physical and spiritual realities is not only possible but undeniable. James specifically goes on to link anointing to *spiritual* renewal—forgiveness of sins. After indicating that the prayer that accompanies the anointing "will save the one who is sick" and insisting that "the Lord will raise him up," James says, "And if he has committed sins, he

42. Patrick J. Hartin, *James*, SP 14 (Collegeville, MN: Liturgical Press, 2003), 268.
43. Dale C. Allison Jr., *James*, ICC (London: Bloomsbury T&T Clark, 2013), 317.
44. Allison, *James*, 461.
45. Again, see Allison, *James*, 638, who explains that the meaning "must be eschatological."
46. Allison, *James*, 766.

will be forgiven" (James 5:15). *The forgiveness of sins, then, is directly connected with the anointing of the sick person.* Although it is also connected to confession in the next verse, one cannot neatly isolate remission of sins from the power of the anointing prayer.

Frederick Puller is therefore wrong when he writes of James's instructions, "He mentions no effect besides the healing of the sick."[47] For Puller, viewing the language of "salvation" in James 5 as multifaceted represents "a strained attempt to combine two very different meanings under one word."[48] However, this neglects the overall context of the passage. It also ignores more broadly the way physical and spiritual healing are bound up together in the scriptures, which inform James's teaching. To insist that James's affirmation that the sick person will be "saved" refers *only* to bodily healing, therefore, fails to do justice to the text.

It is no wonder Christian tradition has read James's instructions as indicative that anointing the sick involves *both* physical and spiritual effects. Conformity to the Lord is among them: James indicates that the believer will be "raised up," using language the early Church associated with Christ's resurrection. As we have seen, it is improbable that James thought death could be perpetually avoided by receiving anointing. So regardless of whether or not the believer is "saved" from physical death through anointing, the believer always has hope in resurrection. And although James 5 does not spell this out, Christian theology rightly reads this hope in terms of participation in Christ's own risen life.

Healing as Conformity to Christ

Although it is perfectly consonant with James 5 to speak of anointing of the sick as a sacrament of "healing," we should note that James never actually uses that word. Rather, the author speaks of how the person who is anointed and prayed over will be "saved." While this is certainly associated with forgiveness of sins, we should be careful not to limit salvation to remission of sins alone. In context, it is specifically linked to being "raised up." Again, while the immediate context suggests the language refers first to physical healing, the passage cannot be reduced to this.

47. Frederick W. Puller, *The Anointing of the Sick in Scripture and Tradition* (London: SPCK, 1904), 12.

48. Puller, *Anointing of the Sick*, 17.

For Christian theology, salvation cannot be viewed simply in negative terms—that is, it cannot be reducible to what the believer is delivered *from* in Christ. It also entails a positive dimension; the believer is not just saved *from* threatening realities (sin, death, judgment, etc.), but the believer is also saved *for* a purpose. To speak analogously, one does not simply talk of delivering a letter *from* the letter writer but one also describes the letter's *destination*—namely, *to whom* it is delivered. What, then, is the goal of salvation? Jesus indicates that the goal of the Christian life is nothing less than to become *like God*: "Be perfect, therefore, as your heavenly Father is perfect" (Matt. 5:48). Going on, the New Testament writers indicate that this *theomimesis*—imitation of God—is understood by looking at Christ himself. In the Fourth Gospel, Jesus declares: "Whoever has seen me has seen the Father" (John 14:9). Likewise, Colossians explains that Jesus is "the *image* [*eikōn*] of the *invisible* God" (Col. 1:15). Humanity is created in the "image" and "likeness" of God in Genesis, but only in Jesus do we find what it truly means to "image" the Father.

As we have seen, Paul therefore explains that God's saving plan is ultimately ordered so that believers may "be conformed to the image of his Son" (Rom. 8:29). Likewise, in Ephesians, we read, "*Be imitators of God*, as beloved children, and *walk in love just as Christ loved us* and gave himself for our sake, an offering and a sweet-smelling sacrifice to God" (Eph. 5:1–2). To be an "imitator of God" is to love as Christ did, who offered his life as a "sacrifice." The goal of salvation, then, is nothing less than conformity to Christ.

The vital point is this: Christ is the model of salvation. He reveals what humanity is called to be. As the Second Vatican Council puts it, "Christ the new Adam . . . fully reveals humanity to itself and brings to light its very high calling."[49] Romanus Cessario thus speaks of spiritual healing in Christ as "image-restoration." Christ not only heals the wounds of sin but "bestows new life from his own divinity." Salvation is not simply healing from sin, but *true healing is becoming what he is*. Furthermore, Cessario stresses that for Christian faith this "image-restoration" in Christ occurs through the sacraments.[50] This conviction is anchored in Paul's teaching, which, as we have detailed, connects participation in Christ to baptism and the eucharist

49. Second Vatican Council, *Gaudium et spes* (The Hope and Joy), Pastoral Constitution on the Church in the Modern World (December 7, 1965), §22; in Flannery, *Vatican Council II*, 185.

50. Cessario, *Seven Sacraments*, 48.

(Rom. 6:3–4; 1 Cor. 10:16–17). It is through the sacraments that believers are "in Christ" and therefore made "partakers of the divine nature" (2 Pet. 1:4).

Yet if true healing is being conformed to Christ, this healing can also be understood in terms of sharing in his royal, priestly, and prophetic identity. As I have argued, Scripture shows that those who are "in Christ" have a participation in these aspects of Jesus's messianic mission. Christians are initiated into Christ's threefold office by virtue of their baptism. The Council of Trent says that anointing of the sick brings to "consummation" the baptized's vocation. The sacrament brings spiritual healing from sin, and in this believers share in Christ's reign over sin and its aftereffects. This can possibly include physical healing since sin and sickness are understood to be among the consequences of sin. The sacrament also enables the sick to offer his or her suffering in union with Christ's, thus fulfilling his or her call to present oneself as a "living sacrifice . . . acceptable to God" (Rom. 12:1). In this, believers exercise a share in Christ's priesthood. Finally, the sacrament enables the sick, by faithfully enduring their suffering, to share in Christ's prophetic witness. In these ways, the sacrament brings about a deeper conformity of the believer to Christ, finding true healing in him. This is fitting since the sacrament involves "anointing"—the sick becomes a "christ" in Christ.

Healed to Die and Rise in Christ

Finally, as we have seen, the book of Acts continues the story of Jesus's work from the Gospel of Luke: what Jesus did in his personal body during his public ministry continues in the life of the Church (see above, pp. 111–16). Christian faith recognizes that this story does not end in Acts 28. Jesus's active presence is continued through the life of the Church today. This is realized particularly (though not exclusively) in her sacramental ministry.

Leo the Great writes, "What was visible in our Savior has passed over into his mysteries."[51] The term "mysteries" here is used to refer to the sacraments of the Church. Catholic teaching therefore holds that the saving realities that were visible in Christ's public life are realized in the life of the believer through the sacraments. The Church teaches:

> Jesus' words and actions during his hidden life and public ministry were already salvific, for they anticipated the power of his Paschal mystery. They announced

51. Leo the Great, *Sermon* 74.2; translation from CCC 1115.

> and prepared what he was going to give the Church when all was accomplished. The mysteries of Christ's life are the foundations of what he would henceforth dispense in the sacraments, through the ministers of his Church.[52]

The believer encounters the mysteries of Christ's life through the sacraments. To understand the sacraments, then, one must go back and read the Gospels. What happens in Christ's life illuminates our understanding of the sacraments. We can illustrate this approach with baptism.

The Christian can understand what happens at his or her baptism by reflecting on the accounts of Jesus's baptism. As the Spirit came upon Jesus at his baptism (Mark 1:10), the believer likewise receives the gift of the Spirit in his or her baptism (1 Cor. 6:11), where he or she is clothed with Christ (Gal. 3:27) and is therefore anointed in the Spirit in him (2 Cor. 1:21–22). As Jesus is identified as the Father's "Son" at his baptism (Mark 1:11), the baptized person becomes a child of God through union with the divine Son, becoming not only a child of God but a "co-heir" with him (see Rom. 8:17; Gal. 3:27–29). Finally, Jesus's baptism foreshadows his death. Interpreters of Mark have long noted that the two scenes of Jesus's baptism and crucifixion are tied together with the imagery of the heavens and temple veil being "torn" (*schizō*) open (Mark 1:10; 15:38).[53] Indeed, baptism is used as a symbol of death in the Gospels (Mark 10:38–39; Luke 12:50). Paul therefore indicates that the believer dies and rises with Christ in baptism (Rom. 6:3–6; Col. 2:12). Thus, heaven is opened to the baptized.

A similar reflection may also be made of anointing of the sick. Prior to Jesus's death, he is anointed with literal oil (Matt. 26:6–13; Mark 14:3–9; John 12:1–8). In Matthew, Mark, and John, Jesus responds to the woman who anoints him by identifying her act with his death (Matt. 26:12; Mark 14:8; John 12:7). Luke omits this saying, but he nevertheless notes that when Jesus dies, women prepare materials to anoint his body with ointment (Luke 23:56; cf. Mark 16:1). Jesus's death is therefore connected to anointing.

Because these stories of anointing do not involve the use of oil or the Greek verb *chriō*, which are used in the sacral anointing scenes involving royal figures, some commentators suggest no reference to Jesus's messianic identity is

52. CCC 1115.

53. See C. Clifton Black, *Mark's Gospel: History, Theology, Interpretation* (Grand Rapids: Eerdmans, 2023), 223–25, who also points out that the language of Jesus breathing his last on the cross (*exepneusen*; Mark 15:37) might be seen as also evoking the descent of the "spirit" at Jesus's baptism (*pneuma*; Mark 1:10).

intended in these stories.[54] This, however, imagines that Greek writers could attach messianic significance only to one particular substance or one particular verb for anointing. This is demonstrably not the case.

The early Christian writer Ignatius of Antioch alludes to the scene of Jesus being anointed by the woman at Bethany and connects it explicitly to Jesus's identity as *Christ*. He writes:

> The Lord accepted the *ointment* [*myron*] upon his head for this reason: that he might breathe incorruptibility upon the church. Do not be *anointed* [*aleiphō*] with the stench of the teaching of the ruler of this age, lest he take you captive and rob you of the life set before you. Why do we not all become wise by receiving God's knowledge, which is Jesus *Christ*?[55]

Ignatius connects Jesus's role as "Christ" to his anointing with *myron*. The absence of olive oil in the Gospel accounts does not disrupt the messianic connection he wants to draw out of the scene. He goes on to insist that believers should not be "anointed" with the "stench" of false teaching. The implication is that believers *should be* "anointed" as Christ was. That the next line identifies Jesus as "Christ"—the word that means "Anointed One"—completes the thought. There can be no question, then, that the context of Ignatius's teaching involves *messianic* allusions.[56]

Here is the key point: Ignatius does not seem bothered by the fact that different words are used for anointing *or* that *myron* is used by the woman instead of olive oil. We should therefore not insist that Mark's audience could not have connected messianic significance to the story of Jesus's anointing at Bethany because the evangelist did not use the "right" Greek word. Instead, Mark is best read as subtly drawing different strands together in his narrative. In Mark 14, the anointing at Bethany is said to anticipate Jesus's *death* (Mark 14:8). Later, in Mark 16, after Jesus's death, women go to the tomb to "anoint" (*aleipsōsin*) Jesus's body (16:1). Mark, then, repeatedly emphasizes

54. See, e.g., Robert H. Stein, *Mark*, BECNT (Grand Rapids: Baker Academic, 2008), 635.

55. Ignatius, *To the Ephesians* 17:1–2, in Holmes, *Apostolic Fathers*, 197 (emphasis added).

56. Ignatius underscores Jesus's messianic identity by linking him to Davidic hopes: "Jesus the Christ was conceived by Mary according to God's plan, both from the seed of David and of the Holy Spirit" (*To the Ephesians* 18:2, in Holmes, *Apostolic Fathers*, 197). Ignatius connects Jesus's role as "Christ" to both his being born of the line of "David" and his being conceived through the "Holy Spirit." This seems related to imagery of anointing as well since the New Testament identifies the Spirit as the "anointing" Jesus received (Luke 4:18; Acts 10:38; see also Isa. 61:1).

the motif of anointing in connection with Jesus's death—which, for the evangelist, includes the climactic affirmation of Jesus's identity as the messianic Son of God (15:39).[57] In fact, in all four canonical Gospels, *Jesus's death is inseparably bound up with anointing*.

Adela Yarbro Collins is therefore correct when she observes that the scene of Jesus's anointing at Bethany has many connotations.[58] The scene certainly points forward to Jesus's death, in which his identity as the messianic divine Son of God is made manifest. The evidence from Ignatius allows us to think that Greek readers would also catch the allusion to Jesus's identity as "Christ"—the "Anointed One"—in the story of the anointing at Bethany. That the apostles "anoint" people in Mark 6—a passage that uses the same Greek terminology as is found in Mark 16:1 (*aleipsōsin*)—brings that passage also into the larger narrative of Jesus's identity as "Anointed One."

Yet the anointing of Jesus by a woman signifies something invisible and spiritual: his anointing ultimately points to his identity as the "Anointed One," the "Christ," the one anointed by the Spirit (Acts 10:38). It is not difficult to understand why Matthew, Mark, and John felt it necessary to stress this identity just prior to narrating his death, lest there be any doubt about it. After all, that the Messiah himself would suffer was not anticipated by his disciples (Matt. 16:21–22//Mark 8:31–32) and had the effect of leading some to doubt he had fulfilled his messianic mission (Luke 24:19–27).

The spiritual reality signified by Jesus's anointing at Bethany is also realized in the sacrament of anointing of the sick.[59] Believers are anointed in the same Spirit and made "christs" in Christ (2 Cor. 1:21–22). In the face of great affliction, they are physically anointed, which signifies the strength and power of the Spirit, who confirms their hope and enables them to be faithful as Christ himself remained faithful in his passion.

Moreover, Christ overcame the temptation to subject the divine will to his human will at the Mount of Olives, at the place known as Gethsemane—which literally means "the oil press." Anointing oil came, of course, from olives. Patristic sources saw profound symbolism here; it was appropriate

57. Many believe that the Roman centurion's declaration of Jesus's identity as God's son is ironic. Even if this is the case, however, the reason it is ironic is because Mark views it as proclaiming the truth of Jesus's identity. See, e.g., Nathan Eubank, "Dying with Power: Mark 15,39 from Ancient to Modern Interpretation," *Biblica* 95, no. 2 (2014): 247–68.

58. Adela Yarbro Collins, *Mark*, Hermeneia (Minneapolis: Fortress, 2007), 642.

59. See, e.g., Paul Jerome Keller, *101 Questions and Answers on the Sacraments of Healing: Penance and Anointing of the Sick* (New York: Paulist Press, 2010), 132–33.

that Christ, the Anointed One, be associated with the Mount of Olives.[60] The scene of Jesus's prayer in Gethsemane is given particular emphasis by Maximus the Confessor, who finds in it the essence of Christ's saving work. Christ saves humanity as a human, subjecting his human will to the divine will, enabling those in him to do the same.[61] Christ, the true olive tree, the source of the anointing received by believers, is *pressed*—but he overcomes.

Grave illness also serves to press Jesus's disciples. Yet believers too can overcome temptations against faith, hope, and love in their affliction through the sacrament of anointing. Moreover, they offer their suffering with Christ, presenting their bodies in union with the sacrifice of Christ's body (Rom. 12:1; Col. 1:24). The gift of the Spirit bestowed in anointing empowers them to suffer faithfully as Christ did, sharing in the sonship of the divine Son. As Paul explains: "The Spirit himself bears witness with our spirit that we are the children of God, and if children also heirs, heirs of God and co-heirs with Christ, *provided we suffer together with him*, that we may also be glorified with him" (Rom. 8:16–17). This is what constitutes healing in Christ in its truest sense. Like Christ, they are anointed, but also like Christ, they will be raised in glory. True healing is found in dying and rising in Christ.

60. See, e.g., Augustine, *Tractates on John* 33.3.

61. See Maximus the Confessor, *Opuscula I ad Marinum* (PG 91:12–28); *Disputatio cum Pyrrho* (PG 91:309).

Acknowledgments

This book is the fruit of many years of research, study, and prayerful contemplation. It would never have been completed without the support and prayers of numerous individuals. I apologize to those I cannot mention by name. Of course, all the shortcomings of this study must be attributed to me. But without the assistance I received from so many, this book would have been greatly diminished—or never even published at all. This is especially true given the unexpected circumstances that surrounded its completion.

In January 2024, I learned that my institution, the Augustine Institute, would take the unprecedented step of relocating all of its faculty, staff, and students from Colorado to Missouri. Suffice it to say, this would involve a massive upheaval not only professionally but also personally. As I write this acknowledgments section in the summer of 2024, we are still in the process of that transition. While I believe the move is providential and is the right thing for both the Augustine Institute and for my family, it has entailed countless difficulties that greatly delayed the completion of this book. Jim Kinney and the good people at Baker Academic have been incredibly patient with me throughout it all. I am profoundly thankful for their many kindnesses and for allowing me to finish this work without compromising its integrity.

I also wish to thank those at my institution for supporting this project: Christopher Blum, Israel McGrew, Elizabeth Klein, Mark Giszczak, Sean Innerst, Christopher Mooney, Carl Vennerstrom, Scott Hefelfinger, Arielle Harms, Curtis Mitch, and Lucas Pollice. Whether in brief conversations in the hallway or in longer sit-down discussions about topics treated here, engagement with my colleagues greatly improved this study. I must make special mention of Jim Prothro, who kindly engaged in lengthy exchanges about issues addressed in this book. I am profoundly grateful for his friendship, support, and many insightful recommendations.

In addition, I express my gratitude to other biblical scholars, theologians, and academic friends who read this manuscript in draft form or who in other ways assisted me in thinking through important areas treated in this book: Matthew Levering, Dale Allison, John Kincaid, Isaac Morales, OP, Amy-Jill Levine, Nathan Eubank, Khaled Anatolios, Edith Humphrey, Leslie Baynes, Daniel Cardó, Dominic Legge, OP, Timothy Brookins, Sam Johnson, Bill Wright, Joshua Smith, Joseph Dodson, Matthew Monnig, SJ, Reginald Lynch, OP, Douglas Bushman, Joshua Jipp, Jason Staples, Craig Keener, Paul Wheatley, Daniel Gurtner, Anders Runesson, David Augustine, Andrew Hofer, OP, Christopher Skinner, Rafael Rodriguez, Tom Harmon, and Andrew Younan. I extend particular gratitude to Brant Pitre for being an invaluable sounding board from the time of this project's inception to its completion. Moreover, I am grateful to Dominic Langevin, OP, for taking time to offer thoughts on an early draft of this book.

I also wish to thank the numerous priests that spoke with me about their experiences and/or pastoral concerns surrounding the sacrament, allowing this book to take a fuller form than it otherwise would have had. I especially thank the wonderful priests at my family's beloved and longtime parish in Colorado, Our Lady of Loreto—namely, Fr. David Bluejacket and Fr. Kevin Kasel. Likewise, thank you to Fr. James Claver, who served as the full-time chaplain of the Augustine Institute Graduate School in our final years in Denver.

I would be remiss not to offer a special word of thanks to the series editors, Tim Gray and John Sehorn, for their support for my work. I will forever be grateful to Tim for his vision for this series, for thinking of me for this topic, and for his encouragement as I worked on it. John Sehorn's exceptional editorial work on this project deserves specific comment. John helped me think through this project from its very inception. Along the way, he made many superb suggestions that vastly improved this work. In addition, he helped streamline my presentation, trimming down footnotes and technical discussions that would have been obstacles to nonacademic readers. I must also thank Tim West and Amy Donaldson at Baker Academic for their excellent work copyediting this book, which greatly improved it and saved me from many embarrassments.

I thank my family members for being a reservoir of prayer and support for me as I worked on this project: my parents, Patrick and Theresa; my siblings, Noree, Tracee, Julia and her husband—my brother-in-law—Ivan, Marita, and Georgie; my aunts and uncles—Rita (Lala), Marty, Bill and Kathy, Terry and Danielle; my wonderful parents-in-law, Tom and Illene.

My amazing children—Michael, Matthew, Molly, Thomas, Susanna, and Simon—also deserve special thanks. This book would not have ever been able to move from the word processor to the printed page without their patience, joyful encouragement, and prayers.

Above all, I thank my wonderful wife, Kim, for all the many sacrifices she made as I worked on this project. As it neared completion, she took on so many of the responsibilities regarding our move to St. Louis, which allowed me to finish the manuscript. Somehow she also found the time to read an early draft carefully, offering invaluable edits and suggestions. My dear, you are truly my best friend—I love you and am grateful to God beyond words for you.

Obviously, I also must include a word of thanks to the Lord for the grace of working on and completing this study. May the name of Jesus the Lord be praised now and forever.

Finally, I end these acknowledgments by mentioning my uncle, Fr. Peter Irving (Uncle Pete), who—since I was very young—has been a vital supporter of my work in academic theology. (He gave me my first book on New Testament Greek when I was about thirteen!) As I wrote this study, my thoughts frequently turned to him. He, like so many faithful priests, has anointed countless thousands of individuals, administering anointing of the sick to people in their most desperate hour. Time and time again, I have watched him set aside his own plans and priorities to respond urgently, selflessly, and lovingly to a sick call from someone in his or her ultimate trial. This book is dedicated to him.

The Solemnity of St. Peter and St. Paul
June 29, 2024

Suggested Resources

Allison, Dale C., Jr. *James*. ICC. London: Bloomsbury T&T Clark, 2013.

Catechism of the Catholic Church §§1499–1535.

Gusmer, Charles W. *And You Visited Me: Sacramental Ministry to the Sick and the Dying*. Rev. ed. Studies in the Reformed Rites of the Church 6. Collegeville, MN: Liturgical Press, 1989.

Kasza, John C. *Understanding Sacramental Healing: Anointing and Viaticum*. Chicago: Hillenbrand Books, 2007.

Levering, Matthew. "Surrender: Anointing of the Sick." In *Dying and the Virtues*, 135–47. Grand Rapids: Eerdmans, 2018.

Novenson, Matthew V. *The Grammar of Messianism: An Ancient Jewish Political Idiom and Its Users*. Oxford: Oxford University Press, 2017.

Palmer, Paul F. "The Purpose of Anointing of the Sick: A Reappraisal." *TS* 19 (1958): 309–44.

Pastoral Care of the Sick: Rites of Anointing and Viaticum. Totowa, NJ: Catholic Book Publishing, 1983.

Selected Bibliography

Adler, William. "On the Priesthood of Jesus." In *New Testament Apocrypha: More Noncanonical Scriptures*, edited by Tony Burke and Brent Landau, 1:69–83. Grand Rapids: Eerdmans, 2016.

Allison, Dale C., Jr. *The Intertextual Jesus: Scripture in Q*. Harrisburg, PA: Trinity Press International, 2000.

———. *James*. ICC. London: Bloomsbury T&T Clark, 2013.

———. *The New Moses: A Matthean Typology*. Minneapolis: Fortress, 1993.

Anatolios, Khaled. *Deification through the Cross: An Eastern Christian Theology of Salvation*. Grand Rapids: Eerdmans, 2020.

Anderson, Gary A. *Christian Doctrine and the Old Testament: Theology in the Service of Biblical Exegesis*. Grand Rapids: Baker Academic, 2017.

———. *The Genesis of Perfection: Adam and Eve in Jewish and Christian Imagination*. Louisville: Westminster John Knox, 2001.

———. *Sin: A History*. New Haven: Yale University Press, 2009.

———. *That I May Dwell among Them: Incarnation and Atonement in the Tabernacle Narrative*. Grand Rapids: Eerdmans, 2023.

Augustine. *The City of God*. Translated by William Babcock. WSA I/7. Hyde Park, NY: New City Press, 2012–13.

———. *Commentary on the Lord's Sermon on the Mount with Seventeen Related Sermons*. Translated by Denis J. Kavanaugh. FC 11. Washington, DC: Catholic University of America Press, 1951.

———. *Expositions of the Psalms 121–150*. Translated by Maria Boulding. WSA III/20. Hyde Park, NY: New City Press, 2000.

———. *Homilies on the First Epistle of John*. Translated by Boniface Ramsey. WSA I/14. Hyde Park, NY: New City Press, 2008.

———. *Homilies on the Gospel of John 1–40*. Translated by Edmund Hill. WSA III/12. Hyde Park, NY: New City Press, 2009.

———. *Homilies on the Gospel of John 41–124*. Translated by Edmund Hill. WSA III/13. Hyde Park, NY: New City Press, 2020.

———. *Letters 1–99*. Translated by Roland Teske. WSA II/1. Hyde Park, NY: New City Press, 2001.

———. *Letters: Volume 3 (131–164)*. Translated by Wilfrid Parsons. FC 20. Washington, DC: Catholic University of America Press, 1953.

———. "Second Discourse on Psalm 26." In *St. Augustine: On the Psalms*. Vol. 1, *Psalms 1–29*, translated by Scholastica Hebgin and Felicitas Corrigan, 260–83. ACW 29. New York: Paulist Press, 1960.

———. *Sermons 184–229Z*. Translated by Edmund Hill. WSA III/6. New Rochelle, NY: New City Press, 1993.

———. *Treatises on Various Subjects*. Translated by Mary Sarah Muldowney. FC 16. Washington, DC: Catholic University of America Press, 1952.

Aune, David E. *Revelation 1–5*. WBC 52A. Dallas: Word, 1997.

Baert, Barbara. *The Heritage of Holy Wood: The Legend of the True Cross in Text and Image*. Leiden: Brill, 2004.

Baltzer, Klaus. *Deutero-Isaiah*. Translated by Margaret Kohl. Hermeneia. Minneapolis: Fortress, 2001.

Barber, Michael Patrick. "The Bible, the New Ressourcement, and Peter's Priestly Keys." *New Ressourcement* 1, no. 2 (2024): 271–313.

———. "A Catholic Perspective." In *Four Views on the Role of Works at the Final Judgment*, edited by Alan Stanley, 161–84. Grand Rapids: Zondervan, 2013.

———. *The Historical Jesus and the Temple: Memory, Methodology, and the Gospel of Matthew*. Cambridge: Cambridge University Press, 2023.

———. "Thomas Aquinas's Exegesis of Paul and the Eucharist as *Panis Angelicus*: Typology and Transubstantiation." In *Thomas Aquinas and the Eucharist*, edited by Michael A. Dauphinais, Andrew Hofer, and Roger W. Nutt. Ave Maria, FL: Sapientia Press, 2025.

Barr, James. *The Garden of Eden and the Hope of Immortality*. Minneapolis: Fortress, 1992.

———. "Is God a Liar? (Genesis 2–3)—and Related Matters." *JTS* 57 (2006): 1–22.

Bauckham, Richard. *James*. NTR. London: Routledge, 1999.

Baxter, Wayne S. "Healing and the 'Son of David': Matthew's Warrant." *NovT* 48, no. 1 (2006): 36–50.

Beale, G. K. *The Book of Revelation*. NIGTC. Grand Rapids: Eerdmans, 1999.

———. *The Temple and the Church's Mission: A Biblical Theology of the Dwelling Place of God*. Downers Grove, IL: IVP Academic, 2004.

Beattie, Derek. "What Is Genesis 2–3 About?" *ExpTim* 92 (1980): 8–10.

Bede the Venerable. *Commentary on the Seven Catholic Epistles*. Translated by Dom David Hurst. Kalamazoo, MI: Cistercian Publications, 1985.

———. *On the Tabernacle*. Translated by Arthur G. Holder. Liverpool: Liverpool University Press, 1994.

Behr, John, ed. and trans. *Origen: On First Principles*. Vol. 1. OECT. Oxford: Oxford University Press, 2017.

Benedict XVI. *The Sacrament of Charity*. Ijamsville, MD: The Word Among Us Press, 2007.

Best, Ernest. *Ephesians*. ICC. London: T&T Clark, 1998.

Bissias, David G. *The Mystery of Healing: Oil, Anointing, and the Unity of the Local Church*. Rollinsford, NH: Orthodox Research Institute, 2008.

Black, C. Clifton. *Mark: Images of an Apostolic Interpreter*. 1994. Reprint, Minneapolis: Fortress, 2001.

———. *Mark's Gospel: History, Theology, Interpretation*. Grand Rapids: Eerdmans, 2023.

Blackwell, Ben C. *Christosis: Engaging Paul's Soteriology with His Patristic Interpreters*. Grand Rapids: Eerdmans, 2016.

Blenkinsopp, Joseph. *Isaiah 56–66*. AB 19B. New York: Doubleday, 1988.

Botner, Max. *Jesus Christ as the Son of David in the Gospel of Mark*. SNTSMS 174. Cambridge: Cambridge University Press, 2019.

Boyle, John F. "Saint Thomas Aquinas on the Anointing of the Sick (Extreme Unction)." In *Recovering Aquinas and the Sacraments: Studies in Sacramental Theology*, edited by Matthew Levering and Michael Dauphinais, 76–84. Chicago: Hillenbrand Books, 2009.

Bradshaw, Paul F., Maxwell E. Johnson, and L. Edward Phillips. *The Apostolic Tradition*. Hermeneia. Minneapolis: Fortress, 2002.

Brodie, Thomas L. "Luke 7,36–50 as an Internalization of 2 Kings 4,1–37: A Study in Luke's Use of Rhetorical Imitation." *Biblica* 64 (1983): 457–85.

———. "A New Temple and a New Law: The Unity and Chronicler-Based Nature of Luke 1:1–4:22a." *JSNT* 5 (1979): 21–45.

Brown, Raymond E. *The Epistles of John*. AB 30. Garden City, NY: Doubleday, 1982.

Brown, Sherri, and Francis J. Moloney. *Interpreting the Gospel and Letters of John: An Introduction*. Grand Rapids: Eerdmans, 2017.

Brzana, Stanislaus J. *Remains of Sin and Extreme Unction according to Theologians after Trent*. Rome: Catholic Book Agency, 1953.

Bullard, Roger A., and Howard A. Hatton. *A Handbook on the Wisdom of Solomon*. United Bible Societies' Handbooks. New York: United Bible Societies, 2004.

Calvin, John. *Institutes of the Christian Religion*. Edited by John T. McNeill. Translated by Ford Lewis Battles. 2 vols. Philadelphia: Westminster, 1960.

Campbell, R. Alastair. *The Elders: Seniority within Earliest Christianity*. Edinburgh: T&T Clark, 1994.

Cappello, Felix M. *Tractatus Canonico-Moralis de Sacramentis*. Vol. 3. 3rd ed. Taurini: Marietti, 1949.

Carroll, John T. *Luke: A Commentary*. NTL. Louisville: Westminster John Knox, 2012.

Cessario, Romanus. *The Seven Sacraments of the Catholic Church*. Grand Rapids: Baker Academic, 2023.

Cheriavely, John F. "25th Year of the Rite of Anointing of the Sick: Challenges and Perspectives." *Questions liturgiques* 78 (1997): 164–75.

Cogan, Mordechai. *I Kings*. AB 10. New York: Doubleday, 2001.

Cogan, Mordechai, and Hayim Tadmor. *II Kings*. AYB 11. New Haven: Yale University Press, 2008.

Collins, Adela Yarbro. *Mark*. Hermeneia. Minneapolis: Fortress, 2007.

Collins, John J. *Daniel*. Hermeneia. Minneapolis: Fortress, 1993.

———. *The Scepter and the Star*. ABRL. New York: Doubleday, 1995.

Collins, Raymond F. *1 & 2 Timothy and Titus*. NTL. Louisville: Westminster John Knox, 2002.

Connell, Martin. *Church and Worship in Fifth-Century Rome: The Letter of Innocent I to Decentius of Gubbio*. GLS 50. Piscataway, NJ: Gorgias, 2010.

Cuschieri, Andrew. *Anointing of the Sick: A Theological and Canonical Study*. Lanham, MD: University Press of America, 1993.

Cyril of Jerusalem. *The Works of Saint Cyril of Jerusalem*. Translated by Leo P. McCauley and Anthony A. Stephenson. 2 vols. FC 61–62. Washington, DC: Catholic University of America Press, 1969–70.

Dahood, Mitchell. *Psalms I: 1–50*. AB 16. Garden City, NY: Doubleday, 1965.

Daly-Denton, Margaret. *David in the Fourth Gospel: The Johannine Reception of the Psalms*. Leiden: Brill, 2000.

Danneels, Godfried. "Current Challenges for Sacramental Theology." *Antiphon* 5, no. 2 (2000): 44–45.

Davids, Peter H. *James*. NIGTC. Grand Rapids: Eerdmans, 1982.

Davies, W. D., and D. C. Allison. *A Critical and Exegetical Commentary on the Gospel according to Saint Matthew*. 3 vols. ICC. London: T&T Clark, 1988–1997.

de Jonge, Marinus, and Johannes Tromp. *The Life of Adam and Eve and Related Literature*. Sheffield: Sheffield Academic, 1997.

Denzinger, Heinrich. *Compendium of Creeds, Definitions, and Declarations on Matters of Faith and Morals*. Edited by Peter Hünermann. 43rd ed. San Francisco: Ignatius, 2012.

Deppe, D. B. *The Sayings of Jesus in the Epistle of James*. Chelsea, MI: Bookcrafters, 1989.

deSilva, David A. *The Jewish Teachers of Jesus, James, and Jude: What Earliest Christianity Learned from the Apocrypha and Pseudepigrapha*. Oxford: Oxford University Press, 2012.

DiNoia, J. Augustine, and Joseph Fox. "Priestly Dimensions of the Sacrament of Anointing of the Sick." *The Priest* 62 (2006): 10–13.

Douglas, Mary. *Leviticus as Literature*. Oxford: Oxford University Press, 1999.

Dunn, Geoffrey D. *Tertullian*. The Early Church Fathers. London: Routledge, 2004.

Dunn, James D. G. *The Epistles to the Colossians and to Philemon*. NIGTC. Grand Rapids: Eerdmans, 1996.

———. *The Theology of Paul the Apostle*. Grand Rapids: Eerdmans, 1998.

Dvořáček, Jiří. *The Son of David in Matthew's Gospel in the Light of Solomon as Exorcist Tradition*. WUNT 2/415. Tübingen: Mohr Siebeck, 2016.

Edelman, Diana Vikander. *King Saul in the Historiography of Judah*. Sheffield: JSOT Press, 1991.

Edwards, J. Christopher. *The Ransom Logion in Mark and Matthew: Its Reception and Its Significance for the Study of the Gospels*. WUNT 2/327. Tübingen: Mohr Siebeck, 2012.

Ehrman, Bart, and Zlatko Pleše. *The Apocryphal Gospels*. Oxford: Oxford University Press, 2011.

Eldridge, Michael D. *Dying Adam with His Multiethnic Family*. SVTP 16. Leiden: Brill, 2001.

Elliott, J. K. *The Apocryphal New Testament: A Collection of Apocryphal Christian Literature in an English Translation*. Oxford: Oxford University Press, 1993.

Elliott, John H. "Elders as Shared Household Heads and Not Holders of 'Office' in Earliest Christianity." *BTB* 33, no. 2 (2003): 77–82.

———. *First Peter*. AB 37B. New York: Doubleday, 2000.

Empereur, James L. *Prophetic Anointing: God's Call to the Sick, the Elderly, and the Dying*. Wilmington, DE: Michael Glazier, 1982.

Eubank, Nathan. "Dying with Power: Mark 15,39 from Ancient to Modern Interpretation." *Biblica* 95, no. 2 (2014). 247–68.

———. *Wages of Cross-Bearing and Debt of Sin*. Berlin: De Gruyter, 2013.

Evans, Craig A. "Luke's Use of the Elijah/Elisha Narratives." *JBL* 106 (1987): 75–83.

Eve, Eric. *The Jewish Context of Jesus' Miracles*. JSNTSup 231. London: Sheffield Academic, 2002.

Feingold, Lawrence. *Touched by Christ: The Sacramental Economy*. Steubenville, OH: Emmaus Academic, 2021.

Ferguson, Everett. *Baptism in the Early Church: History, Theology, and Liturgy in the First Five Centuries*. Grand Rapids: Eerdmans, 2009.

Finn, Thomas M. "The Sacramental World in the *Sentences* of Peter Lombard." *TS* 69 (2008): 557–82.

Fitzmyer, Joseph A. *The Acts of the Apostles*. AB 31. New Haven: Yale University Press, 2008.

———. *Romans*. AB 33. New York: Doubleday, 1993.

Flannery, Austin. *Vatican Council II: The Basic Sixteen Documents, Constitutions, Decrees, Declarations*. Rev. ed. Collegeville, MN: Liturgical Press, 2014.

Fletcher-Louis, Crispin H. T. *All the Glory of Adam: Liturgical Anthropology in the Dead Sea Scrolls*. STDJ 42. Leiden: Brill, 2002.

Foster, Paul. *Colossians*. BNTC. London: Bloomsbury T&T Clark, 2016.

Francis. *Meeting Jesus in the Sacraments*. Huntington, IN: Our Sunday Visitor, 2015.

Friebel, Kelvin G. *Jeremiah's and Ezekiel's Sign Acts: Rhetorical Nonverbal Communication*. JSOTSup 283. Sheffield: Sheffield Academic, 1999.

Fritz, Volkmar. *1 & 2 Kings*. Translated by Anselm Hagedorn. CC. Minneapolis: Fortress, 2003.

Gadenz, Pablo T. *The Gospel of Luke*. CCSS. Grand Rapids: Baker Academic, 2018.

Gaillardetz, Richard R. "Preface." In *The Cambridge Companion to Vatican II*, edited by Richard R. Gaillardetz, xv–xvii. Cambridge: Cambridge University Press, 2020.

Geddert, Timothy J. *Mark*. BCBC. Scottdale, PA: Herald, 2001.

Gillingham, S. E. "The Messiah in the Psalms: A Question of Reception History and the Psalter." In *King and Messiah in Israel and the Ancient Near East: Proceedings of the Oxford Old Testament Seminar*, edited by John Day, 209–37. LHBOTS 270. 1998. Reprint, London: Bloomsbury T&T Clark, 2013.

Goldingay, John. *Old Testament Theology*. Vol. 1, *Israel's Gospel*. Downers Grove, IL: IVP Academic, 2003.

———. *Psalms*. BCOT. 3 vols. Grand Rapids: Baker Academic, 2006–7.

Gorman, Michael J. *Inhabiting the Cruciform God: Kenosis, Justification, and Theosis in Paul's Narrative Soteriology*. Grand Rapids: Eerdmans, 2009.

Grossberg, Daniel. "Judge." In *Eerdmans Dictionary of the Bible*, edited by David N. Freedman, Allen C. Myers, and Astrid B. Beck, 752–54. Grand Rapids: Eerdmans, 2000.

Gusmer, Charles W. *And You Visited Me: Sacramental Ministry to the Sick and the Dying*. Rev. ed. Studies in the Reformed Rites of the Church 6. Collegeville, MN: Liturgical Press, 1989.

Häring, Bernard. *The Sacraments and Your Everyday Life*. Liguori, MO: Liguori Publications, 1976.

Harrison, Carol. *Augustine: Christian Truth and Fractured Humanity*. CTC. Oxford: Oxford University Press, 2000.

Hartin, Patrick J. *James*. SP 14. Collegeville, MN: Liturgical Press, 2003.

———. *James and the Q Sayings of Jesus*. JSNTSup 47. Sheffield: Sheffield Academic, 1991.

Hays, Richard B. *Echoes of Scripture in the Gospels*. Waco: Baylor University Press, 2016.

Heine, Ronald E. *Origen: An Introduction to His Life and Thought*. Eugene, OR: Cascade Books, 2019.

Hengel, Martin. "Sit at My Right Hand!" In *Studies in Early Christology*, translated by Rollin Kearns, 148–58. London: T&T Clark, 1995.

Hillers, Delbert R. *Lamentations*. AB 7A. New York: Doubleday, 1992.

Himmelfarb, Martha. *Ascent to Heaven in Jewish and Christian Apocalypses*. Oxford: Oxford University Press, 1993.

Hippolytus of Rome. *On the Apostolic Tradition*. Translated by Alistair Stewart-Sykes. 2nd ed. PPS 54. Yonkers, NY: St. Vladimir's Seminary Press, 2015.

Holmes, Michael W. *The Apostolic Fathers: Greek Texts and English Translations.* 3rd ed. Grand Rapids: Baker Academic, 2007.

Hooker, Morna D. *The Signs of a Prophet: The Prophetic Actions of Jesus.* Harrisburg, PA: Trinity Press International, 1997.

Hopkins, Stephen C. E. "The Legend of the Holy Rood Tree: A New Translation and Introduction." In *New Testament Apocrypha: More Noncanonical Scriptures*, edited by Tony Burke, 2:145–59. Grand Rapids: Eerdmans, 2020.

Horstmanshoff, Manfred. "Aelius Aristides: A Suitable Case for Treatment." In *Paideia: The World of the Second Sophistic*, edited by Barbara E. Borg, 277–90. Berlin: De Gruyter, 2004.

Humphrey, Edith. *Mediation and the Immediate God: Scriptures, the Church, and Knowing God.* Yonkers, NY: St. Vladimir's Seminary Press, 2023.

Izbicki, Thomas M. "Saint Geneviève and the Anointing of the Sick." *CHR* 104, no. 3 (2018): 393–414.

Janowski, Bernd. "He Bore Our Sins: Isaiah 53 and the Drama of Taking Another's Place." In *The Suffering Servant: Isaiah 53 in Jewish and Christian Sources*, edited by Bernd Janowski and Peter Stuhlmacher, translated by Daniel P. Bailey, 48–74. Grand Rapids: Eerdmans, 2004.

Jensen, Steven J. *The Human Person: A Beginner's Thomistic Psychology.* Washington, DC: Catholic University of America Press, 2018.

Jerome. *The Homilies of Saint Jerome (1–59 on the Psalms).* Translated by Marie Liguori Ewald. FC 48. Washington, DC: Catholic University of America Press, 1964.

Jewett, Robert. *Romans.* Hermeneia. Minneapolis: Fortress, 2007.

Jipp, Joshua. *Christ Is King: Paul's Royal Ideology.* Minneapolis: Fortress, 2015.

———. *The Messianic Theology of the New Testament.* Grand Rapids: Eerdmans, 2020.

John Chrysostom. *On the Priesthood.* Translated by Graham Neville. PPS. Crestwood, NY: St. Vladimir's Seminary Press, 1964.

Johnson, Luke Timothy. *The First and Second Letters to Timothy.* AB 35A. New York: Doubleday, 2001.

———. *The Letter of James.* AB 37A. New York: Doubleday, 1995.

———. *Prophetic Jesus, Prophetic Church: The Challenge of Luke-Acts to Contemporary Christians.* Grand Rapids: Eerdmans, 2011.

Justin Martyr. *Dialogue with Trypho.* Translated by Thomas B. Falls. Revised by Thomas P. Halton. FC 3. Washington, DC: Catholic University of America Press, 2003.

Kasza, John C. "Anointing of the Sick." In *The Oxford Handbook of Sacramental Theology*, edited by Hans Boersma and Matthew Levering, 558–71. Oxford: Oxford University Press, 2005.

———. *Understanding Sacramental Healing: Anointing and Viaticum.* Chicago: Hillenbrand Books, 2007.

Keener, Craig S. *Acts: An Exegetical Commentary*. 4 vols. Grand Rapids: Baker Academic, 2012–15.

———. *1 Peter: A Commentary*. Grand Rapids: Baker Academic, 2021.

Keller, Paul Jerome. *101 Questions and Answers on the Sacraments of Healing: Penance and Anointing of the Sick*. New York: Paulist Press, 2010.

Kern, Joseph. *De sacramento extremae unctionis: Tractatus dogmaticus*. Ratisbonae: Pustet, 1907.

Klawans, Jonathan. *Purity, Sacrifice, and the Temple: Symbolism and Supersessionism in the Study of Ancient Judaism*. Oxford: Oxford University Press, 2006.

Klijn, A. F. J. *The Acts of Thomas: Introduction, Text, and Commentary*. 2nd rev. ed. NovTSup 108. Leiden: Brill, 2003.

Knowles, Michael. *Jeremiah in Matthew's Gospel: The Rejected-Prophet Motif in Matthean Redaction*. JSNTSup 68. Sheffield: Sheffield Academic, 1993.

Koester, Craig R. *Hebrews*. AB 36. New Haven: Yale University Press, 2001.

———. *Revelation*. AYB 38A. New Haven: Yale University Press, 2014.

Kollmann, Bernd. "Sickness and Disease." In *T&T Clark Encyclopedia of Second Temple Judaism*, edited by Daniel M. Gurtner and Loren T. Stuckenbruck, 2:736–38. London: Bloomsbury T&T Clark, 2020.

Konradt, Matthias. *The Gospel according to Matthew: A Commentary*. Translated by M. Eugene Boring. Waco: Baylor University Press, 2020.

Korner, Ralph. *The Origin and Meaning of Ekklēsia in the Early Jesus Movement*. AGJU 98. Leiden: Brill, 2017.

Kubiś, Adam. "The Current Debate on the Relationship between Sin and Sickness in John 5:14." *Biblical Annals* 12, no. 2 (2022): 203–32.

Lamb, William R. S., ed. *The Catena in Marcum: A Byzantine Anthology of Early Commentary on Mark*. TENTS 6. Leiden: Brill, 2012.

Langevin, Dominic. *From Passion to Paschal Mystery: A Recent Magisterial Development concerning the Christological Foundation of the Sacraments*. Fribourg: Academic Press Fribourg, 2015.

Larson-Miller, Lizette. *The Sacrament of Anointing of the Sick*. Lex Orandi Series. Collegeville, MN: Liturgical Press, 2005.

Larsson, Gary. *Bound for Freedom: The Book of Exodus in Jewish and Christian Traditions*. Peabody, MA: Hendrickson, 1999.

Lauterbach, Jacob Z., ed. and trans. *Mekilta de-Rabbi Ishmael*. 3 vols. Philadelphia: Jewish Publication Society of America, 1933.

Laws, Sophie. *The Epistle of James*. BNTC. London: Adam & Charles Black, 1980.

Leeming, Bernard. *Principles of Sacramental Theology*. London: Longmans, Green, 1956.

———. "Recent Trends in Sacramental Theology." *ITQ* 23 (1956): 195–217.

Leo the Great. *Sermons*. Translated by Jane Patricia Freeland and Agnes Josephine Conway. FC 93. Washington, DC: Catholic University of America Press, 1996.

Levering, Matthew. *Dying and the Virtues*. Grand Rapids: Eerdmans, 2018.

Levine, Amy-Jill. "Bearing False Witness: Common Errors Made about Early Judaism." In *The Jewish Annotated New Testament*, edited by Amy-Jill Levine and Mark Zvi Brettler, 759–63. 2nd ed. Oxford: Oxford University Press, 2017.

———. "Concluding Reflections: What's Next in the Study of Matthew?" In *Matthew within Judaism: Israel and the Nations*, edited by Anders Runesson and Daniel M. Gurtner, 449–66. Early Christian Literature. Atlanta: SBL Press, 2019.

Levine, Amy-Jill, and Marc Zvi Brettler. *The Bible with and without Jesus: How Jews and Christians Read the Same Stories Differently*. New York: HarperOne, 2020.

Levine, Amy-Jill, and Ben Witherington III. *The Gospel of Luke*. NCBC. Cambridge: Cambridge University Press, 2018.

Levison, John R. "Adam and Eve in Romans 1.18–25 and the Greek *Life of Adam and Eve*." *NTS* 50 (2004): 519–34.

———. *The Greek Life of Adam and Eve*. CEJL. Berlin: De Gruyter, 2023.

Li, Soeng Yu. *Paul's Teaching on the* Pneumatika *in 1 Corinthians 12–14: Prophecy as the Paradigm of* ta Charismata ta Meizona *for the Future-Oriented* Ekklēsia. WUNT 2/455. Tübingen: Mohr Siebeck, 2017.

Litwa, M. David. *We Are Being Transformed: Deification in Paul's Soteriology*. Berlin: De Gruyter, 2012.

Litwak, Kenneth D. "Sanhedrin." In *T&T Clark Encyclopedia of Second Temple Judaism*, edited by Daniel M. Gurtner and Loren T. Stuckenbruck, 2:706–8. London: Bloomsbury T&T Clark, 2020.

Luther, Martin. *On the Babylonian Captivity of the Church*. Vol. 36 of *Luther's Works*, translated by A. T. W Steinhäuser, F. C. Ahrens, and A. R. Wentz. Philadelphia: Fortress, 1959.

Lynch, Reginald M. *The Cleansing of the Heart: The Sacraments as Instrumental Causes in the Thomistic Tradition*. Thomistic Ressourcement Series 9. Washington, DC: Catholic University of America Press, 2017.

Macaskill, Grant. *Union with Christ in the New Testament*. Oxford: Oxford University Press, 2013.

MacDonald, Alex. "Sacramental Causality." *AER* 22, no. 6 (1900): 574–85.

MacDonald, Margaret Y. *The Pauline Churches: A Socio-Historical Study of Institutionalization in the Pauline and Deutero-Pauline Writings*. SNTSMS 60. Cambridge: Cambridge University Press, 1988.

Maimonides, Moses. *The Guide of the Perplexed*. Translated by Shlomo Pines. 2 vols. Chicago: University of Chicago Press, 1963.

Marley, Euan. Review of *The Elders: Seniority within Earliest Christianity*, by R. Alastair Campbell. *New Blackfriars* 78, no. 914 (1997): 203.

Martin, Ralph P. *James*. WBC 48. Dallas: Word, 1988.

Martos, Joseph. *Deconstructing Sacramental Theology and Reconstructing Catholic Ritual*. Eugene, OR: Wipf & Stock, 2015.

———. *Doors to the Sacred: A Historical Introduction to Sacraments in the Catholic Church*. Garden City, NY: Doubleday, 1981.

Mason, Eric. *"You Are a Priest Forever": Second Temple Jewish Messianism and the Priestly Christology of the Epistle to the Hebrews*. STDJ 74. Leiden: Brill, 2008.

Matera, Frank J. *New Testament Theology: Exploring Diversity and Unity*. Louisville: Westminster John Knox, 2007.

McCarter, P. Kyle, Jr. *I Samuel*. AYB 8. New Haven: Yale University Press, 2008.

McDonough, Sean M. *Yhwh at Patmos: Rev 1:4 in Its Hellenistic and Early Jewish Setting*. WUNT 2/107. Tübingen: Mohr Siebeck, 1999.

McKnight, Scot. "Jesus and Prophetic Actions." *BBR* 10, no. 2 (2000): 201–5.

McVey, Kathleen E. *Ephrem the Syrian: Hymns*. New York: Paulist Press, 1989.

Meier, John P. *Matthew*. New Testament Message 3. Wilmington, DE: Michael Glazier, 1980.

Mersch, Émile. *The Theology of the Mystical Body*. Translated by Cyril Vollert. London: Herder, 1952.

Meyendorff, Paul. *The Anointing of the Sick*. The Orthodox Liturgy 1. Crestwood, NY: St. Vladimir's Seminary Press, 2009.

Meyers, Carol L., and Eric M. Meyers. *Haggai, Zechariah 1–8*. AYB 25B. New Haven: Yale University Press, 2008.

Miura, Yuzuru. *David in Luke-Acts*. WUNT 2/232. Tübingen: Mohr Siebeck, 2005.

Moessner, David P. *Luke the Historian of Israel's Legacy, Theologian of Israel's "Christ": A New Reading of the "Gospel Acts" of Luke*. BZNW 182. Berlin: De Gruyter, 2016.

Morales, Isaac Augustine. "Baptism and Union with Christ." In *"In Christ" in Paul: Explorations in Paul's Theology of Union and Participation*, edited by Michael J. Thate, Kevin J. Vanhoozer, and Constantine R. Campbell, 157–77. WUNT 2/384. Tübingen: Mohr Siebeck, 2014.

Morales, L. Michael. *The Tabernacle Pre-Figured: Cosmic Mountain Ideology in Genesis and Exodus*. BTS 15. Leuven: Peeters, 2012.

Moran, William L. *The Amarna Letters*. Baltimore: Johns Hopkins University Press, 1992.

Moscicke, Hans. *The New Day of Atonement: A Matthean Typology*. WUNT 2/517. Tübingen: Mohr Siebeck, 2020.

Moye, Richard H. "In the Beginning: Myth and History in Genesis and Exodus." *JBL* 109 (1990): 577–98.

Müller, Reinhard. "The Blinded Eyes of the Wise: Sapiential Tradition and Mosaic Covenant in Deut 16:19–20." In *Wisdom and Torah: The Reception of "Torah" in the Wisdom Literature in the Second Temple Period*, edited by Bernd U. Schipper and D. Andrew Teeter, 9–33. Leiden: Brill, 2013.

Nicolas, Jean-Hervé. *Catholic Dogmatic Theology: A Synthesis*. Vol. 3. Translated by Matthew K. Minerd. Washington, DC: Catholic University of America Press, 2024.

Novenson, Matthew V. *The Grammar of Messianism: An Ancient Jewish Political Idiom and Its Users*. Oxford: Oxford University Press, 2017.

Nutt, Roger W. *General Principles of Sacramental Theology*. Washington, DC: Catholic University of America Press, 2017.

———. *To Die Is Gain: A Theological (re-)Introduction to the Sacrament of Anointing of the Sick for Clergy, Laity, Caregivers, and Everyone Else*. Steubenville, OH: Emmaus Academic, 2022.

Omre, Nicholas. *Medieval Children*. New Haven: Yale University Press, 2001.

O'Neill, Colman E. *Meeting Christ in the Sacraments*. Rev. ed. Staten Island, NY: Alba House, 1991.

Origen. *Commentary on the Epistle to the Romans, Books 1–5*. Translated by Thomas Scheck. FC 103. Washington, DC: Catholic University of America Press, 2001.

———. *Contra Celsum*. Translated by Henry Chadwick. Cambridge: Cambridge University Press, 1953.

———. *Homilies on Leviticus 1–16*. Translated by Gary Wayne Barkley. FC 83. Washington, DC: Catholic University of America Press, 1990.

Osheim, Amanda C. "The Christian Faithful." In *The Cambridge Companion to Vatican II*, edited by Richard R. Gaillardetz, 211–31. Cambridge: Cambridge University Press, 2020.

Palmer, Paul F. "The Purpose of Anointing of the Sick: A Reappraisal." *TS* 19 (1958): 309–44.

———. *Sacraments and Forgiveness: History and Doctrinal Development of Penance, Extreme Unction and Indulgences*. SCT 2. Westminster, MD: Newman Press, 1959.

———. "The Theology of the *Res et Sacramentum* with Particular Emphasis on Its Application to Penance." In *Readings in Sacramental Theology*, edited by C. Stephen Sullivan, 104–23. Englewood Cliffs, NJ: Prentice Hall, 1964.

Pastoral Care of the Sick: Rites of Anointing and Viaticum. Totowa, NJ: Catholic Book Publishing, 1983.

Patterson, Todd L. *The Plot-Structure of Genesis*. BIS 160. Leiden: Brill, 2018.

Paul, Shalom M. *Isaiah 40–66: Translation and Commentary*. ECC. Grand Rapids: Eerdmans, 2012.

Piotrowski, Nicholas G. *Matthew's New David at the End of Exile: A Socio-Rhetorical Study of Scriptural Quotations*. NovTSup 170. Leiden: Brill, 2016.

Pitre, Brant. *Jesus and Divine Christology*. Grand Rapids: Eerdmans, 2024.

Pitre, Brant, Michael P. Barber, and John A. Kincaid. *Paul, a New Covenant Jew: Rethinking Pauline Theology*. Grand Rapids: Eerdmans, 2019.

Porter, J. Roy. "Oil in the Old Testament." In *Oil of Gladness: Anointing in the Christian Tradition*, edited by Martin Dudley and Geoffrey Rowell, 35–45. London: SPCK, 1993.

Poschmann, Bernard. *Penance and the Anointing of the Sick*. Translated by Francis Courtney. New York: Herder & Herder, 1964.

Power, David N., Regis Duffy, and Kevin Irwin. "Sacramental Theology: A Review of Literature." *TS* 55 (1994): 657–705.

Prothro, James B. *The Bible and Reconciliation: Confession, Repentance, and Restoration*. CBTS. Grand Rapids: Baker Academic, 2023.

———. *Both Judge and Justifier: Biblical Legal Language and the Act of Justifying in Paul*. WUNT 2/461. Tübingen: Mohr Siebeck, 2018.

———. *A Pauline Theology of Justification: Forgiveness, Friendship, and Life in Christ*. Lectio Sacra. Eugene, OR: Cascade Books, 2023.

Puller, Frederick W. *The Anointing of the Sick in Scripture and Tradition*. London: SPCK, 1904.

Raphael, Rebecca. "Sickness and Disease." In *The Eerdmans Dictionary of Early Judaism*, edited by John J. Collins and Daniel C. Harlow, 1228–30. Grand Rapids: Eerdmans, 2010.

Rashkover, Randi. "Christology." In *The Jewish Annotated New Testament*, edited by Amy-Jill Levine and Marc Zvi Brettler, 754–56. 2nd ed. Oxford: Oxford University Press, 2017.

Reid, Barbara, and Shelly Matthews. *Luke*. Wisdom Commentary 43A–B. 2 vols. Collegeville, MN: Liturgical Press, 2021.

Rigby, Paul. "Original Sin." In *Augustine through the Ages: An Encyclopedia*, edited by Allan D. Fitzgerald, 607–14. Grand Rapids: Eerdmans, 1999.

Runesson, Anders, Donald Binder, and Birger Olsson. *The Ancient Synagogue from Its Origins to 200 C.E.: A Source Book*. AJEC 72. Leiden: Brill, 2008.

Sanders, E. P. *Judaism: Practice and Belief, 63 BCE–66 CE*. Philadelphia: Trinity Press International, 1992.

———. *Paul: The Apostle's Life, Letters, and Thought*. Minneapolis: Fortress, 2015.

Sarna, Nahum M. *Exodus*. JPS Torah Commentary. Philadelphia: Jewish Publication Society, 1991.

Schmidt, A. Jordan. *Wisdom, Cosmos, and Cultus in the Book of Sirach*. Deuterocanonical and Cognate Studies 42. Berlin: De Gruyter, 2019.

Schmidt, T. C., and Nick Nicholas. *Hippolytus of Rome: Commentary on Daniel and "Chronicon."* Gorgias Dissertations 67. GSECP. Piscataway, NJ: Gorgias, 2017.

Scholer, John M. *Proleptic Priests: Priesthood in the Epistle to the Hebrews*. JSNTSup 49. Sheffield: JSOT Press, 1991.

Schwartz, Daniel R. "Introduction: Was 70 C.E. a Watershed in Jewish History? Three Stages of Modern Scholarship, and a Renewed Effort." In *Was 70 C.E. a Watershed in Jewish History? On Jews and Judaism before and after the Destruction of the Second Temple*, edited by Daniel R. Schwartz, Zeev Weiss, and Ruth A. Clements, 1–19. Leiden: Brill, 2012.

Smith, Mark S. *The Genesis of Good and Evil: The Fall(out) and Original Sin in the Bible*. Louisville: Westminster John Knox, 2019.

Snodgrass, Klyne. *Stories with Intent: A Comprehensive Guide to the Parables of Jesus*. 2nd ed. Grand Rapids: Eerdmans, 2018.

Sperry-White, Grant, trans. *The Testamentum Domini*. GLS 22. Piscataway, NJ: Gorgias, 2010.

Staples, Jason. "'Lord, Lord': Jesus as Yhwh in Matthew and Luke." *NTS* 64 (2018): 1–19.

Stein, Robert H. *Mark*. BECNT. Grand Rapids: Baker Academic, 2008.

Stone, Michael E. "The Angelic Prediction in the Primary Adam Books." In *Literature on Adam and Eve: Collected Essays*, edited by Gary A. Anderson, Michael E. Stone, and Johannes Tromp, 111–31. Leiden: Brill, 2000.

Sumney, Jerry L. *Colossians*. NTL. Louisville: Westminster John Knox, 2008.

Szkredka, Slawomir. *Sinners and Sinfulness in Luke: A Study of Direct and Indirect References in the Initial Episodes of Jesus' Activity*. WUNT 2/434. Tübingen: Mohr Siebeck, 2017.

Talbert, Charles H. *Literary Patterns, Theological Themes and the Genre of Luke-Acts*. SBLMS 20. Missoula, MT: Scholars Press, 1974.

Tanner, Norman, ed. *The Decrees of the Ecumenical Councils*. 2 vols. Washington, DC: Georgetown University Press, 1990.

Thomas Aquinas. *Commentary on the Gospel of Matthew, Chapters 1–12*. Translated by Jeremy Holmes and Beth Mortensen. Latin/English Edition of the Works of St. Thomas Aquinas 33. Lander, WY: The Aquinas Institute for the Study of Sacred Doctrine, 2013.

———. *Commentary on the Letters of Saint Paul to the Philippians, Colossians, Thessalonians, Timothy, Titus, and Philemon*. Edited by John Mortensen and Enrique Alarcón. Latin/English Edition of the Works of St. Thomas Aquinas 40. Lander, WY: The Aquinas Institute for the Study of Sacred Doctrine, 2012.

———. *Summa Contra Gentiles, Books III–IV*. Translated by Laurence Shapcote. Latin/English Edition of the Works of St. Thomas Aquinas 12. Green Bay, WI: The Aquinas Institute for the Study of Sacred Doctrine, 2018.

———. *Summa Theologiae, Prima Pars, 1–49*. Translated by Laurence Shapcote. Latin/English Edition of the Works of St. Thomas Aquinas 13. Lander, WY: The Aquinas Institute for the Study of Sacred Doctrine, 2012.

———. *Summa Theologiae, Tertia Pars, 60–90*. Translated by Laurence Shapcote. Latin/English Edition of the Works of St. Thomas Aquinas 20. Lander, WY: The Aquinas Institute for the Study of Sacred Doctrine, 2012.

Thompson, Alexander Phillip. *Recognition and the Resurrection Appearances of Luke 24*. BZNW 225. Berlin: De Gruyter, 2023.

Tilling, Chris. *Paul's Divine Christology*. Grand Rapids: Eerdmans, 2015.

Twelftree, Graham H. "Sanhedrin." In *Dictionary of Jesus and the Gospels*, edited by Joel B. Green, Scot McKnight, and I. Howard Marshall, 728–32. Downers Grove, IL: InterVarsity, 1992.

Vagaggini, Cyprian. *Theological Dimensions of the Liturgy: A General Treatise on the Theology of the Liturgy*. Translated by Leonard J. Doyle and W. A. Jurgens. Rev. ed. Collegeville, MN: Liturgical Press, 1976.

VanderKam, James. *The Dead Sea Scrolls and the Bible*. Grand Rapids: Eerdmans, 2012.

Vogels, Walter. "The Cultic and Civil Calendars of the Fourth Day of Creation (Gen 1:14b)." *SJOT* 11, no. 2 (1997): 163–80.

von Rad, Gerhard. *Genesis: A Commentary*. Translated by John H. Marks. OTL. Philadelphia: Westminster, 1972.

von Wahlde, Urban C. *The Gospel and Letters of John*. 3 vols. ECC. Grand Rapids: Eerdmans, 2010.

Weinfeld, Moshe. *Deuteronomy and the Deuteronomic School*. Oxford: Clarendon, 1972.

———. *The Place of the Law in the Religion of Ancient Israel*. VTSup. Leiden: Brill, 2004.

Weinrich, William C., trans. and ed. *Latin Commentaries on Revelation: Victorinus of Petovium, Apringius of Beja, Caesarius of Arles, and Bede the Venerable*. ACT. Downers Grove, IL: IVP Academic, 2011.

Wenham, Gordon. *Genesis 1–15*. WBC 1. Nashville: Nelson, 1987.

White, Thomas Joseph. *Exodus*. BTCB. Grand Rapids: Brazos, 2016.

———. *The Incarnate Lord: A Thomistic Study in Christology*. Thomistic Ressourcement Series 5. Washington, DC: Catholic University of America Press, 2017.

Whybray, Norman. *Reading the Psalms as a Book*. Sheffield: Sheffield Academic, 1996.

Williams, Catrin H. *I Am He: The Interpretation of* 'Anî Hû' *in Jewish and Early Christian Literature*. WUNT 2/113. Tübingen: Mohr Siebeck, 2000.

Williams, Travis B., and David G. Horrell. *1 Peter*. 2 vols. ICC. London: Bloomsbury T&T Clark, 2023.

Winston, David. *The Wisdom of Solomon*. AB 43. New York: Doubleday, 1979.

Ziegler, John J. *Let Them Anoint the Sick*. Collegeville, MN: Liturgical Press, 1987.

Zwingli, Huldrych. *Writings*. Vol. 2, *In Search of True Religion: Reformation, Pastoral and Eucharistic Writings*, translated by H. Wayne Pipkin. Eugene, OR: Pickwick, 1984.

Subject Index

Scripture and Other Ancient Sources Index

Old Testament

Genesis

Exodus

Leviticus

Romans

1 Corinthians

2 Corinthians

Galatians

Ephesians

Philippians